A ZUNI ATLAS

A ZUNI ATLAS

BY T. J. FERGUSON

AND E. RICHARD HART

New Cartography by Ronald Stauber and Troy Lucio

UNIVERSITY OF OKLAHOMA PRESS : NORMAN AND LONDON

BOOKS BY E. RICHARD HART

Newe: A Western Shoshone History, with Beverly Crum, et al. (Reno, Nevada, 1976)
I Will Die an Indian (editor) (Sun Valley, Idaho, 1979)
FARM: The Future of Agriculture in the Rocky Mountains (editor) (Salt Lake City, 1980)
That Awesome Space: Human Interaction with the Intermountain Landscape (editor) (Salt Lake City, 1981)
A Zuni Atlas, with T. J. Ferguson (Norman, 1985)

BOOKS BY T. J. FERGUSON

A Zuni Atlas, with E. Richard Hart (Norman, 1985)

Library of Congress Cataloging-in-Publication Data

Ferguson, T. J. (Thomas John), 1950–
A Zuni atlas.
(The Civilization of the American Indian Series; v. 172)
Bibliography: p. 141.
Includes index.
1. Zuñi Indians—Maps. 2. Southwest, New—Maps. 3. Zuñi Indians—History—Maps. 4. Zuñi Indians—Antiquities—Maps. 5. Zuñi Indians—Economic conditions—Maps. 6. Zuñi Indians—Reservations—Maps. 7. Indians of North America—New Mexico—Maps. 8. Indians of North America—Arizona—Maps. I. Hart, E. Richard. II. Stauber, Ron. III. Lucio, Troy.
IV. title. V. Series.
G1496.E1F4 1985 912′.79 85–40474
ISBN 0–8061–1945–4 (cloth)
ISBN 0–8061–2287–0 (pbk.)

The paper in this book meets the guidelines for permanence and durability of the Committee on Production Guidelines for Book Longevity of the Council on Library Resources Inc. ∞

CONTENTS

MAPS AND FIGURES

Maps

Figures

ILLUSTRATIONS

"On the mud roofs of Zuni," ca. 1890. Photograph by Ben Wittick, courtesy School of American Research Collections in the Museum of New Mexico (Neg. No. 2446).

PREFACE

A Zuni Atlas is the collaborative summary of many years of work by the authors that outlines, through map, image, and text, the archaeology, ethnohistory, history, ethnography, and current condition of the Zuni tribe in relationship to its geographical environment. The authors themselves are not Zunis. However, the substantive new archaeological, historical, and ethnohistorical material presented herein has been seen and approved by Zuni political and religious leaders, and much of it was done either at the request of or under contract for the Zuni Tribal Council. Indeed, much of the new ethnographic material (note especially the 234 documented Zuni land-use sites in appendices 1 and 2) originates from the Zunis themselves and has been made available to the public after long discussion and deliberation among Zuni leaders.

A considerable amount of the material in this book was originally presented, in an earlier format and different context, to the United States Court of Claims as evidence in behalf of the Zuni Tribe, supporting a suit against the United States that seeks payment for lands taken from the tribe without compensation—*Zuni Indian Tribe v. United States*, Docket No. 161-79L (Ct. Cl., filed April 27, 1979). Both authors presented written testimony to the court and testified in person during the trial. Mr. Hart has been engaged by the tribe since 1972 to study patterns of Zuni land use and spent the year 1980 studying Zuni ethnohistory thanks to a fellowship from the National Endowment for the Humanities. Mr. Ferguson, before his testimony, spent five years living on the Zuni Reservation, engaged in research, excavation, and fieldwork with the Zuni Archaeology Program, serving as Director of that tribal program from 1977–81. Identification of the more than two hundred Zuni land-use sites was carried out principally through the fieldwork of Mr. Ferguson, in collaboration with Zuni witnesses, and Edmund J. Ladd, who played an important role as interpreter. Twelve of these Zuni witnesses later testified or provided depositions to the Court as a part of the litigation, or both.

Following the trial, which took place in March, 1982, in Salt Lake City, the New Mexico Humanities Council provided a grant to the Zuni History Project, for the purpose of interpreting the technical material submitted to the Court as expert testimony, in order that it might be presented in a more accessible form for the public and the Zunis themselves. As a result of this project, which received additional support from the Institute of the American West, an exhibit of land-use maps was prepared. A conference on Zuni history was sponsored, and a tabloid publication was produced. Many of the maps included in this book were originally drafted by Ronald Stauber and Troy Lucio of the Zuni Archaeology Program for presentation as a part of the Zuni land-use exhibit. Unless otherwise noted, Mr. Lucio and Mr. Stauber, under the direction of the authors, completed the maps included in this atlas. Some of the land-use maps drew upon the work of Ms. Catherine J. Patrillo, who drafted larger versions at the American West Center, at the University of Utah, for use in the Zuni litigation. The heavy borders on the land-use maps and the map titled "Areas and Dates of Zuni Land Taken" were drafted originally on USGS maps by Mr. Hart, based on the cumulative available body of ethnohistorical evidence.

The atlas bibliography is necessarily selective—the authors have some two thousand citations in their working bibliography. It is not possible to list all of those interviewed, though important contributors are listed in the Acknowledgments. For more complete citations and descriptions of findings, see the written testimony submitted in behalf of the tribe in the land-claim litigation.

With the help of Wilfred Eriacho, principal of the Zuni Elementary School, the authors have attempted to standardize the spellings of Zuni words. Zuni is a separate language group, and many variations in common Zuni words have been used during the past century. The spellings used here are tribally approved and are intended to be usable in the Zuni schools and by the general public. The Map of Archaeological Sites uses spellings of place names as rendered in the archaeological literature.

A final word should be included about the value of Zuni tradition. To an extent much greater than many other tribes and ethnic cultures, the Zunis have maintained, learned, and passed on their tribal traditions. Often learned by rote and passed down with great accuracy over the space of centuries, these diverse and sometimes dynamic traditions represent a rich storehouse of knowledge of great value in the study of many subjects. Their origin and migration narratives have been compared to the epics of Homer, with a resource of knowledge in history and poetics. The relationship of the Zunis to their environment cannot be adequately captured in an atlas, or, indeed, in a shelf of books. The depth of feeling, the human experience, expression, symbolism, and values are as deep as the human condition.

Albuquerque, New Mexico — T. J. Ferguson
Hailey, Idaho — E. Richard Hart

Schoolteacher T. F. Ealy and his assistant, Jennie Hammaker, with a group of schoolchildren in front of former Zuni governor Pedro Pino's house, 1879. Photograph courtesy the Museum of the American Indian, Heye Foundation (Neg. No. 35030).

ACKNOWLEDGMENTS

THE AUTHORS have had the fortunate opportunity to exchange scholarly ideas with a number of people during work on this project. These persons include Floyd A. O'Neil, Ward Alan Minge, Myra Ellen Jenkins, Fred Eggan, Triloki Nath Pandey, S. Lyman Tyler, John Baxter, and Kathryn Mackay, who worked as experts in the Zuni land-claim litigation or supported the experts' work. Stephen G. Boyden was principal attorney for the tribe and had many suggestions and questions. He was joined by attorneys John S. Boyden, Jr., and G. Richard Hill.

Robert White, at the USGS office, was helpful in providing materials for use in preparing the atlas. Jon Barton, in 1973, drafted an early map showing land-use sites located by Mr. Hart. C. Gregory Crampton was helpful to Hart in his early research and introduced him to much of the Zuni area in the early 1970s. Barbara J. Mills has provided intellectual assistance throughout the project.

Zunis who testified or gave depositions in the litigation were Tom Awelagte, Oscar Nastacio, Fred Bowannie, Chester Mahooty, Frank Vacit, Alonzo Hustito, Ralph Quam, Theodore Edaakie, Mecalito Wytsalucy, Sefferino Eriacho, Chester H. Gaspar, Alvin L. Nastacio, and Robert E. Lewis. Edmund J. Ladd acted as interpreter during legal proceedings and compiled the list of Zuni place names in that capacity when depositions were taken. Other Zunis who supported the work were Wilfred Eriacho, Alex Boone, the late Quincy Panteah, Edison Laselute, the late Lorenzo Chavez, the late Nathaniel Nasheboo, the late Andrew Napetcha, Alex Seowtewa, and Calbert Seciwa.

The staff at the American West Center at the University of Utah was particularly helpful, as was the staff at the Zuni Archaeology Program.

Other institutions that made resources available to the authors during the research on the atlas were the Smithsonian Institution, the National Archives, the Denver Federal Center, the Southwest Museum, the New Mexico State Archives, the Library of Congress, the University of New Mexico Library, and the Huntington Library.

We are particularly grateful for the financial support we received from the New Mexico Humanities Council, the National Endowment for the Humanities, and the Institute of the American West.

Most of all, we wish to acknowledge the hospitality and friendship for which the Zunis have been known for centuries, and which they have shown to us during the last decade.

A ZUNI ATLAS

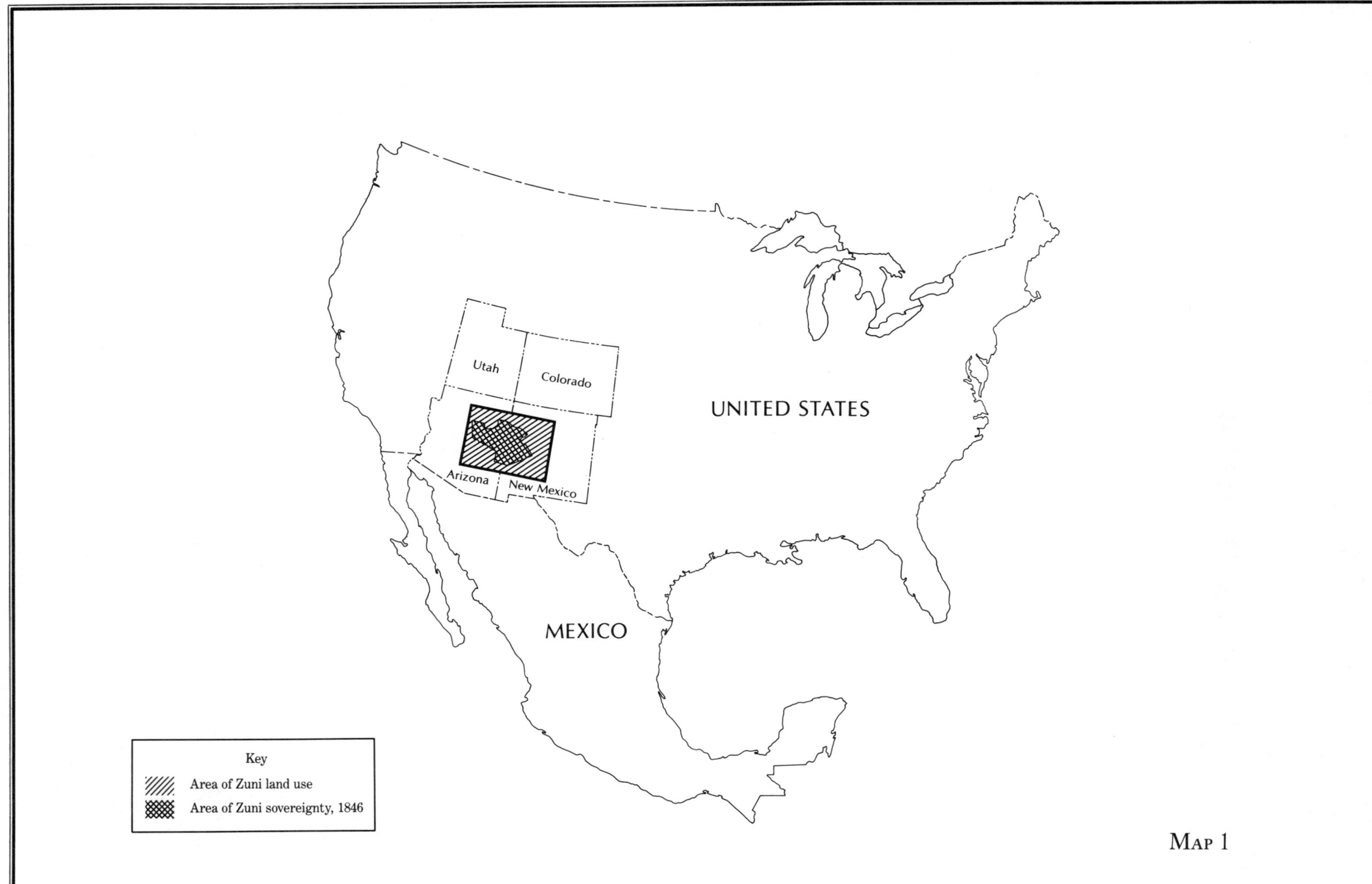

MAP 1

LOCATION OF ZUNI AREA

1. LOCATION OF THE ZUNI AREA

THE ZUNI AREA is located in the southwestern United States in what is today east-central Arizona and west-central New Mexico. The traditional area of Zuni land use extends over a large region stretching from the Grand Canyon in the west to the Rio Grande in the east. Within this extensive area is a smaller but still sizable territory over which the Pueblo of Zuni had control or sovereignty in 1846, when the United States sent military forces to occupy the Southwest. Although the Zuni villages were concentrated in a core area of settlement along the Zuni River, the Zuni people made use of a wide range of valuable resources throughout the area of Zuni sovereignty and beyond.

As mapped in this atlas, the Zuni area lies in eastern Arizona and western New Mexico, between 106 degrees and 112 degrees west longitude and 32 degrees and 37 degrees north latitude. This area encompasses the land regularly and extensively used by the Zuni Indians to sustain their traditional way of life. The oral traditions of the Zuni people and the historic documentary record indicate that the Zunis had an intimate knowledge of this region, based on ancient, historic patterns of land use.

The Zunis occasionally traveled well beyond this area for a variety of purposes. For instance, the Zunis hunted large game at Blue Mountain (Sierra Abajo) in Utah; conducted religious observances at Mesa Verde in Colorado; hunted buffalo in the plains of eastern New Mexico; traded with other Indians in western and southern Arizona and northern Mexico; and made religious pilgrimages to the Pacific Ocean. Thus, this depiction of the Zuni area does not encompass the total range traversed or visited by the tribe, but it does contain the region of greatest Zuni land use and the majority of important individual places used by Zunis.

It was the extensive use of the Zuni area that enabled the Zunis to be self-sufficient and to live in large, stable communities where a rich cultural life could be enjoyed. During the last 150 years, much of the Zuni territory has been encroached upon by non-Zuni peoples, and the total area available for Zuni use has been substantially reduced (see Map 32, Areas and Dates of Zuni Land Taken). As a result, the Zunis have become less self-sufficient. Zuni land holdings have been restricted to a small Indian Reservation of approximately 640 square miles in New Mexico, held in trust by the United States Government (see Zuni Reservation Changes: 1949–82, Map 35). Even so, the Zunis regularly continue to use many places outside the reservation, exercising their religious traditions and practices while sustaining their culture and way of life throughout the Zuni area.

The Zuni Mission in 1873. Photograph by Timothy O'Sullivan, courtesy the Maxwell Museum (Neg. No. 4.ZI.3).

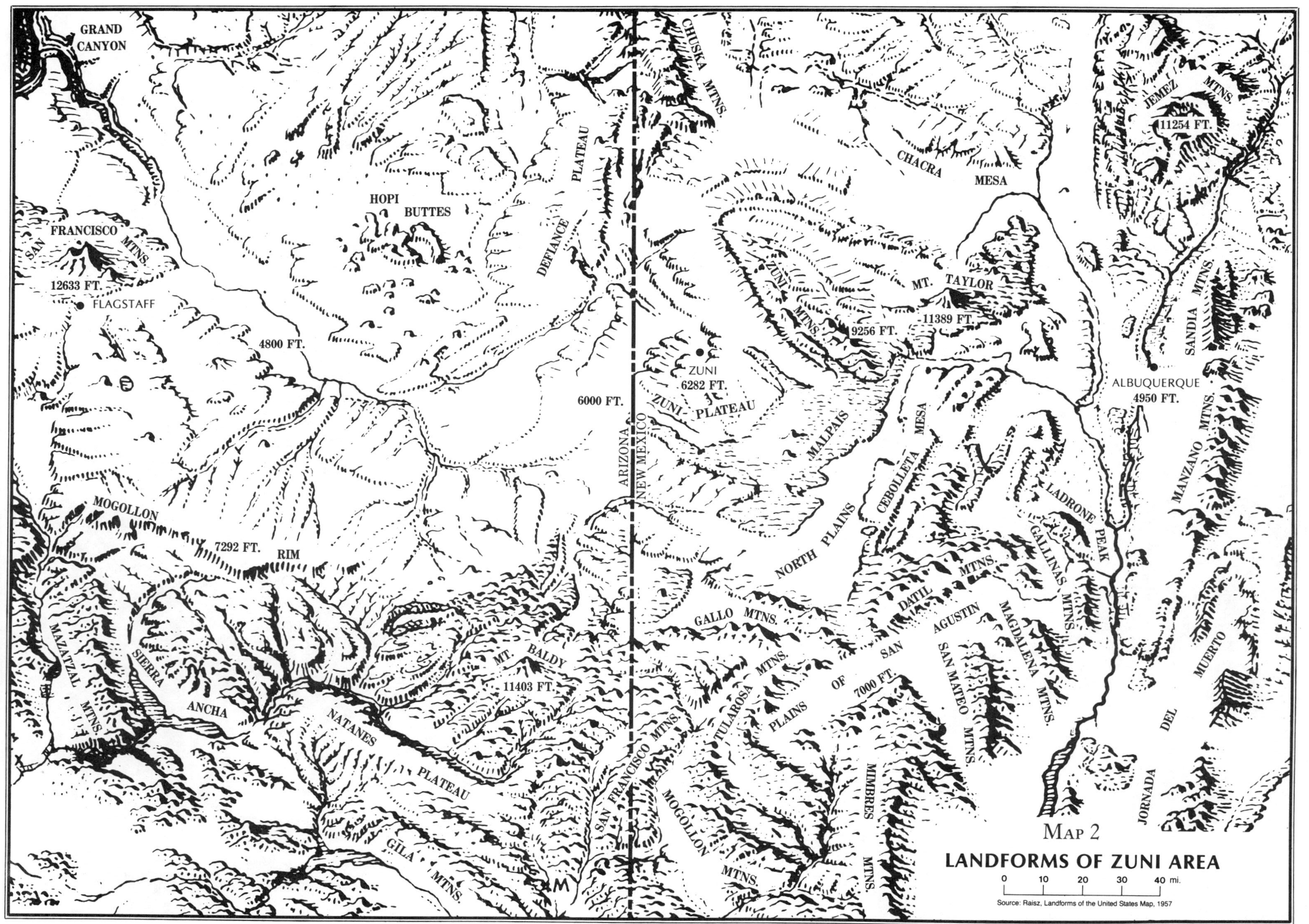

Map 2

LANDFORMS OF ZUNI AREA

2. LANDFORMS OF THE ZUNI AREA

THE ZUNI AREA is situated primarily in the southeastern section of the Colorado Plateau, a large physiographic province covering parts of Arizona, New Mexico, Colorado, and Utah. The Zuni portion of the Colorado Plateau is drained by the Little Colorado River and its tributaries, including the Zuni River. Within this area, the geological processes of deposition, erosion, volcanism, and tectonic activity have produced a broad plateau of tableland that generally slopes downward from east to west, ranging in altitude from about nine thousand to forty-five hundred feet. This plateau is extensively dissected by streams and washes, resulting in a topography featuring landforms of broad, flat plains and mesas, isolated buttes, and usually dry river valleys, occasionally broken by low mountain ranges. The vistas in this part of the Colorado Plateau offer panoramic horizons, often ringed by multihued sandstone buttes and mesas. In the northwest corner of the Zuni area, the Grand Canyon of the Colorado River has been deeply eroded, at the bottom cut to an elevation of twenty-six hundred feet.

To the east of Zuni Pueblo, the Colorado Plateau has been subject to extensive tectonic activity. Here the Zuni Mountains are the result of an uplift that began about seventy million years ago. This uplift produced an oval-shaped geological formation seventy-five miles long and thirty miles wide, with the axis of the mountain crest running from the northwest to the southeast. The gently sloped dome of the Zuni Mountains rises to an elevation of 9,256 feet, providing about 2,000 feet of local vertical relief from the surrounding plateau. The uplift of the Zuni Mountains has a diverse pattern of faults and joints, and is the most faulted of the uplifts on the Colorado Plateau.

The east and west sides of the Colorado Plateau in the Zuni area are marked by high volcanic peaks. Mt. Taylor, sitting on top of Cebolleta Mesa at the east end of the Zuni Mountains, rises to an elevation of 11,389 feet. A large malpais, or lava flow (sometimes called the Malpais), from Mt. Taylor separates the Zuni Mountains from Cebolleta Mesa. Some 150 miles west of Zuni Pueblo, the San Francisco Peaks rise dramatically from the Plateau and are landmarks visible from great distances.

In the western Zuni area, the southern edge of the Colorado Plateau is defined by the steep slopes of the Mogollon Rim, an old fault line. The Colorado Plateau slopes gently upward to the Mogollon Rim, where the land forms a prominent escarpment. Lying below the Mogollon Rim is a rugged and heavily dissected region of low mountains that form a physiographic transition between the tablelands of the Colorado Plateau and the long, broad valleys and mountain ranges of the Basin and Range physiographic province to the south and east.

The eastern end of the Mogollon Rim is obscured by geologically recent volcanic mountain ranges that cover it to a depth of several thousand feet in places. The White Mountains in Arizona are the first of these mountain ranges, and their highest peak, Mt. Baldy, rises to an elevation of 11,403 feet. To the south and east of the White Mountains are many other mountain ranges in a region known as the Mogollon Slope. The steeply pitched mountain ranges of the Mogollon Slope attain elevations as high as 10,244 feet, and include the San Francisco, Mogollon, Tularosa, Datil, Gallinas, Magdelena, and San Mateo Mountains. These mountains enclose the Plains of San Agustin, an ancient playa (lake) that is still a closed basin.

To the east of the mountainous Mogollon Slope are the long, parallel mountain ranges and broad river basins of the Basin and Range Province, encompassing the Rio Grande valley. At the northern end of the Rio Grande valley are high mountains that are part of the southern Rocky Mountains physiographic province. The Jemez Mountains, rising to an elevation of 11,254 feet in the northeast part of the Zuni area, represent the southern extension of this landform.

The landforms of the Zuni area provide a varied topography encompassing plateaus, mesas, mountains, and river basins. Between the bottom of the Grand Canyon and the highest mountain peaks there is a vertical relief of over ten thousand feet. The range of diversity in the physical landscape of the Zuni area constitutes an important source of environmental variability in the resources important for human life.

Zuni women sitting on flagstone steps, ca. 1912-15. Photograph by Pennington Studio, Durango, Colorado, courtesy the Maxwell Museum (Neg. No. 4.ZI.22).

3. GEOLOGY OF THE ZUNI AREA

MANY different types of rocks formed in many different geological periods are exposed in the surface geology of the Zuni area. These rocks cover a time span from the Precambrian Period 2.5 billion years ago to the Quaternary Period of the last 2 million years. During this long time span, this part of the surface of the earth has undergone many changes while the shapes and sizes of continental land masses, oceans, and large lakes were being altered several times.

The earliest rocks exposed in the area consist of Precambrian granite, plutonic rocks that cooled from magma (molten rock) at great depths in the earth. This granite is believed to underlie the entire area, but it is exposed only where there has been considerable uplift and where the overlying rocks have been eroded, as they have been on the Continental Divide in the Zuni Mountains.

During Precambrian time, more than 570 million years ago, this area was under the sea, and various rock materials (sediments) were deposited; but since then, these deposits have been deeply buried and subjected to heat and stress, which has metamorphosed (changed) them into very complex rocks that are called simply metamorphics. These can be seen in many of the same places as the Precambrian granites. Sometimes the metamorphics are changed into very fine clays.

After the Precambrian deposition, and perhaps later depositions, the whole area was uplifted above sea level and massive erosion took place, removing much of the geologic record. It is only for the Pennsylvanian time period, ca. 320 million years ago, that we again have a record with the beginning of the deposition of marine and deltaic limestones and sandstones. The area continued to receive sequential marine and terrestrial (continental) deposits for the next 250 million years, during the Permian, Jurassic, and Cretaceous periods, as the ancient ocean advanced and retreated across the land. This process built up thousands of feet of sediment, including the red and white sandstone expressed on the mesa walls around Zuni.

The great uplift of the Colorado Plateau began about 70 million years ago during the Cretaceous period. This uplift radically altered the geological environment, producing many of the land features we see today. The Zuni Mountains were formed into a long oval dome during this geological activity. The characteristic mesas of the Zuni area were formed by wind and water erosion of these upthrown blocks. At the edges of the Colorado Plateau there was considerable faulting, which caused huge blocks of the earth to sink down and mountains to be raised up.

The area is still geologically active, and the uplift may still be occurring, as the various recent volcanoes testify. Mt. Taylor is very young; it began building only about 7 million years ago, during the Tertiary period, with flows as recent as one million years ago. The lava flows at Blackrock and the Malpais and the cinder cones at and near Bandera Crater were all formed in the last 2 million years during the Quaternary period. The famed Zuni Salt Lake is cradled in a volcanic crater (maar) formed during this same period.

Different soils of various depths have been derived from the geological deposits exposed at the earth's surface. The soils in the Zuni River valley have been classified as excellent for irrigated agriculture, and consist of some of the best soils in the Zuni area. Mineral deposits formed by geological processes in the Zuni area have provided resources traditionally collected and used by the Zunis, including clays, pigments, obsidian, salt, and turquoise.

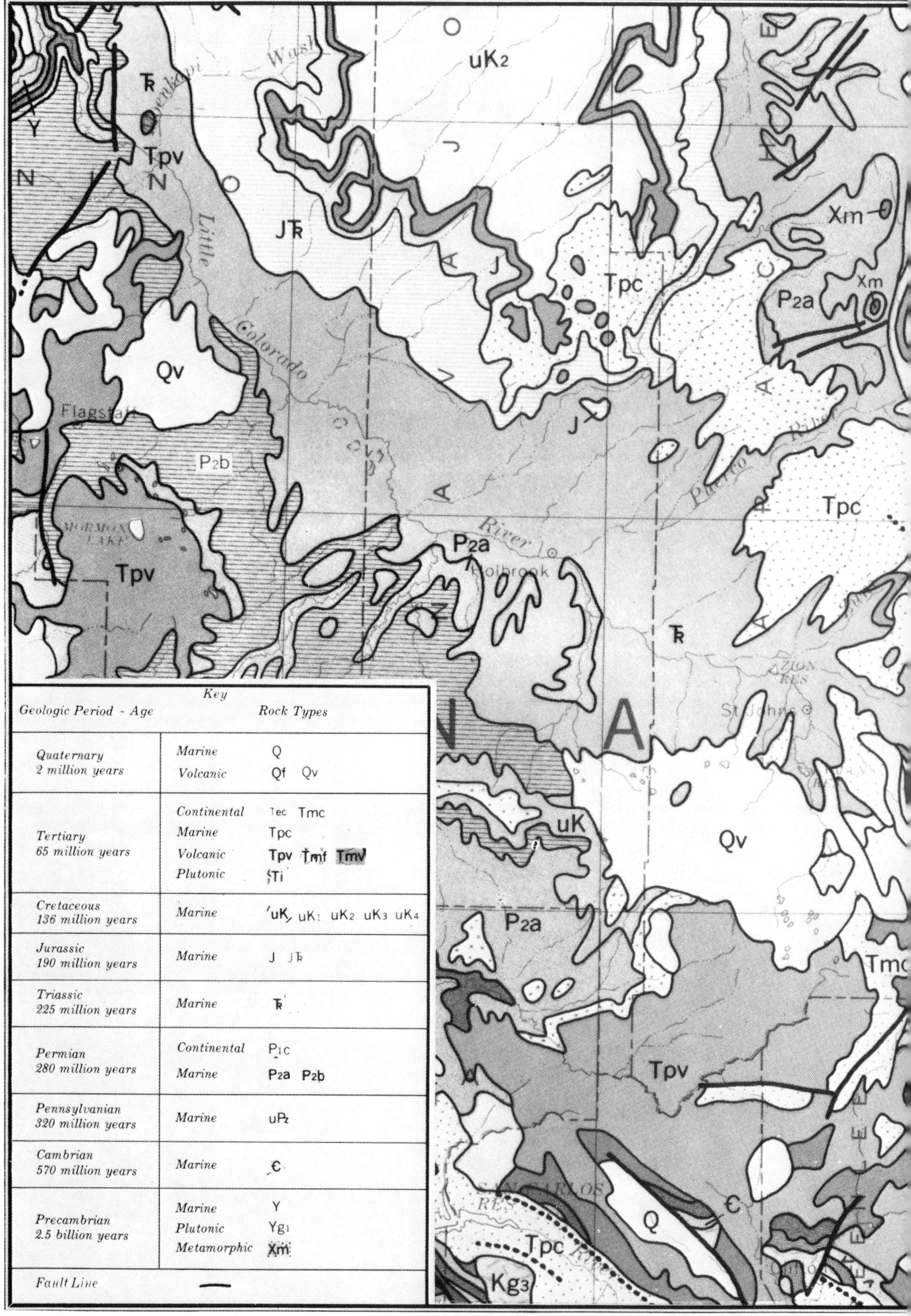
Wash
Little
Colorado
River
Flagstaff
MORMON LAKE
Holbrook
Puerco River
ZION RES
St Johns
SAN CARLOS RES
Key
Geologic Period - Age
Rock Types
Quaternary 2 million years
Marine Q
Volcanic Qf Qv
Tertiary 65 million years
Continental Tec Tmc
Marine Tpc
Volcanic Tpv Tmf Tmv
Plutonic Ti
Cretaceous 136 million years
Marine uK uK1 uK2 uK3 uK4
Jurassic 190 million years
Marine J JTR
Triassic 225 million years
Marine TR
Permian 280 million years
Continental P1c
Marine P2a P2b
Pennsylvanian 320 million years
Marine uPz
Cambrian 570 million years
Marine €
Precambrian 2.5 billion years
Marine Y
Plutonic Yg1
Metamorphic Xm
Fault Line

Map 3
GEOLOGY OF ZUNI AREA
0 10 20 30 40 mi.
Source: U.S. Geological Survey, Geological Map of the United States, 1974

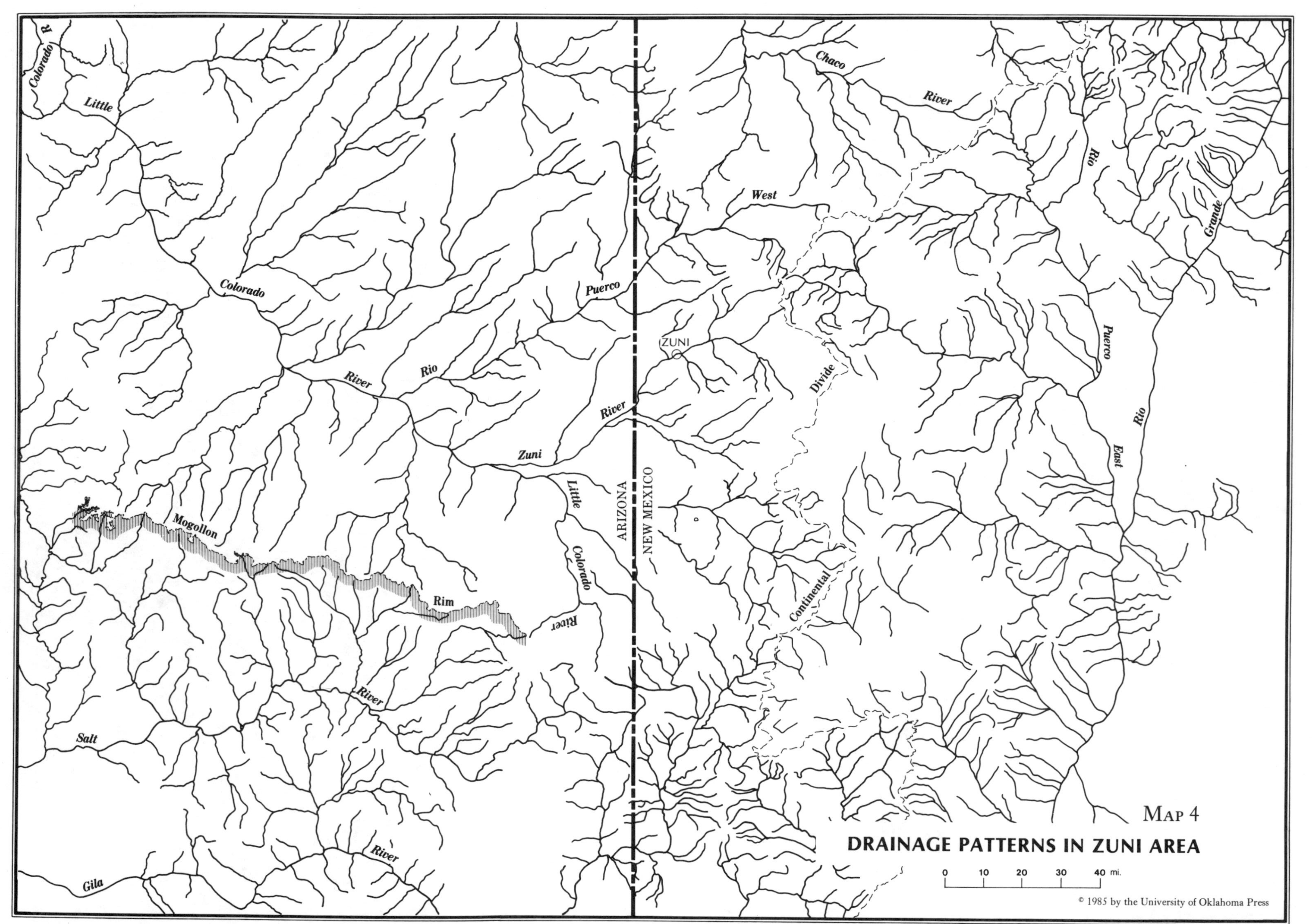

MAP 4
DRAINAGE PATTERNS IN ZUNI AREA

4. DRAINAGE PATTERNS IN THE ZUNI AREA

THE drainages of the Zuni region are separated into east- and west-flowing streams by the Continental Divide. To the east, streams flow toward the Rio Grande. To the west, they flow towards the Colorado, Salt, and Gila rivers. The Plains of San Agustin and the North Plains are closed basins; water flows into them, but no water flows out.

The major tributary river and stream basins adding to the water flow of the upper Little Colorado River include the drainages of the Carrizo Wash, Zuni River, Puerco River, Leroux Wash, and Pueblo Colorado Wash feeding into the Little Colorado River from the north, and the drainages of Concho Creek, Show Low Creek, Silver Creek, and Chevelon Creek draining the area south of the Little Colorado River to the Mogollon Rim. Today, many of the streams and rivers on the Colorado Plateau run only intermittently, and are nearly dry for long periods of the year. In the past, many of these streams probably carried a more continuous water flow than they do at present.

South of the Mogollon Rim, and in the mountains of the Mogollon Slope, the drainages feed the Salt and Gila rivers, which are tributary to the Colorado River. A number of important streams and rivers in this region flow year-round through the narrow valley bottoms. East of the Continental Divide, the drainage of the Rio San Jose flows into the Rio Puerco, which, like the Rio Salado and Jemez River, flows into the Rio Grande. The Rio Grande, originating in the high Rocky Mountains in southern Colorado, has a permanent water flow.

Important areas of water resources include all of the high mountain peaks in and around the Zuni region. The winter snows on these mountain peaks provide an important source of both surface water from runoff during the spring melt and recharge of subterranean aquifers. In general, water resources in the Zuni area become increasingly scarce at lower elevations.

Traditionally, surface runoff and stream flow were important sources of usable water throughout the Zuni area. Another origin of water available for human use was ground water exploited through wells or natural springs. In some parts of the Zuni region the underground water table is quite high, and can be tapped with shallow wells. In other areas, ground water is discharged through springs and seeps caused by faults and other geological structures. Before the advent of deep, drilled wells, human land use was in large measure governed by the availability of surface runoff and high water tables.

With respect to the hydrology of the Zuni area, it should be noted that the drainage of the Zuni Mountains, with a large watershed and heavily faulted geological structure, provides an area of relatively stable and accessible water resources, in contrast to many other parts of the arid Southwest. Runoff from the snowpack of the Zuni Mountains during the spring provides an important source of water, augmented by the output of copious springs at such places as Nutria, Pescado, and Ojo Caliente. In places along the Zuni River, the water table is less than twenty-five feet deep, and therefore easily accessible through hand-dug wells. Thus, while the Zuni River does not have a large and permanent stream flow along its whole length, the area it drains does encompass many important water resources.

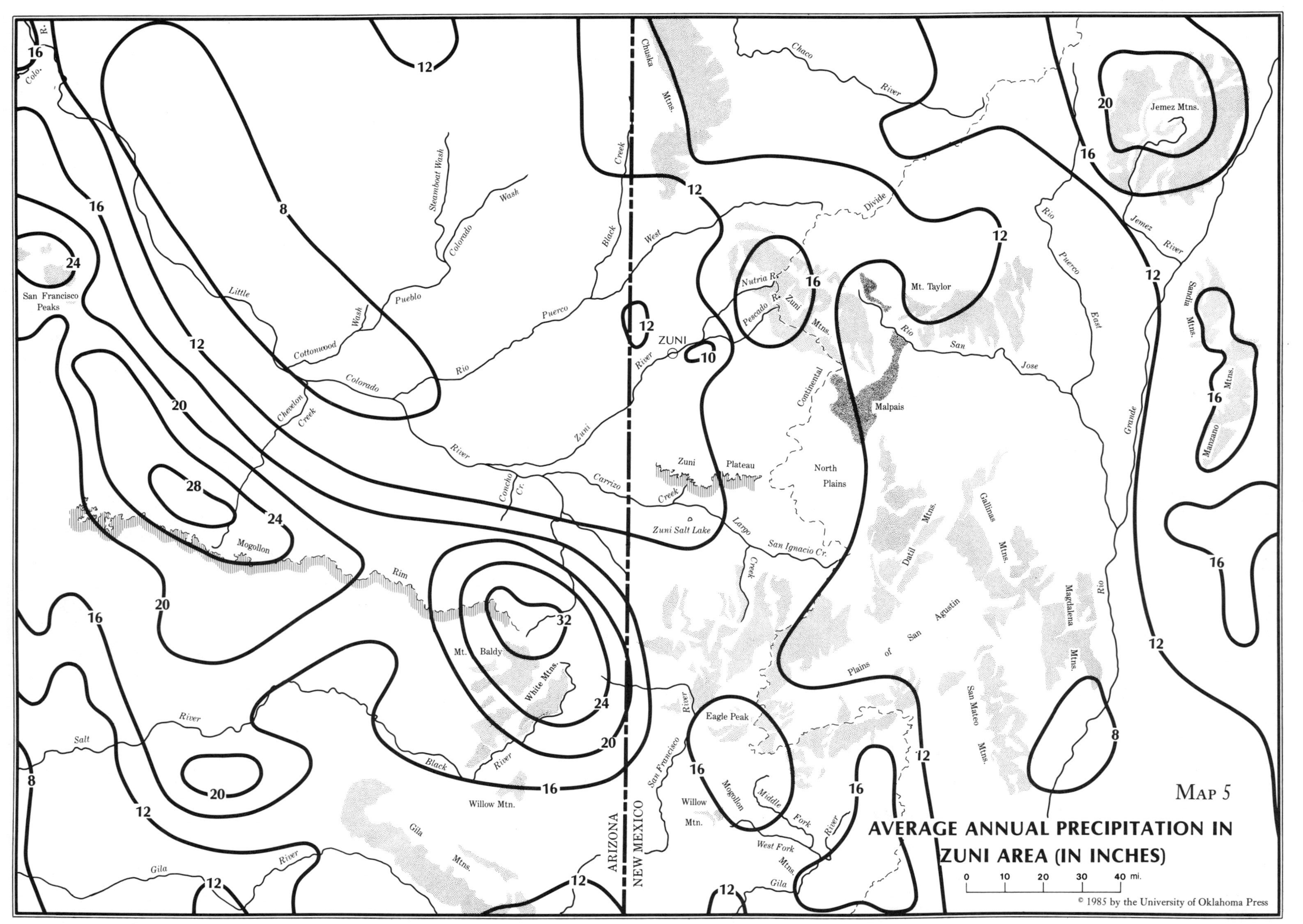

Map 5
AVERAGE ANNUAL PRECIPITATION IN ZUNI AREA (IN INCHES)

5. AVERAGE ANNUAL PRECIPITATION IN ZUNI AREA

PRECIPITATION in the form of rain and snow is one of the two most important aspects of the climate in the Zuni region. Temperature is the other. In general, the climate of this area can be characterized as being semi-arid and temperate. Much of the variability in climate is a result of the diverse topography of the landforms in the region.

There is a close geographical correspondence between elevation and precipitation in the Zuni territory, with the higher elevations receiving more rain and snow. Within the Zuni area, the highest average annual precipitation occurs in the mountain ranges above eight thousand feet elevation. Here the precipitation ranges from twenty-six to forty inches or more. Within the most favorable zone for human occupation, the valleys at six to seven thousand feet elevation that form an edge along the Colorado Plateau where it meets the mountain ranges, the annual precipitation averages from eleven to sixteen inches a year. The lowest amounts of precipitation occur in the western part of the Colorado Plateau where the elevations are less than fifty-five hundred feet. Here the annual precipitation averages eight inches or less a year.

In all parts of the Zuni area, the highest amounts of precipitation currently occur in July, August, and September, when forty to fifty percent of the precipitation falls in the form of late afternoon or evening thundershowers. These summer rainstorms can be very localized, torrential downpours, dumping so much water on such small areas that it runs off rapidly. Unless this rapid runoff is controlled, under certain conditions it can cause soil erosion and arroyo downcutting. The snowfall that occurs in the higher elevations from November to March also contributes important amounts of moisture. Winter precipitation often occurs as a slow drizzle that can last for days, resulting in heavy snowfall at high elevations. Winter precipitation allows moisture to be gradually absorbed by the soil, with a slow runoff as the snowpack melts in the spring. In general, the lowest amounts of precipitation fall in May and June.

One of the most important characteristics of precipitation in the Zuni area is its variability from year to year, regardless of elevation. Various locales in the Zuni region can erratically receive either much more or much less than the annual average they usually receive. For example, for the period 1951–60, precipitation recorded at Blackrock, five miles east of Zuni Pueblo, usually averaging 11.79 inches, ranged from 5.24 to 16.31 inches.

The areas affected by increased or decreased precipitation can be small and isolated, or they can be quite large. In addition to the great variability in annual rainfall between various places in the Zuni area, there are also longer-term climatic cycles of increasing or decreasing moisture, which have affected the entire region. The Zuni region and various sections of it have been subject to a number of severe droughts during the prehistoric and historic periods. This variability in precipitation requires human populations to be culturally and economically flexible if they are to successfully exploit the area on a long-term basis.

Zuni men at a "watermelon feast," near Hawikku in 1919. Photograph by F. W. Hodge, courtesy the Museum of the American Indian, Heye Foundation (Neg. No. 5822).

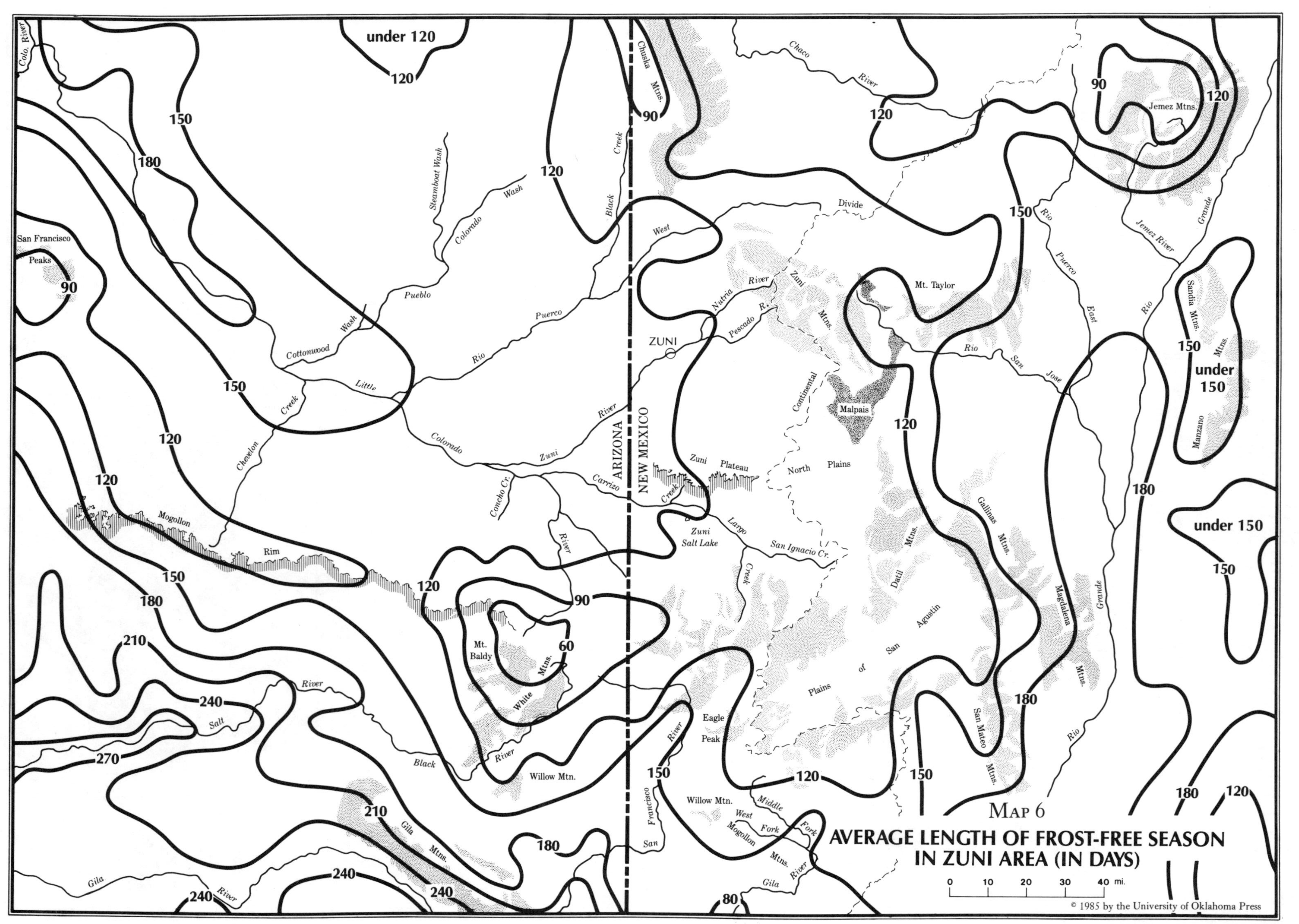

Map 6

AVERAGE LENGTH OF FROST-FREE SEASON IN ZUNI AREA (IN DAYS)

6. AVERAGE LENGTH OF FROST-FREE SEASON

TEMPERATURE is an important factor in the climate of the Zuni area because it controls the growth of vegetation and rate of evaporation. In the Zuni region, temperature has a much greater regularity than other environmental variables such as precipitation. The average temperatures are largely defined by latitude and altitude, with altitude being more important within the Zuni area. For every rise of a thousand feet in elevation, there is a decrease of 3.3 degrees F. in average annual temperature, with a corresponding lag of ten days of seasonal biological advance.

In general, the highest temperatures occur in July, the lowest in January. Daily temperature ranges are great, as much as 40 degrees or more, because of the clear, dry air that permits rapid gain and loss of heat. As measured at Blackrock, five miles east of Zuni Pueblo, the average daily temperature in the winter is 32 degrees F., while the average daily temperature in the summer is 69 degrees F., for a mean annual temperature of 50 degrees F. Average temperatures in areas of higher elevation are correspondingly lower, while the average temperature of areas at lower elevation are correspondingly higher.

Frost occurs when the temperature drops below 32 degrees F., important to the Zunis' agricultural pursuits because it kills annual plants and crops if severe enough. The length of the frost-free season between the last day of freezing temperature in the spring and the first day of freezing temperature in the fall provides one measure of the annual growing season. Zuni Pueblo, at 6,282 feet elevation, has an average frost-free season of close to 150 days. However, it should be noted that the actual growing season is somewhat less than the frost-free period, for plant growth generally will not occur below 40 degrees F., and the season with temperatures higher than this is shorter than the frost-free season.

The length of the frost-free season depends partially on elevation, and it is generally longer in the lower, western part of the Zuni region and along the lower Rio Grande. Frost is also highly dependent on local wind conditions and terrain, and the length of the frost-free season in a particular locale can be greatly decreased by topography that acts as a cold air drainage, or by exposure to freezing winds. Like precipitation, and actually associated with it, the length of the frost-free season is quite variable from year to year. In general, years of greater than normal precipitation are accompanied by a shorter than average frost-free season, while years of less than normal precipitation are accompanied by a longer than average frost-free season.

While the difference in the length of the frost-free season among the various locales in the Zuni area is sometimes slight, over the long run it can be very significant. A difference of a few days in the length of the frost-free season can be vital to the production of agricultural crops such as corn, which has a long maturation period. An average frost-free season of at least 120 days is generally considered necessary for corn agriculture to be successfully practiced in the Southwest.

In the semi-arid climate of the Southwest, temperature also has a great effect on evaporation of moisture from soils and plants, and this too can affect natural vegetation and agriculture. High temperatures during the spring and summer, augmented by strong dry winds that also cause evaporation, tend to dessicate vegetation and dry up available moisture. As a result, in areas with long growing seasons, sufficient moisture for agriculture is often lacking. The factors of altitude, terrain, and winds, in conjunction with patterns of precipitation, often produce adverse conditions for the growth of vegetation in the Zuni area. Long-term agriculture can be successfully practiced in only a few select locations.

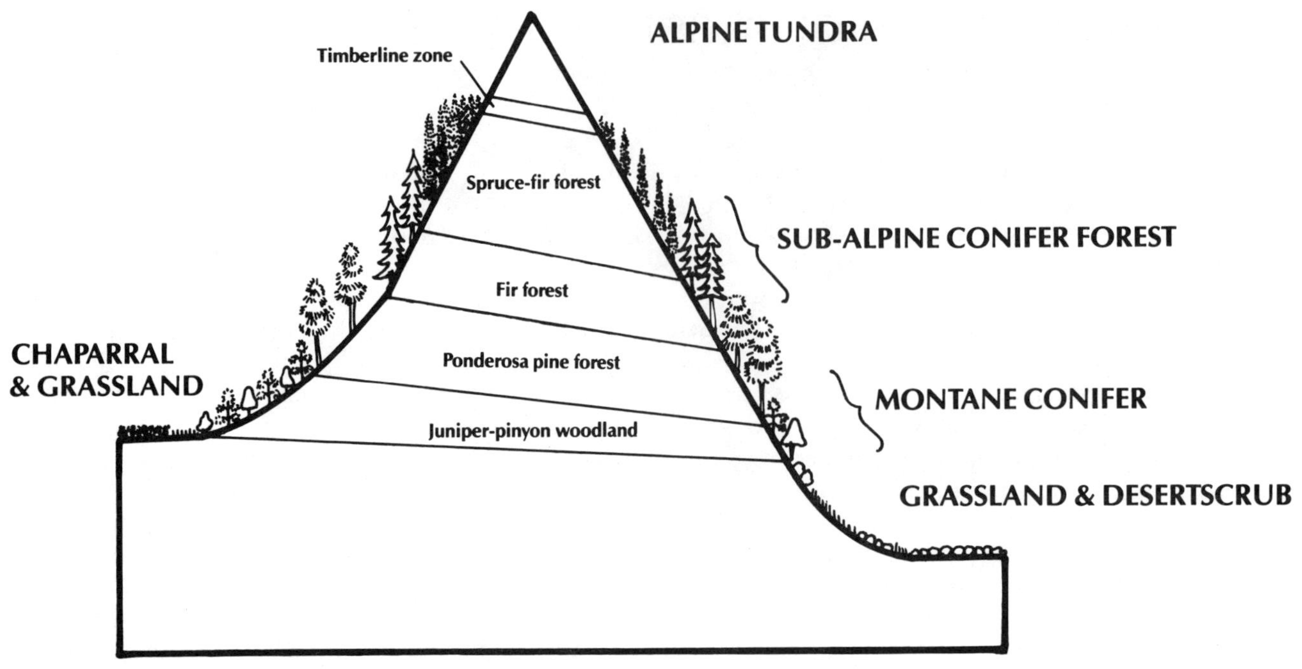

FIGURE 1. *Schematic Profile of typical biotic communities based on elevation and dominant vegetation. Adapted from Charles H. Lowe,* Arizona's Natural Environment, *University of Arizona Press, 1964.*

7. BIOTIC COMMUNITIES OF ZUNI AREA

PLANTS and animals live and function together in natural biotic communities. Because native perennial vegetation is a sensitive and mappable indicator of environmental controls such as climate, soil, and topography, plants provide a way to classify environments also inhabited by animals—hence the entire biotic community. In the Southwest, biotic communities are organized hierarchically, largely on the basis of temperature and available moisture. In general, total precipitation (and available moisture) increases and temperature decreases as elevation increases. Thus, in the Southwest, biotic communities are primarily structured by altitude. The classification used to map biotic communities is based upon the ecological formation of vegetation into tundra, forest, woodland, scrubland, and grassland, and is differentiated on the basis of dominant types of vegetation.

Ten biotic communities are found in the primary area of Zuni land use, and an additional six biotic communities are located in adjacent lands. Each biotic community contains many species of plants and animals distributed in a mosaic of associations. Specific plants dominant in one biotic community often occur as minor associations in other communities. Similarly, the rich animal and bird life of the Zuni area often ranges into two or more biotic communities. The biotic diversity of the Zuni area provides many valuable plant and animal resources for human use. The following discussion of biotic communities in the Zuni area is organized by elevation, beginning with the highest landscapes.

Alpine tundra makes up a small fraction of the total Zuni area, and is located only on the San Francisco Peaks above the tree line, which varies from 11,000 to 11,500 feet, based on exposure. The extreme cold of the high altitude tundra decreases the moisture available for plants, and permits only low shrubs, lichens, and mosses to grow.

Below the alpine tundra is the moister *sub-alpine conifer* forest consisting of Douglas fir–white fir (8,000 to 10,000 feet) and spruce fir–alpine fir (8,500 to 11,500 feet) forest, with tall trees and closed canopies that shelter an understory of various shrubs, herbs, and grasses. These two types of coniferous forests intermingle in the high mountains ringing the Zuni area, including the San Francisco Peaks, White Mountains, Chuska Mountains, Mogollon Slope, Mt. Taylor, Sandia, and Jemez Mountains.

The *montane conifer forest,* composed of ponderosa pine accompanied by many shrubs, herbs, grasses, and occasional oak, juniper, and pinyon trees, covers a large portion of the Zuni area between six and nine thousand feet elevation. The montane conifer forest covers much of the mountain landscape along the Mogollon Rim and the Mogollon Slope, as well as in the Zuni, Cebolleta, and Jemez Mountains.

Below the montane conifer forest, at an elevation from five to seven thousand feet, is the *Great Basin conifer* woodland consisting of relatively small, widely-spaced juniper and pinyon trees, often occurring in open savannahs with grasses and herbs. The juniper-pinyon woodland covers much of the Colorado Plateau and also occurs beneath the Mogollon Rim and along the Mogollon Slope,

The *Madrean evergreen woodland,* dominated by an oak-juniper association of trees accompanied by numerous chapparal shrubs, occurs in small amounts at the edge of the mountainous zone between the Mogollon Rim and Mogollon Slope and the Basin and Range Province. A riparian woodland characterized by cottonwood, willow, and walnut trees occurs along watercourses throughout the Zuni area.

The *Great Basin montane scrub vegetation* consisting of oak and other small trees and shrubs occurs in a very small area on the west slope of the Sandia Mountains. The related dense shrubby growth of California chaparral and interior chaparral occurs at an elevation of between four and six thousand feet outside the primary Zuni area below the Mogollon Rim, and in a small area east of the Magdelena Mountains.

The *Plains and Great Basin grassland* occurs at five to seven thousand feet of elevation in a large area of the Colorado Plateau, as well as in the Plains of San Agustin and the Rio Grande valley. This well developed grassland includes grasses like gramma, fescue, dropseed, wheatgrass, muhly, brome, and galleta. Above seven thousand feet a sub-alpine grassland exists in open areas of the coniferous forest. Below five thousand feet in the Rio Grande valley and south of the Mogollon Rim, semi-desert grassland contains large areas of bare ground. Today, many overgrazed grasslands are being invaded by shrubs like sage and rabbitbrush and trees like juniper and pinyon.

On the lower parts of the Colorado Plateau, at an elevation of three to six thousand feet, the Great Basin desertscrub occurs, characterized by shrubs and grasses separated by areas devoid of vegetation and dominated by sagebrush, mormon tea, greasewood, four-wing saltbush, rabbitbrush, and yucca. This biotic community also occurs in parts of the valleys of the Zuni and Puerco rivers. Growing in a small area at the bottom of the Grand Canyon below thirty-five hundred feet elevation is the Mohave desertscrub, with creosote, bur-sage, yucca, and cacti as the dominant vegetation. The Chihuahuan desertscrub and the Lower Colorado and Arizona Upland subdivisions of the Sonoran desertscrub occur in the Basin and Range country bordering the Zuni area.

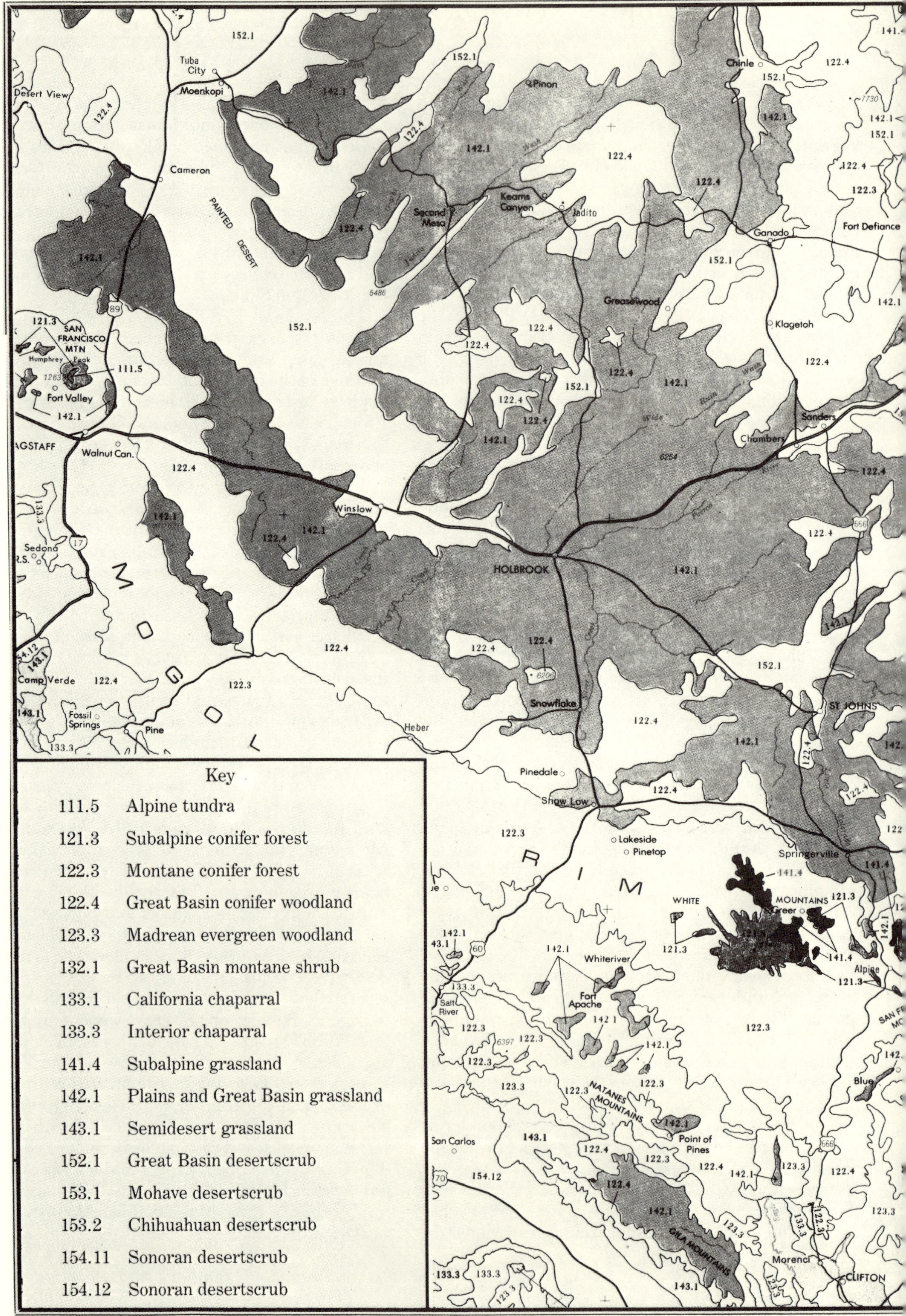
Key
111.5 Alpine tundra
121.3 Subalpine conifer forest
122.3 Montane conifer forest
122.4 Great Basin conifer woodland
123.3 Madrean evergreen woodland
132.1 Great Basin montane shrub
133.1 California chaparral
133.3 Interior chaparral
141.4 Subalpine grassland
142.1 Plains and Great Basin grassland
143.1 Semidesert grassland
152.1 Great Basin desertscrub
153.1 Mohave desertscrub
153.2 Chihuahuan desertscrub
154.11 Sonoran desertscrub
154.12 Sonoran desertscrub
Tuba City
Moenkopi
Desert View
Cameron
PAINTED DESERT
Pinon
Chinle
Keams Canyon
Jadito
Second Mesa
Ganado
Fort Defiance
Greasewood
Klagetoh
SAN FRANCISCO MTN
Humphrey Peak
Fort Valley
Walnut Can.
Winslow
Sanders
Chambers
Sedona
Camp Verde
Fossil Springs
Pine
Heber
HOLBROOK
Snowflake
ST JOHNS
Pinedale
Show Low
Lakeside
Pinetop
Springerville
WHITE MOUNTAINS
Greer
Alpine
Whiteriver
Fort Apache
Salt River
NATANES MOUNTAINS
Point of Pines
San Carlos
GILA MOUNTAINS
Morenci
CLIFTON
Blue
M O G O L L O N R I M

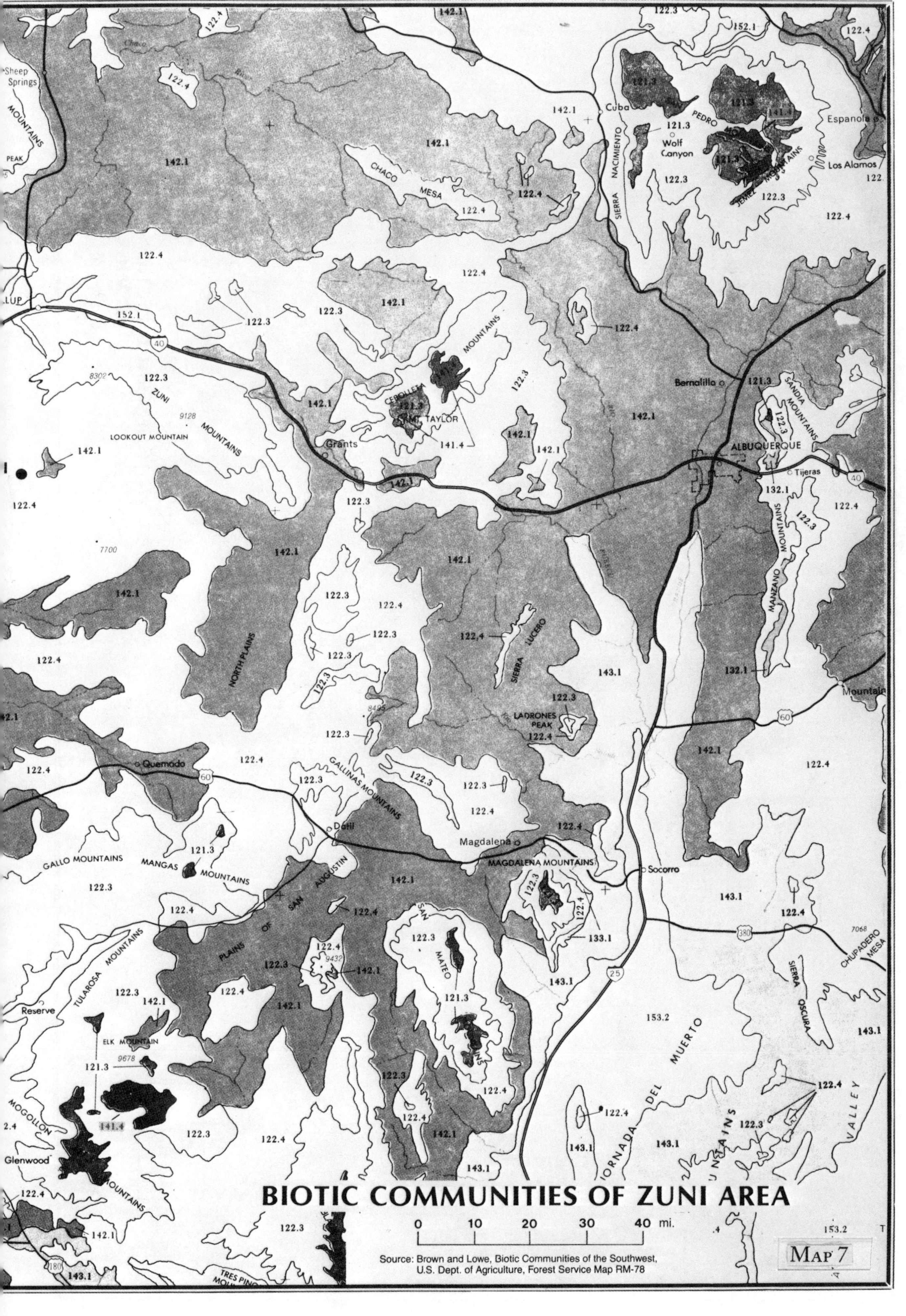

BIOTIC COMMUNITIES OF ZUNI AREA

MAP 7

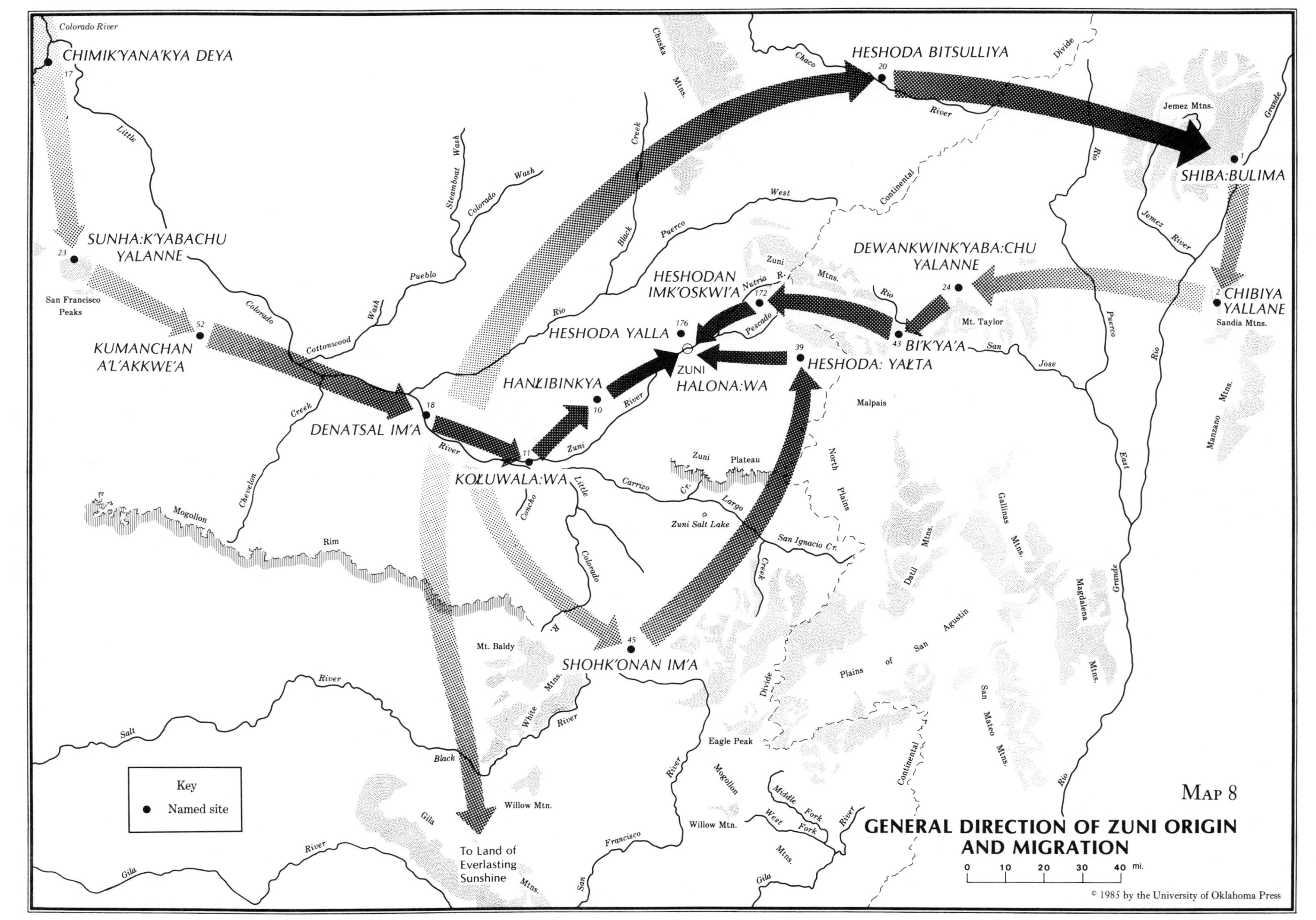
CHIMIK'YANA'KYA DEYA
17
SUNHA:K'YABACHU
YALANNE
23
San Francisco
Peaks
KUMANCHAN
A'L'AKKWE'A
52
DENATSAL IM'A
18
KOŁUWALA:WA
11
HANŁIBINKYA
10
HESHODA YALLA
176
ZUNI
HALONA:WA
HESHODAN
IMK'OSKWI'A
172
HESHODA: YAŁTA
39
BI'K'YA'A
43
DEWANKWINK'YABA:CHU
YALANNE
24
HESHODA BITSULLIYA
20
SHIBA:BULIMA
1
CHIBIYA
YALLANE
2
SHOHK'ONAN IM'A
45
To Land of
Everlasting
Sunshine
Colorado River
Little
Colorado
Steamboat Wash
Colorado Wash
Pueblo
Wash
Cottonwood
Creek
Chevelon
Mogollon
Rim
Black Creek
Puerco
Rio
West
Chuska Mtns.
Chaco
River
Divide
Continental
Jemez Mtns.
Grande
Rio
Jemez River
Puerco
Rio
Sandia Mtns.
Manzano Mtns.
East
Mt. Taylor
San Jose
Rio
Zuni Mtns.
Nutria R.
Pescado
Zuni River
Malpais
Zuni Plateau
Carrizo Cr.
Largo
Zuni Salt Lake
San Ignacio Cr.
Creek
Concho
Little Colorado R.
North Plains
Datil Mtns.
Gallinas Mtns.
Magdalena Mtns.
Plains of San Agustin
San Mateo Mtns.
Divide
Continental
Mt. Baldy
White Mtns.
River
Salt River
Black
Willow Mtn.
Gila
Gila River
San Francisco
Mtns.
Eagle Peak
Mogollon
Willow Mtn.
Middle Fork
West Fork
River
Mtns.
Gila
Key
Named site
Map 8
GENERAL DIRECTION OF ZUNI ORIGIN AND MIGRATION
0 10 20 30 40 mi.

8. GENERAL DIRECTION OF ZUNI ORIGIN AND MIGRATION

THERE are two sources of knowledge about the origin of the Zuni people and their migration to the middle place of Zuni Pueblo. The first source consists of oral traditions handed down within the tribe, and these are the subject of Map 8. The second source consists of archaeological research, a subject treated separately in Map 9. The Zuni accounts of tribal origin and migration, the *chimik'yanakona penane,* are known in general outline by all tribal members and in greater detail by members of the several religious groups. Each religious group recites its own origin account that summarizes early tribal history and provides the religious sanction for their organization and rituals. Thus, instead of a single origin account there are many accounts, accentuating and elaborating on different aspects of the same general story according to the special knowledge of individual narrators. The basic tenets common to the various origin accounts create an overall concordance between them. The origin accounts of the *chimik'yanakona penane* embody sacred truth, and as such are differentiated by the Zuni people from folk tales or *telapnane.*

Map 8 provides a graphic summary of the migration of the Zuni people as it can be reconstructed from the several versions of the Zuni origin account that have been recorded. It is a composite depiction of the routes of early migration, combining features that are described in different versions of the origin account. Two important characteristics of the information illustrated in Map 8 should be kept in mind to assure that the map is not misinterpreted or taken to represent more than it is intended to mean.

First, Map 8 illustrates a simplified and generalized synthesis of the information contained in the Zuni origin accounts. It is simplified because there are many more places mentioned in the religious prayers that preserve the origin accounts than appear on Map 8, but the exact locations of many of these places are no longer known. For instance, in the prayers there are over thirty springs and stopping places mentioned between the place of emergence, *Chimik'yana'kya deya,* and the middle place of Zuni Pueblo, or *Halona:Itiwana.* Only six of these places, whose locations are well known, are illustrated in Map 8. Since different versions of the origin account occasionally describe a particular event as occurring at different places, it was necessary to generalize the main thrust of direction. For instance, most origin and migration accounts describe a time when the tribe split into subgroups before continuing the search for the middle place, with one group going south never to return. This event is described variously as occurring at *Kumanchan A'l'akkwe'a, Denatsal Im'a, Kołuwala:wa, Hanłibinkya.* What is important in terms of Map 8 is that all of these places are located to the west of Zuni in the valley of the upper Little Colorado River, and it is in this general area that the split is depicted.

Second, the referents to the places mentioned in the origin and migration account are more metaphorical than literal. For example, while some origin accounts tell of the emergence of the Zuni into this world through a hole in the Grand Canyon and other accounts place the emergence further down the Colorado River in the Mohave Desert, both places are referred to as *Chimik'yana'kya deya,* the Place of Beginning. What is important is the powerful use of metaphor and not the fact that two separate places of emergence are given in the different versions of the origin accounts. The *chimik'yanakona penane* make the important point that all life, including that of humans, ultimately derives from the earth. The essentially symbolic nature of the origin and migration accounts is recognized by many Zuni elders who know and explain the origin talks. After providing a list of the places referenced in his origin account, one Zuni religious leader commented, "These are the places that are mentioned and places that are discussed as a trail, but it is a religious idea, or religious trail that is recited in the prayer and not an actual path of people walking on the trail." Another religious leader in a similar circumstance remarked, "The trail or the road is one of . . . symbolic nature. The place names along the symbolic trail are the ones we have been talking about, the actual road is not the same as the symbolic road."

The symbolic character of the origin and migration accounts do not lessen their power and value. The *chimik'yanakona penane* create a symbolic bond between the Zuni people and their environment and provide an "historical" context for their tribal customs and organization. The following is a brief general account of the Zuni origin and migration, focusing on the sweeping direction of movement.

The Zuni people were created and first noticed in the fourth and innermost world or womb. When fire was first discovered and light first lit up this dark, deep place, the people discovered they were covered with slime, had webs on their hands and feet, had tails, and that their genitals were improperly placed on their foreheads. It was a great struggle for the Zunis, as their immortal gods led them up through the third womb, then the second womb, and finally through the first womb and into the light of the Sun Father on the surface of Earth Mother. After the Zunis emerged into the bright day, the slime was washed from their bodies, the webs of their hands and feet were split, and the people were finally rearranged until they appeared as people do today.

The Zuni people emerged from the fourth underworld deep within a canyon along the Colorado River.

La'pi'lawa (string-of-feathers) dance at Ojo Caliente, 1919. Photograph by F. W. Hodge, courtesy the Museum of the American Indian, Heye Foundation (Neg. No. 5842).

But the Zuni, or Ashiwi, as they call themselves, were still far from their home. They began a journey through the canyons and deserts of what is now Arizona and New Mexico in search of the middle place, the center of the world, the mid-most spot among all of the great oceans and lands, the spot in the middle of all the heavens of the universe, a spot destined to be their home. As the people traveled from locale to locale, searching for the middle place, they stopped and built villages and stayed in them for "four days and four nights" (which, according to those who know the narratives, actually means four years). Each stream or spring, each ancient village site, each stopping place on the origin trail of the Zunis became a sacred shrine, still remembered in prayers, and at which offerings are still left when the Zuni people return to them.

From *Chimik'yana'kya deya,* or the Place of Origin, the people traveled to *Sunha:k'yabachu Yalanne,* or the San Francisco Peaks, where the Zunis were given certain medicine plants. From there they traveled westward up the valley of *Kyawanahononnai,* "red river" or the Little Colorado River, to *Kumanchan A'l'akkwe'a,* and from there to *Denatsal Im'a,* at which another important medicine plant is found. While staying at one of the origin places in the Little Colorado River valley, the Zuni people were given a choice between accepting a gift of a very plain egg or an egg with beautiful blue spots. One group of the Zunis chose the beautiful egg, out of which hatched a black raven, to the dismay of the people. Out of the very plain egg hatched a colorful parrot with spectacular feathers, and the brothers and sisters who had chosen this egg journeyed southward into the Land of Everlasting Sunshine, never to return. The Zunis who had chosen the beautiful egg continued their search for the mid-most place.

As the Zunis resumed their journey they split into three groups. One group continued up the Little Colorado River to where it is joined by the Zuni River. Here is located *Kołuwala:wa,* a lake under which lies the village of *Kokko,* more commonly called *Katchinas,* the gods of the Zunis. After death, Zunis return to *Kołuwala:wa* to live as deities in the pueblo beneath the waters, where colorful dances and beautiful singing take place. Special offerings are still made and prayers are still given during regular quadrennial pilgrimages of religious leaders to *Kołuwala:wa.*

From *Kołuwala:wa,* the group journeying directly to the middle place went to *Hanłibinkya,* and here the Zuni clans were named. The petroglyph symbols of the clans are still visible in the sandstone canyon of *Hanłibinkya,* where they were carved in ancient times. Also at *Hanłibinkya,* the *Ahayuda,* or twin gods of war, were created by the Sun Father in the foam of a water freshet cascading over the steep cliffs of the canyon. The twin War Gods assisted the Zuni people as they moved from *Hanłibinkya* to the next place, for there were already people at *Heshoda Yalla,* and they tried violently to oppose the Zunis on their quest for the middle place. In an epic battle the Zuni people overcame these other people, with the assistance of the War Gods, taking some of them into the Zuni tribe. While *Heshoda Yalla* was close to the middle place, it was not the middle place, and thus the Zunis continued their journey until they settled *Halona:Itiwana,* the middle place, now called Zuni Pueblo.

As the central body of Zunis journeyed directly from *Kołuwala:wa* to *Halona:Itiwana,* other groups followed a different trail. To the south a group of Zunis went with the *Newe:kwe,* or Galaxy Fraternity. This group traveled along the valley of the upper Little Colorado River to the great round valley beneath *Shohk'onan Im'a,* "Flute Mountain" or Escudilla Peak, and from there northward to *Heshoda Yałta,* on top of *A'ts'ina* or El Morro, in the *Aqualhenna:yalla:we,* or the Zuni Mountains. From here the southern group rejoined the central body of the Zunis in the middle place.

To the north went a group of Zunis with the *Lhewe:kwe* and *Make:lhanna:kwe,* the Sword Swallower and Big Fire Societies. This northern group fought their way into *Ukyawanannai,* the valley of the "snow water river" or the Puerco River valley, and continued beyond with the Bow Priests sweeping danger out of the way, stopping in such places as *Heshoda Bitsulliya* or Chaco Canyon. They journeyed to *Shiba:bulima* in the Jemez Mountains, called *He:mushina Yalla:we* by the Zuni people. *Shiba:bulima* is the origin place of many medicine societies, as well as the prey animals. From *Shiba:bulima,* the trail of the northern group led down the Rio Grande, where *Chibiya Yallane,* a place belonging to the *Shu:ma:kwe,* is located in the Sandia Mountains. From there the trail led to *Dewankwink'yaba:chu Yalanne,* or Mt. Taylor, which is an important source of medicine plants, and to the spring called *Bi'k'ya'a* at the east end of the Zuni Mountains. The northern group eventually stopped at *Heshodan Imk'oskwi'a,* where they found the central body of the Zunis dwelling nearby. The northern group rejoined the other Zunis, and the tribe was reunited in the middle place.

When the journey of the Zuni people brought them close to the middle place *K'yan'asdebi,* a water spider, assisted them in finding the exact center point, *Itiwana.* The water spider spread his legs out until he reached the four oceans in the east, west, south, and north, and also touched the zenith and nadir. When he had thus spread out to find the six cardinal directions, his heart was over the long-sought middle place, and it was here that the Zunis settled for the final time. The Zunis had finally ended their quest for the middle place, but all of the spots they visited during the long journey remain sacred to the people.

Zuni woman with olla *(water jar), ca. 1915–18. Photograph by Pennington Studio, Durango, Colorado, courtesy the Maxwell Museum (Neg. No. 4.ZI.24).*

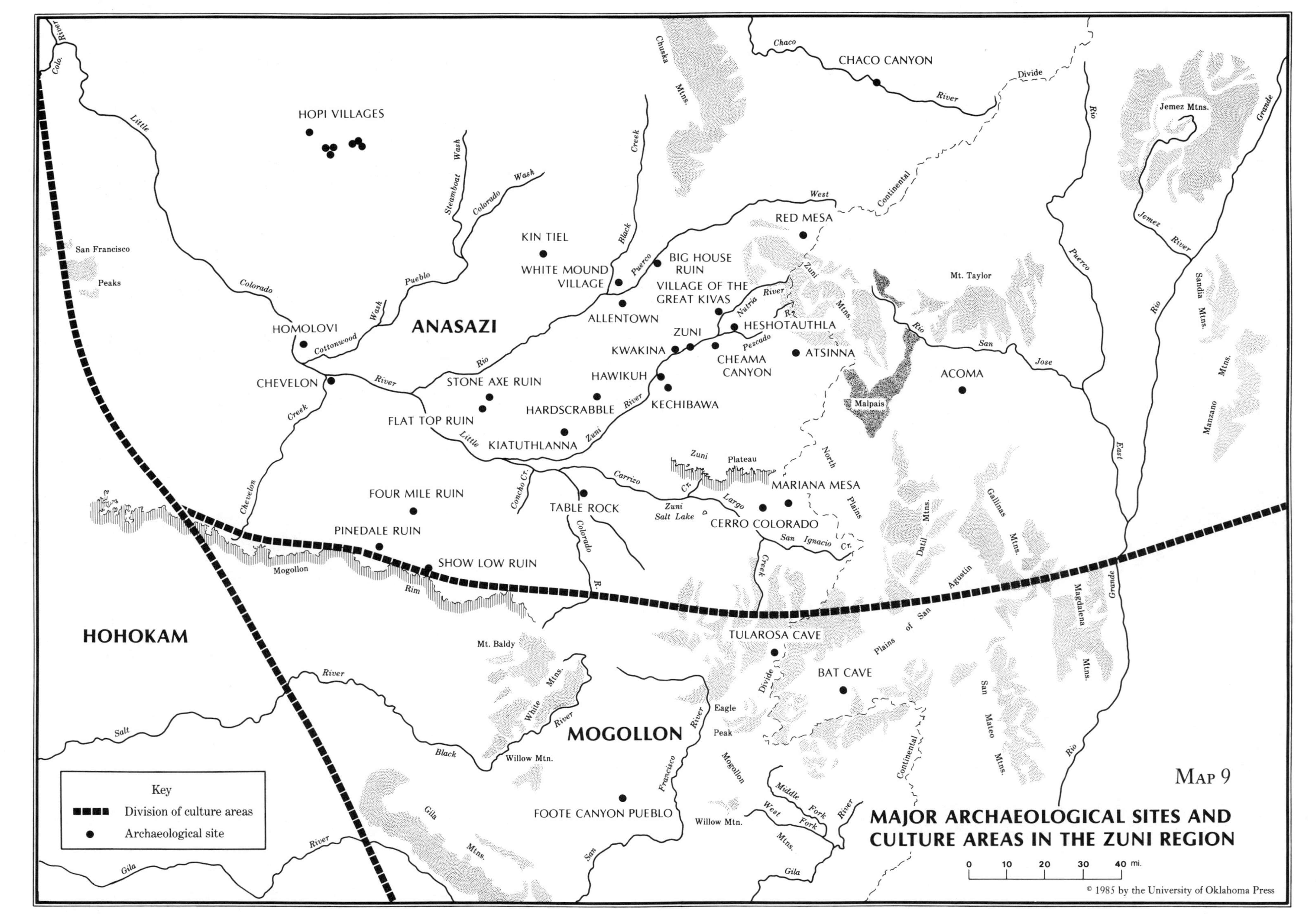

HOPI VILLAGES
KIN TIEL
WHITE MOUND VILLAGE
BIG HOUSE RUIN
VILLAGE OF THE GREAT KIVAS
ALLENTOWN
ZUNI
HESHOTAUTHLA
KWAKINA
ATSINNA
CHEAMA CANYON
HAWIKUH
KECHIBAWA
STONE AXE RUIN
HARDSCRABBLE
FLAT TOP RUIN
KIATUTHLANNA
HOMOLOVI
CHEVELON
CHACO CANYON
RED MESA
ACOMA
ANASAZI
FOUR MILE RUIN
PINEDALE RUIN
SHOW LOW RUIN
TABLE ROCK
MARIANA MESA
CERRO COLORADO
TULAROSA CAVE
BAT CAVE
FOOTE CANYON PUEBLO
HOHOKAM
MOGOLLON
Mt. Taylor
Malpais
Jemez Mtns.
Sandia Mtns.
Manzano Mtns.
Chuska Mtns.
Zuni Mtns.
Zuni Plateau
North Plains
Zuni Salt Lake
Datil Mtns.
Gallinas Mtns.
Plains of San Agustin
Magdalena Mtns.
San Mateo Mtns.
Mt. Baldy
White Mtns.
Willow Mtn.
Eagle Peak
Mogollon Mtns.
Gila Mtns.
Mogollon Rim
San Francisco Peaks
Continental Divide
Key
Division of culture areas
Archaeological site
Map 9
MAJOR ARCHAEOLOGICAL SITES AND CULTURE AREAS IN THE ZUNI REGION
0 10 20 30 40 mi.
© 1985 by the University of Oklahoma Press

9. MAJOR ARCHAEOLOGICAL SITES AND CULTURE AREAS IN THE ZUNI REGION

ARCHAEOLOGISTS study the distribution and patterns of artifacts and other material culture discarded by past peoples. At the present time, archaeologists can only trace the cultural antecedents of the Zuni people on a broad regional basis, because the data and analytical techniques necessary to trace the movement of a particular group of people from site to site in the long prehistoric era have not yet been developed. Given this limitation and the essentially symbolic nature of the Zuni origin accounts, it is not possible to specifically correlate archaeological culture history with the Zuni accounts of origin and migration. In general, however, the Zuni origin accounts and archaeological culture history share certain basic and major themes, including an economic shift from hunting and gathering to corn agriculture, the prevailing movement of people across the landscape, occasional violence and hostility between groups of people, and the assimilation of two cultural traditions with Zuni culture. The following is a brief synopsis of archaeological culture history in the Zuni area.

The earliest evidence for human use of the Zuni area dates to the Paleo-Indian period before 5000 B.C. A few large spear points dating from this period have been found as isolated artifacts on the mesas surrounding Zuni Pueblo, but, in general, Paleo-Indian sites are concentrated in the more open grasslands to the east and west of Zuni in the drainages of the Rio Grande and the Little Colorado rivers and their tributaries. During the Paleo-Indian period, the subsistence economy was based on hunting and gathering, and the population density of the Southwest was relatively low. Small groups of people ranged extensively across the countryside, exploiting animal and plant resources as they became available through the seasons.

During the Archaic period, dating from approximately 5000 B.C. to A.D. 1, the population of the Southwest gradually increased. Hunting and gathering remained the basic way of life, although sometime after 2000 B.C. agriculture came into use as the cultivation of corn, and later beans and squash, was introduced into the Southwest from peoples in highland Mexico. These domesticated plants are found in Archaic sites such as Bat Cave and Tularosa Cave in the mountains of the Mogollon Slope. Agriculture was initially adopted as a backup food production system to supplement the wild food obtained through hunting and gathering, and remained of secondary economic importance throughout the Archaic period. People planted corn, beans, and squash in small amounts, but did not depend on them for their livelihood.

The Archaic period ended about A.D. 1, when agriculture started to become a more important part of the subsistence system. Pit houses, a type of building excavated into the ground and roofed with wood and adobe, appeared at this time, usually accompanied by large storage pits. These architectural features indicate that people were beginning to grow enough food to store, and were probably spending the winters in the vicinity of their farms, while hunting and gathering during other parts of the year. One of these early pit-house sites is located along Hardscrabble Wash, a tributary drainage of the Zuni River. As the land filled up with people through the natural increase in population, the mobility and resources of hunter-gatherers were constrained, and this condition contributed to the gradual development of a sedentary agricultural way of life in the millenium after A.D. 1.

The production of pottery in the Southwest began around A.D. 200, and after this time regional cultures developed that can be distinguished from each other on the basis of material culture. The Anasazi cultural tradition developed in the north part of the Zuni area, and is distinguished by a ceramic complex including grayware utility pottery and black-on-white decorated pottery. The Anasazi cultural tradition also was associated with circular kivas or ceremonial chambers. The Mogollon cultural tradition developed in the southern part of the Zuni area, and was associated with brownware utility pottery, redware decorated pottery, and square kivas. The Hohokam cultural tradition that developed in the Basin and Range Province of southern Arizona was associated with buffware pottery. All of these Southwestern cultural traditions that developed after the advent of pottery shared a trend toward increasing village sedentism and agriculture. The Anasazi and Mogollon cultural traditions probably each encompassed a number of separate tribes that shared a common base of material culture but probably had different customs.

The population that settled in the drainage of the Zuni River was initially part of the Anasazi cultural tradition. By A.D. 650, small villages of pit houses began to be located on mesa benches and other elevated land forms in the immediate vicinity of what later became Zuni Pueblo. These early village settlements were similar to other Anasazi sites such as the Flattop site in the Petrified Forest and the Cerro Colorado site in the Carrizo Creek drainage south of Zuni. By A.D. 700 to 900, Anasazi villages containing deep pit houses with associated above-ground masonry storage bins began to be constructed in the alluvial valley bottoms. At this time, sites in the Zuni drainage were similar to other Anasazi sites in adjacent drainages such as White Mound Village and Allantown, near the Puerco River, and Kiatuthlanna, near the confluence of the Zuni and Little Colorado rivers. The pit-house villages of this time contained many granaries and grinding stones, indicating the increased importance of facilities and tools to store and process agricultural produce, although hunting and the collection of wild plant foods were still important in the overall subsistence system. The presence of jewelry made of shell from the Pacific Ocean and the Gulf of California is evidence that these early pit-house villages were tied into a large regional trade network extending throughout the larger Southwest. In the Zuni area, these villages were associated with a series of decorated black-on-white pottery types known as the Cibola Whitewares.

After A.D. 900 in the Anasazi area, above-ground masonry buildings began to replace pit houses as the most prevalent house form. The masonry pueblos built at this time apparently developed out of the earlier above-ground masonry storage bins. Circular subterranean structures were retained, although their function changed from domestic use to ceremonial use as a kiva. The typical site plan from this period encompassed a small four- to twelve-room house fronted by a circular underground kiva with a trash mound to the south or southeast. The change from pit-house villages to above-ground masonry pueblos can be seen at sites like Kiatuthlanna and Allantown, as well as in the Red Mesa Valley along the Puerco River and in Cheama Canyon, east of Zuni Pueblo. Literally thousands of these small sites were occupied in the Anasazi area at this time, and in the Zuni region most of these sites are associated with Cibola Whitewares and a decorated, red-slipped pottery known as the White Mountain Redware. The large number of these small sites suggests that people shifted their homes around the landscape fairly frequently, perhaps in response to small changes in the amount of annual rainfall or salinization of farm fields.

From A.D. 900 to 1150, many of the small Anasazi house sites in the Zuni drainage appear to have been organized into communities oriented around a large public building with an associated Great Kiva, a very large ceremonial chamber. The Village of the Great Kivas along the Nutria River is one example of this kind of community center. These centers, in turn, were organized into a large regional trade and exchange system, with its center at Chaco Canyon in the San Juan Basin. For reasons not entirely clear, the Chaco System was reorganized during the twelfth century, and the San Juan Basin was abandoned as a location of habitation sites.

After A.D. 1150, the people living in the Zuni drainage reoriented their trade and began to interact more with other people living along the Mogollon Rim and in the mountains of the Mogollon Slope south of Zuni Pueblo. St. Johns Polychrome, a type of White Mountain Redware manufactured in the Zuni area, was widely traded throughout the Southwest at this time. The most prevalent type of settlement consisted of small pueblos.

Between A.D. 1250 and 1300 a major change in settlement pattern occurred as people aggregated into very large and well-planned pueblos ranging in size from 250 to 1,200 rooms. These large pueblos were all oriented around internal plazas and enclosed by a high wall. They extend from Kin Tiel, in the northwest drainage, through Big House Ruin, in Manuelito Canyon along the Puerco River, to Atsinna, at El Morro in the Zuni Mountains. Several of these large pueblos were located on defensible mesa tops, suggesting that warfare or raiding might have been a concern. Evidence of violent conflict, indicated by dismembered bodies, was found in archaeological excavations at a contemporaneous and related large pueblo at Mariana Mesa, east of Zuni Salt Lake.

In the Zuni drainage alone, there were thirty-six large, plaza-oriented pueblos constructed between A.D. 1250 and 1540, extending from Atsinna to Hawikuh. In general, the earliest of these aggregated pueblos were located in the Zuni Mountains, in topographic situations that concentrated surface runoff. The presence of water control features near these pueblos indicates that the people were directing water to their farm fields. This intensification of agriculture enabled the people to concentrate into large pueblos. Later aggregated pueblos were located downstream in areas of good soils where springs or major tributary drainages provided abundant water resources for farming. Zuni Pueblo is one of these later sites, and was probably founded about A.D. 1350.

Two of the types of pottery produced at the large late prehistoric pueblos in the Zuni drainage were distinctive White Mountain Redwares with vitrified paint decoration. The two types are named Heshotauthla Polychrome and Kwakina Polychrome, after the two large pueblos along the Zuni and Pescado rivers. These Zuni ceramics with vitrified paint were traded to contemporaneous pueblos in the Mogollon area, such as Foote Canyon Pueblo, and to pueblos in the Rio Grande valley. The Zuni pottery with vitrified paint, has a ceramic affinity with pottery made at the same time at sites along the Mogollon Rim such as Pinedale, Four Mile, and Show Low Ruins, indicating interaction with the people who lived in that part of the upper Little Colorado River Valley.

In the late prehistoric period, the population living in the upper Little Colorado River valley gradually concentrated into fewer sites. At the same time, the Mogollon area south of Zuni was abandoned as a location for habitations, and at least a few of the Mogollon peoples probably moved into the Little Colorado River valley. Late prehistoric sites in the upper Little Colorado area such as Table Rock Pueblo, Stone Axe Ruin, Chevelon, and Homolovi show cultural affinity to both Hopi and Zuni groups, and may have contributed population to both tribes when they were vacated. The use of both cremation and inhumation as burial practices at the Zuni sites of Hawikuh and Kechibawa, as well as the occurrence of a type of pottery known as Salado Polychrome, are often cited

Excavations at Halona:wa, as seen from the village of Zuni, ca. 1886. Ethnologist Frank H. Cushing's house is in background. Photograph by Victor Mindeleff, courtesy the Smithsonian Institution, National Anthropological Archives (Neg. No. 2348).

by archaeologists as evidence of a migration of people with a Mogollon cultural tradition into Zuni from the west sometime between A.D. 1350 and 1540. This small group of immigrants was assimilated into the Anasazi population, which had been long resident in the Zuni drainage, and modern Zuni culture and society emerged from the amalgam.

By the end of the prehistoric era, the population in the drainage of the Little Colorado River had consolidated at Zuni and Hopi. To the east of Zuni, between the Continental Divide and the Rio Grande valley, only Acoma Pueblo was occupied. The Zuni people had concentrated their settlements into a tightly clustered group of six pueblos along the Zuni River in an optimal area of land and water resources for agriculture. This core area of Zuni settlement was surrounded by a much larger sustaining area used for hunting and collecting wild plant and animal resources. The Little Colorado River valley and the mountains of the Mogollon Slope were important resource procurement areas used for limited activities. The Zuni pueblos at this time served as a nexus in a widespread regional trade network connecting the Colorado River area on the west with the Great Plains to the east, and the Colorado Plateau on the north with the Hohokam, or Pima-Papago area, and northern Mexico to the south.

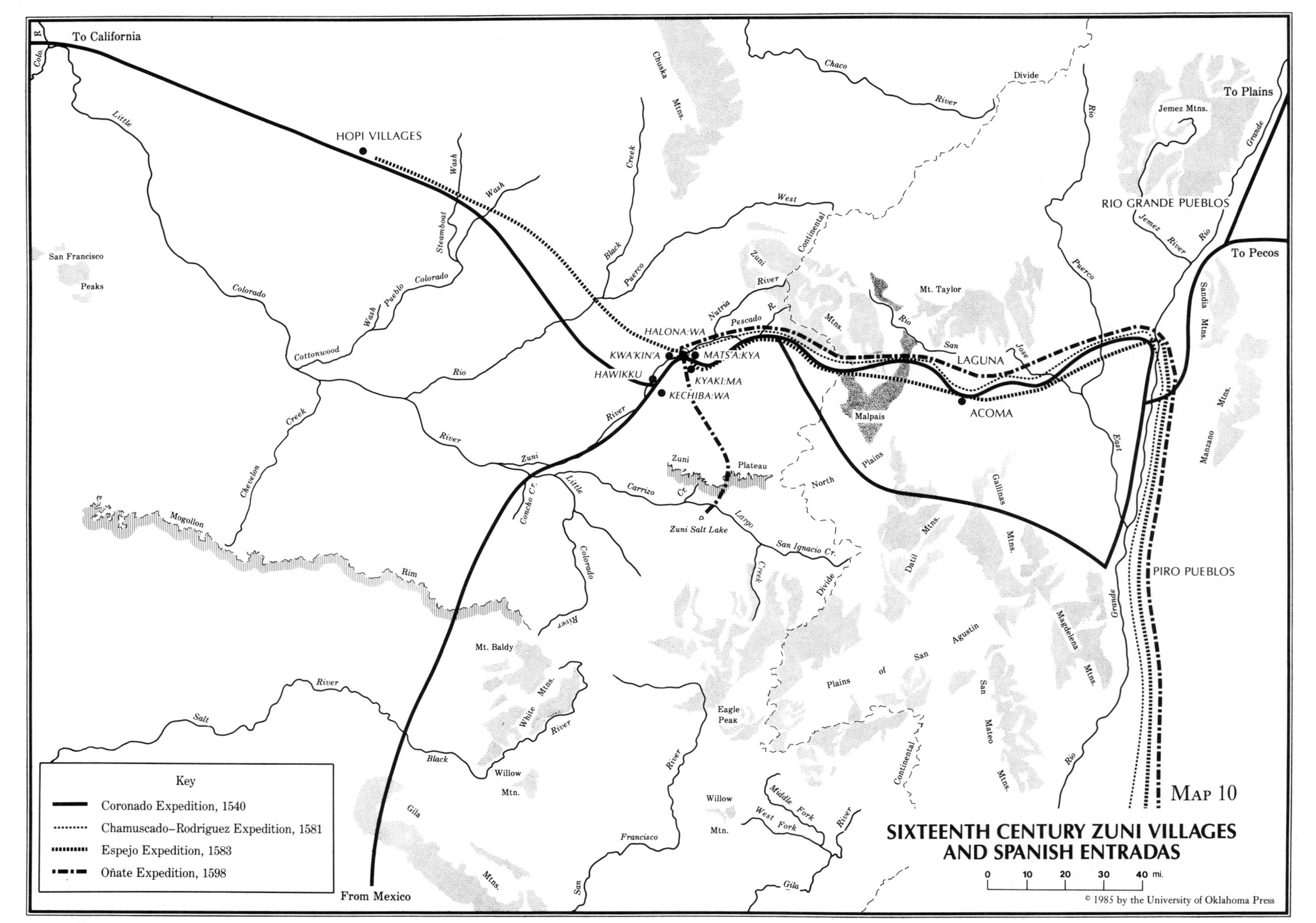
MAP 10
SIXTEENTH CENTURY ZUNI VILLAGES AND SPANISH ENTRADAS
Key
Coronado Expedition, 1540
Chamuscado–Rodriguez Expedition, 1581
Espejo Expedition, 1583
Oñate Expedition, 1598
0 10 20 30 40 mi.
To California
From Mexico
To Plains
To Pecos
HOPI VILLAGES
RIO GRANDE PUEBLOS
PIRO PUEBLOS
HALONA:WA
KWA'KIN'A
MATS'A:KYA
HAWIKKU
KYAKI:MA
KECHIBA:WA
LAGUNA
ACOMA
Zuni Salt Lake
Mt. Taylor
Malpais
Jemez Mtns.
Sandia Mtns.
Manzano Mtns.
Chuska Mtns.
San Francisco Peaks
Mogollon Rim
Mt. Baldy
White Mtns.
Willow Mtn.
Eagle Peak
Datil Mtns.
Gallinas Mtns.
Magdelena Mtns.
San Mateo Mtns.
Plains of San Agustin
Zuni Plateau
North Plains
Continental Divide
Little Colorado
Colorado
Cottonwood Wash
Pueblo Colorado Wash
Steamboat Wash
Black Creek
Puerco
West
Zuni River
Nutria
Pescado R.
Rio San Jose
Rio Puerco
East
Rio Grande
Jemez River
Chaco River
Chevelon Creek
Rio
River
Zuni River
Concho Cr.
Carrizo Cr.
Largo Creek
San Ignacio Cr.
Salt River
Black River
Gila
San Francisco River
Middle Fork
West Fork
Gila River
Colo. R.
© 1985 by the University of Oklahoma Press

10. SIXTEENTH-CENTURY ZUNI VILLAGES AND SPANISH ENTRADAS

Spanish military forces moved on New World wealth with an incredible speed following the European discovery of the Americas. As the Spanish war machine swept across Central and South America in search of gold and silver, stories began to be repeated about the "Seven Cities of Cibola" to the north, first from Nuño de Guzmán and later from the survivors of the Pánfilo de Narváez expedition. Cabeza de Vaca and Esteban, two survivors of the Narvaez shipwreck off the coast of Florida in 1528, had spent nearly a decade wandering across the whole breadth of the continent after their ship went down. It may have been a longstanding Spanish myth concerning seven rich cities that influenced their colorful accounts of the Seven Cities of Cibola to the north, where, it was said, copper was worked in foundries, the people were clothed in cotton, and the land was full of cultivated corn; or their stories may have been based in part on native accounts of Zuni or the Pueblo country in general.

Whatever the roots of the stories were, in 1539, Friar Marcos de Niza set out with Estaban, the black former slave, in search of Cibola. Esteban had taken to wearing an affected costume, adorned with feathers and bells, and to carrying a gourd rattle, all in an effort to impress any natives with whom he came in contact. His attitude and demeanor had quite the opposite effect on the Zunis, who executed him when he tried to appropriate Zuni women and wealth. Friar Marcos escaped back to Mexico, but elaborated on the Seven Cities motif with new stories of gold and precious gems.

The stories of Friar Marcos prompted a major expedition, in 1540, led by Francisco Vásquez Coronado, who journeyed northward in search of the seven golden cities of Cibola. His invasion force included hundreds of men armed for war. Coronado's force reached the province of Zuni and the pueblos along the Rio Grande to the east, but failed to find the wealth that had been promised.

Documents from the Coronado expedition are not completely clear, but most historians now agree that there were probably only six Zuni villages occupied in 1540: Hawikku, Kwa'kin'a, Halona:wa, Mats'a:kya, Kyaki:ma and Kechiba:wa, although a recent archaeological study shows the possibility that the Zuni village of Chalo:wa, located near Kechiba:wa, was also inhabited then. The first Zuni village Coronado arrived at was Hawikku, where he was met by 250 Zuni warriors assembled to protect their pueblo. A brief battle ensued, after which the Zuni forces withdrew and Coronado's forces occupied Hawikku. There were approximately 6,000 Zunis in 1540, but the firepower of the Spaniards was too great for them to overcome. After the Battle of Hawikku the Zunis never again waged a major battle against any European force. Peace was made with Coronado, and subsequent Spanish visitors in the sixteenth century were met with the hospitality for which the Zunis have become famous.

Communication in the Spanish settlements was poor in the sixteenth century, hence the next Spanish Entrada, the Chamuscado-Rodríguez Expedition of 1581, was unaware of Coronado's earlier visit to the Pueblo country. This party, also in search of mythical wealth, came by way of the Rio Grande pueblos to Zuni, where the Spaniards met with the same lack of success in finding great wealth. While the Spaniards did not find gold, they did marvel at the amount of corn cultivated by the Zunis. When the expedition returned to Mexico, two missionaries from the Chamuscado-Rodríguez Expedition, placing themselves in great danger, decided to stay along the Rio Grande and attempt to convert the Indians there to Christianity.

In 1583, Antonio de Espejo heard that two monks needed to be saved from certain peril on the frontier. Espejo saw in this situation an opportunity to improve his position, and he quickly organized a rescue expedition and set off toward the Pueblo country. He was too late to save the missionaries, who had already been killed, but the expedition gave him the opportunity to explore the Pueblo country, including Zuni, which was described in his written account of the expedition. Espejo was the first Spaniard to use the word "Zuni" (the Zunis' own name for themselves is *Ashiwi).* Gold and silver still eluded the Spaniards as they searched through Pueblo country, and Espejo returned to Mexico without acquiring the wealth he had sought.

Zuni was untouched by Spanish contact during the ensuing fifteen years, but in 1598 Juan de Oñate received official permission to colonize the Pueblo frontier. After founding the first Spanish settlement in New Mexico at San Gabriel, along the banks of the Rio Grande, Oñate set out to obtain submission to the Crown from the various Indian pueblos in the province. In November, 1598, Oñate's party reached Zuni and went about obtaining the required Act of Obedience and Vassalage from the peoples' leaders. While there, Oñate watched a communal rabbit hunt involving eight hundred Zunis, remarked on their yucca fiber, and sent a small party to find the fabled Zuni Salt Lake, the salt from which he described as being better than any found in all of Christendom.

When Spaniards established permanent settlements at the end of the sixteenth century, these were located along the Rio Grande. The geographic isolation of Zuni from the Spanish settlements enabled the Zunis to continue their traditional use of land with little

A portion of the excavations of the Hendricks-Hodge Expedition at Hawikku in 1919. Photograph courtesy the Museum of the American Indian, Heye Foundation (Neg. No. 5811).

direct interference. But their relative isolation did not protect them entirely from the invaders. Perhaps the greatest impact of the sixteenth-century Spanish Entradas into Zuni territory was the introduction of European diseases for which the Zunis and other native Americans had no natural immunities. Epidemics of smallpox, measles, and other diseases swept the Pueblo tribes, greatly reducing the population and creating hardship.

Chuba Dommanan, a passageway in the southwestern corner of Zuni Pueblo, 1879. The once prominent Zuni chimneys constructed of stacked pottery jars plastered with mud are visible in the foreground. Photograph by John K. Hillers, courtesy the Smithsonian Institution, National Anthropological Archives (Neg. No. 2267-0).

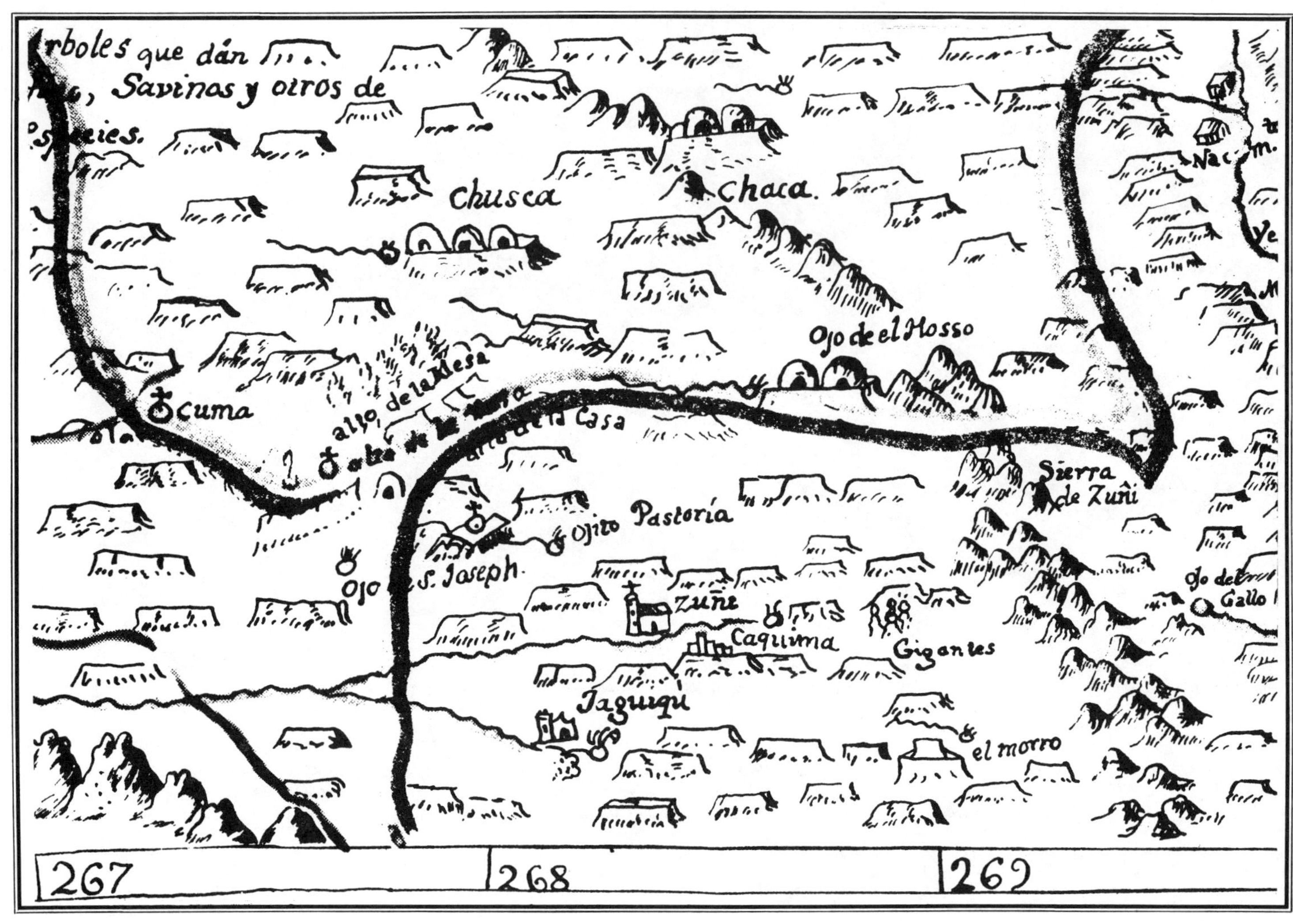

Map 11. Detail from a map by Don Bernardo Miera y Pacheco, 1778. Facsimile, courtesy Utah State Historical Society.

11. THE MAPS OF DON BERNARDO MIERA Y PACHECO 1775–79

DON Bernardo Miera y Pacheco was an officer in the Engineering Corps of the Spanish army who emigrated to Sante Fe sometime between 1754 and 1756. He was a native of Valle De Carriedo, Montanos de Burgos, and originally moved his family from Chihuahua to El Paso in 1743. Evidently his first visit to Zuni came in 1747, when he went through Zuni territory as a member of an expedition against the Apaches. At that time he was listed as an engineer, and captain of the militia, and also served as mapmaker. This expedition left Zuni and traveled south, finding a pass through the mountains and moving on into the Gila drainage, where the Spanish troops, in alliance with Zunis, attacked the Apaches. After serving as mayor of Pecos and Galisteo, in 1758 Miera completed an elaborate map of New Mexico.

In the mid-1770s, some twenty years after moving to the province, Miera was prominent as mapmaker of the region. He accompanied Vélez de Escalante's party to Hopi in 1775 and mapped the route. Then, in 1776, Miera joined Fathers Francisco Dominguez and Vélez de Escalante on their historic journey through what is now Utah. In 1778, Miera completed maps of that journey and large region, and afterwards, in 1779, he drew a map of the province of New Mexico at the request of governor Juan Bautista de Anza. The boundaries shown on this map do not represent tribal boundaries of land, but a Spanish administrative division of the territory.

Miera was not only a soldier and cartographer, but also an artist who on one occasion sold an image of Saint Philip the Apostle to the Indians of the pueblo of San Felipe. His superiors called him a *paisano,* suggesting he had made a homestead and was raising crops or stock. He was also rated as "clever" and "useful." Certainly his maps, though extremely irregular and imprecise by today's standards, give a colorful glimpse of the Spanish perception of the region in the later half of the eighteenth century. The Royal Corps of Engineers was an elite organization, with all members having the rank of officer, but Miera seems to have led a relatively modest life in comparison to some of the other Spanish engineers who were working in the borderlands during the same period.

The series of maps drawn by Miera are consistent in some details. The plains around the Zuni Salt Lake are shown as *"Llanos de la Salina de Zuni,"* at the foot of the mountains that led to Apache country. The Zuni Mountains and Bear Springs *(Ojo de el Osso)* are also located on Miera's maps. Just above Bear Springs, Miera designates an area of mesas that forms a frontier between Zuni and the province of the Navajos *("tierra de Messas y fronteras de la Provincia de Nabajoo).* In the immediate vicinity of Zuni, Miera shows *"Caquima" (Kyaki:ma)* and on some versions also places *"Jaquiqu" (Hawikku)* just to the southwest of the main Zuni pueblo. *Ojo de Gallo,* near present-day Grants, and El Morro are found along the route from Sante Fe to Zuni.

Miera also depicts a number of sites that are more difficult to identify. *"Ojo del Pueblo Redondo,"* Round Pueblo Spring, may have referred to the ruins at Cienaga, or possibly the Zuni village at Lower Pescado, the Village of the Great Kivas, Nutria, or any of a number of other prehistoric or historic settlements with circular structural features in their site plans. Miera places Navajo rancherias at *"Ojo de San Jose de Navajos."* In 1775, Vélez de Escalante reported that there was evidence of Navajo irrigation there, but he made no mention of Navajos in 1776, when he wrote of the springs, which bear the Zuni name *"Kianaituna,"* today's Pine Springs. *"Ojito Pastoria"* is evidently located in the arid plains northwest of Zuni, and *"Alto de la Mesa"* and *"Alto de la Casa"* may be connected to the ruins at Kin Tiel.

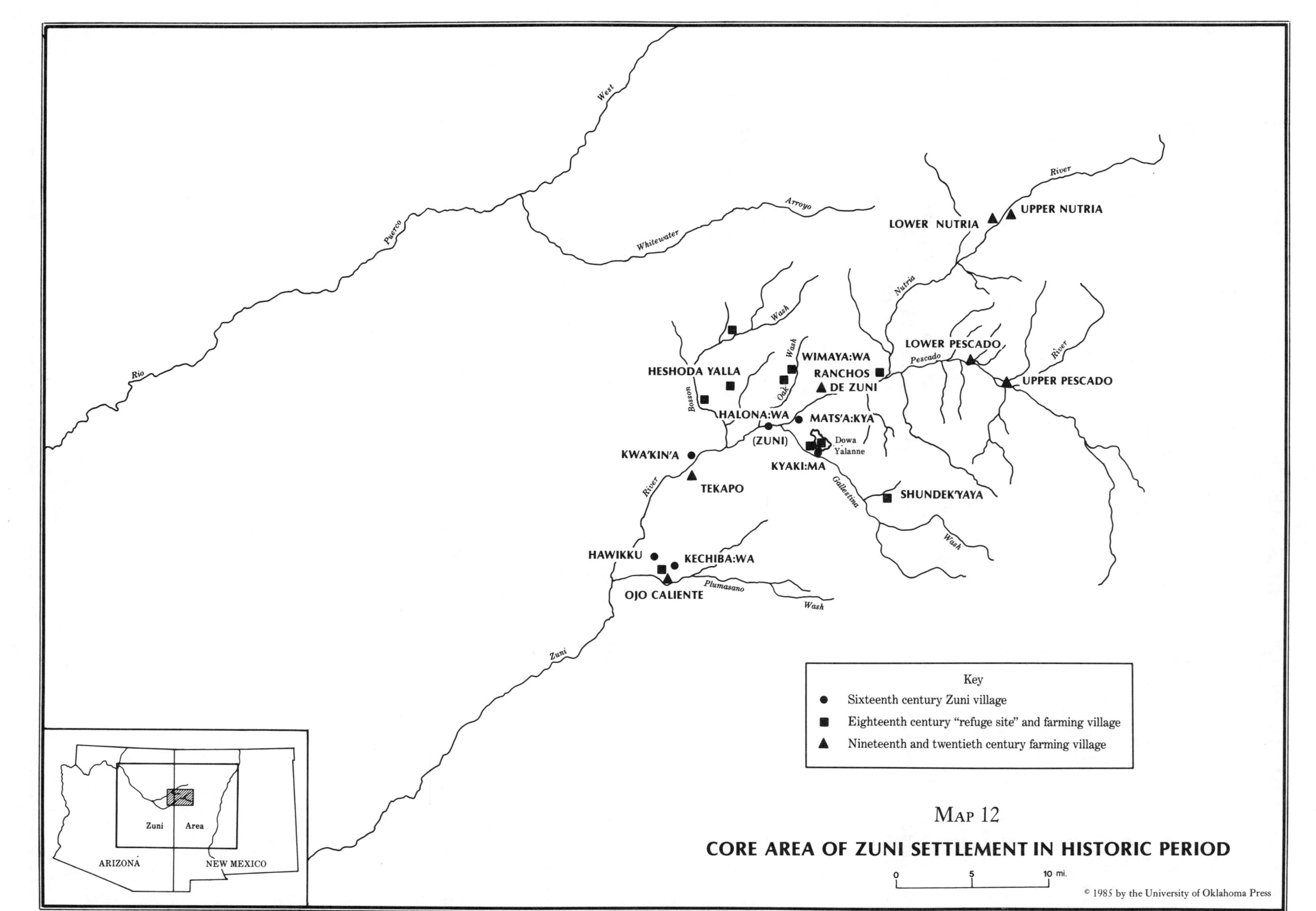

MAP 12

CORE AREA OF ZUNI SETTLEMENT IN HISTORIC PERIOD

12. CORE AREA OF ZUNI SETTLEMENT IN THE HISTORIC PERIOD

DURING the historic period, beginning in 1540, the Zuni Indians maintained a system of land use that was centered around a core area of pueblo villages near prime agricultural lands along the Zuni River and its tributary drainages. This central area of settlement was surrounded by a large sustaining region used for grazing, hunting, and collection of plants and minerals. The pattern of Zuni settlement within the core area has changed several times in the historic period.

When the Spaniards ushered in the historic period, the Zunis lived in six large, permanently occupied pueblos along a fifteen-mile stretch of the Zuni River. These villages—*Hawikku, Kechiba:wa, Kwa'kin'a, Halona:wa, Mats'a:kya,* and *Kyaki:ma*—were all located near major drainages or springs, and were situated on slightly elevated land forms above the floodplain of the Zuni River. This pattern of multiple permanent village settlements continued until 1680, although occupation at one or two of the original pueblos probably became seasonal during this period. In 1680 the Zuni Indians joined all of the other Pueblo Indians in New Mexico in a revolt to drive the Spaniards out of New Mexico, burning the Catholic missions and killing the Spaniards present in their villages. During the Pueblo Revolt the Zunis constructed a number of pueblos on top of the steep-sided mesa Dowa Yalanne to serve as a military stronghold to protect themselves from anticipated Spanish reprisals. In 1692, after the Pueblo Revolt, the Zunis reaffirmed political allegiance to the reestablished Spanish colonial government, and the Zuni population became consolidated into a single permanently inhabited pueblo at *Halona:wa,* or Zuni Pueblo.

In the early eighteenth century the Zunis established a number of seasonally occupied farming villages near peach orchards, such as *Wimaya:wa* and *Heshoda Yalla.* These peach orchard farming villages were also used as outposts for grazing livestock and as places to conduct Zuni religious ceremonies without interference from the Catholic missionaries who had reestablished themselves in Zuni Pueblo. Other sites from this period, like *Shundek'yaya,* are called "refuge sites," and appear to be fortified sheep camps that were used to protect Zuni livestock from Navajo and Apache raids. Thus, while the Zuni people congregated into a single permanently occupied pueblo, they continued to establish and use other settlements throughout the central area.

In the nineteenth century a second set of farming villages was constructed at Ojo Caliente, Nutria, and Pescado to take advantage of the abundant spring water that could be used for irrigation at those locations. The growth of these seasonally occupied farming settlements was associated with an increase in agricultural production as the Zunis began to supply a new market for corn, wheat, and forage created by the United States Army when they established Fort Defiance and Fort Wingate. Small, isolated farm sites were also common in the nineteenth century, many of which, such as *Ranchos de Zuni* near Blackrock, were protected from Navajo and Apache raids by strong circular watchtowers.

Ojo Caliente, Nutria, and Pescado are still in use, as is Tekapo, another farming village founded in the early twentieth century at the end of the irrigation unit established when Blackrock Dam was constructed. After the reservation was fenced in 1934, and grazing areas were formally assigned to stockmen, the Zunis constructed hundreds of small sheep camps to serve as bases of operation for the livestock industry.

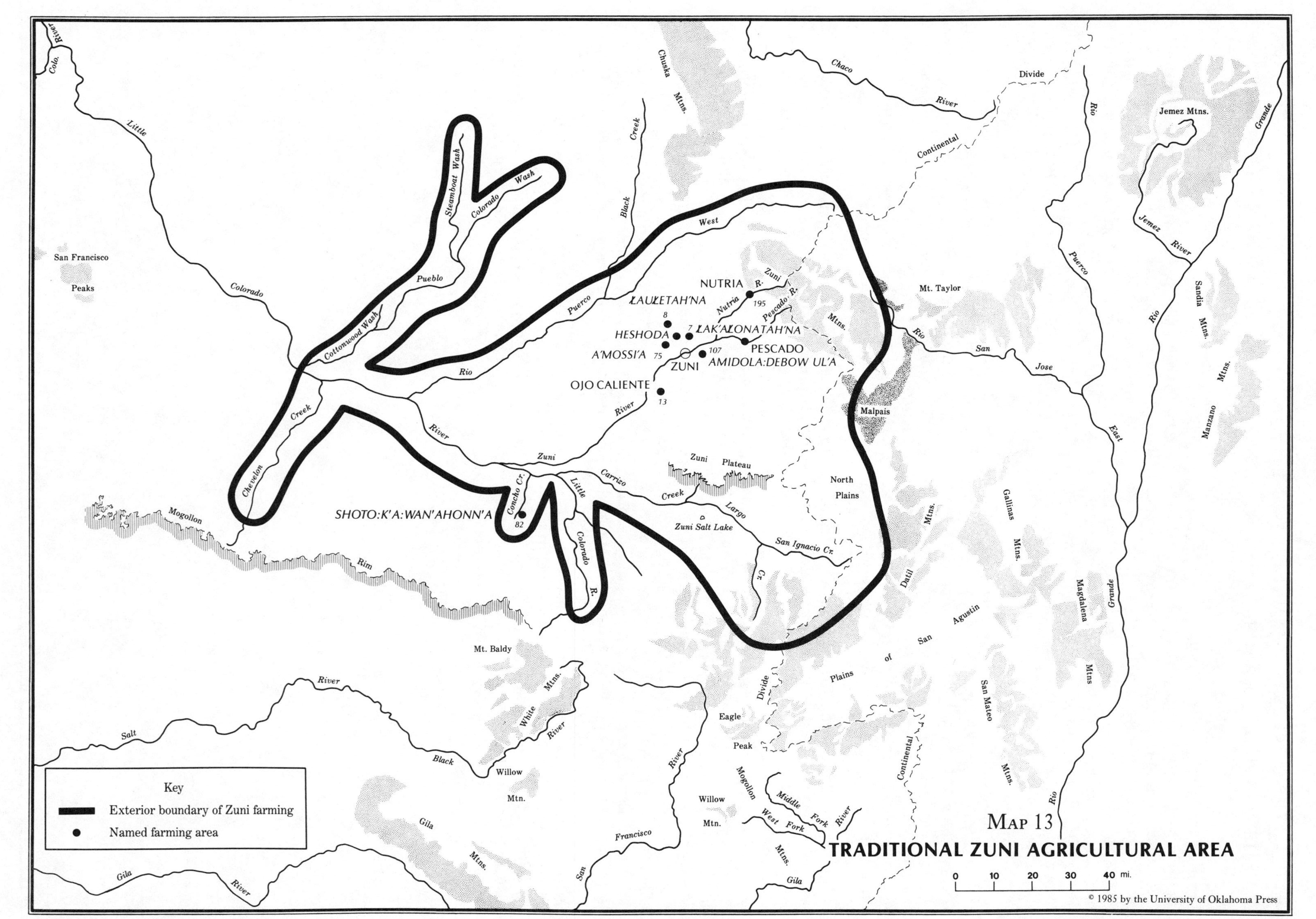

MAP 13
TRADITIONAL ZUNI AGRICULTURAL AREA

13. TRADITIONAL ZUNI AGRICULTURAL AREA

THE historic Zunis inherited an encyclopedic knowledge of their lands, the animals that roamed over them, the plants that grew upon them, and the waterways that flowed across them. Permanent habitation required specialized techniques to use the available resources without depleting them, *even over a very long period of time.* Perhaps the most specialized and sophisticated techniques utilized by the Zunis were their agricultural industries, learned over centuries by the pre-contact Zunis and their ancestors the Anasazi and Mogollon peoples. In an area that was arid and semi-arid, every available source of water had to be wisely used, and all tillable land, well managed.

Much of the water received during the course of a year came in the form of heavy, but brief thunderstorms. The rain fell on the mesas and buttes, quickly rushed down drainages into the valleys, flowed into one of the major river valleys (the Little Colorado or the Rio Puerco), and was gone. There were few permanent springs or streams, so irrigable land was relatively scarce. In response to the climatic conditions of the region they inhabited, the Pueblo Indians in general, and Zunis in particular, developed a system of "floodwater irrigation."

Floodwater irrigation involved the construction of check dams, diversionary dams, and mud walls in order to direct the flow of run-off from rainfall and snowmelt. Elaborate systems were maintained so that corn crops could be grown in the silted areas behind check dams, and so that every drop of moisture was utilized to the greatest extent possible. Floodwater corn fields were found anywhere there was periodic run-off, forming scattered plots, large and small, located across a very wide area. The Zunis grew large crops of corn, cultivating as many as 10,000 acres of floodwater fields annually, including fields at *A'moss'a, Łauletah'na, Łak'ałonatah'na,* and *Amidola:debow Uł'a.* Some fields, such as those at *Shoto:k'a:wan'ahonn'a,* were sixty or more miles distant from the central villages, planted by Zuni sheepherders while they grazed their livestock in distant pastures. Corn was the tribe's most important crop, playing a central role in the spiritual, social and ceremonial life of the Zuni people, but it was not the only crop, by any means.

In the process of maintaining floodwater fields, the Zunis also, in practice, effected erosion control, preventing the loss of topsoil by wind or water and especially by not allowing gullying to take place where large amounts of run-off were frequent. When the Zunis' agricultural practices were restricted in the nineteenth and twentieth centuries, extensive erosion and gullying took place throughout their traditional lands. Other factors also contributed to this devastating cycle.

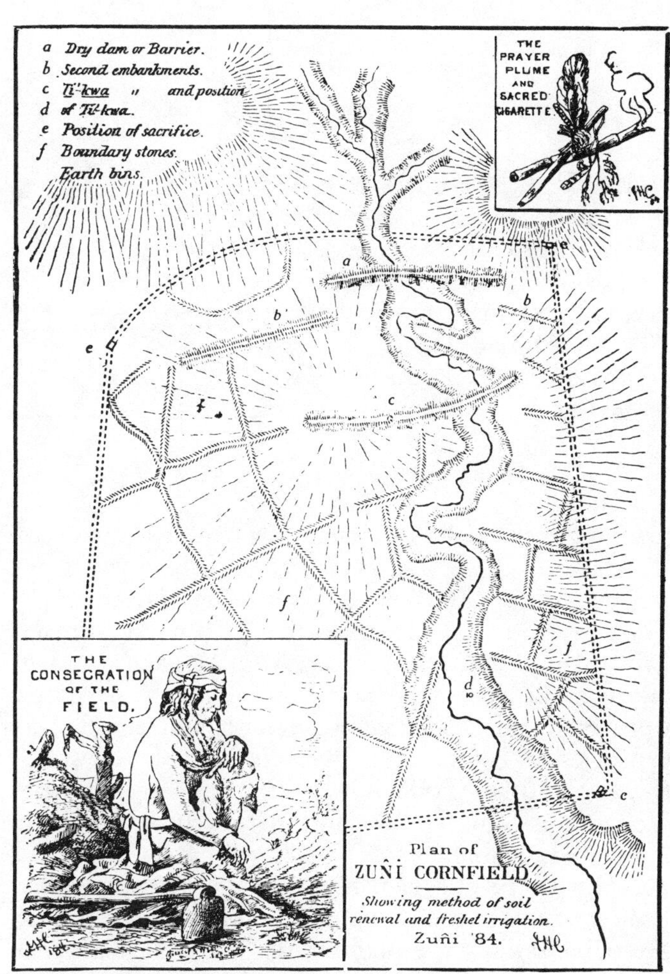

"Plan of a Zuni Cornfield," by Frank Hamilton Cushing, 1884. Reprinted from Frank Hamilton Cushing's Zuni Breadstuff, *Museum of the American Indian, New York, 1920. Photograph courtesy the Museum of the American Indian.*

There were a few permanent sources of water within the Zuni territory, and these were developed to the fullest by the people. Ojo Pescado (Fish Springs), Ojo Caliente (Hot Springs), and Nutria Springs all provided important year-long sources of water and, because of that, were also the areas where the Zunis practiced irrigated agriculture. At the time of contact with the Spaniards, there were reports indicating Zuni use of *acequias,* or canals. By the nineteenth century the Zunis were using hollow logs as aquaducts. After the acquisition of European seed, the Zunis sowed wheat at their ranches around these springs.

Another food the Zunis acquired from the Spaniards was the peach. In the historic period the Zunis planted

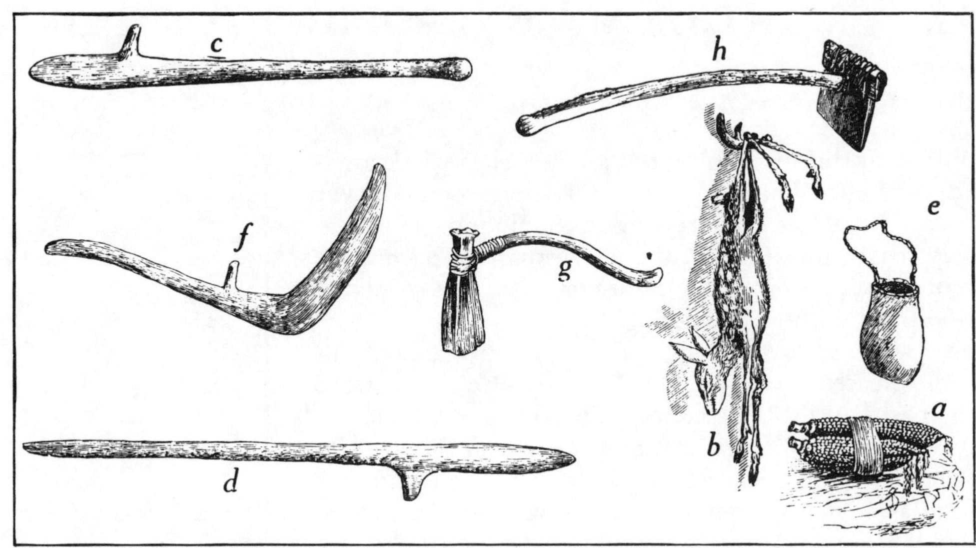

"Planting Implements and other paraphernalia." Reprinted from Frank Hamilton Cushing's Zuni Breadstuff, *Museum of the American Indian, New York, 1920. Photograph courtesy the Museum of the American Indian.*

several peach orchards, including one at the base of their sacred mesa, Dowa Yalanne. Other peach orchards were established at Wimaya:wa and Heshoda Yalla in the mesas to the north of Zuni Pueblo (see Core Area of Zuni Settlement, Map 12), and in other sandy areas as well. Many of these peach orchards were established in the seventeenth and eighteenth centuries and were still in production in the nineteenth century. Today, in 1983, remnants of these orchards are still to be seen, but they have not been cultivated for many years.

A third type of agriculture the Zunis practiced has been frequently mentioned in published accounts of the tribe. This is the planting of "waffle gardens," so named because of their resemblance to waffles. Planted primarily along the banks of the Zuni River at Zuni Pueblo, the waffle gardens were constructed in small squares and rectangles with low mud walls forming cells around each plant to conserve water, regulate temperature, and provide protection from the wind. Higher mud walls surrounded family plots and kept out livestock. Specialty crops such as peppers, onions, squash, melons, pumpkins, and cotton were grown in these plots. Each plant was watered by hand with a ladle, using water carried from a well or from the river in *ollas* on the women's heads. Most of the picturesque and highly productive "waffle gardens" have recently fallen into disuse, although a few are still to

"A Zuni Cornfield with its Scarecrows." Reprinted from Frank Hamilton Cushing's Zuni Breadstuff, *Museum of the American Indian, New York, 1920. Photograph courtesy the Museum of the American Indian.*

A spring with a wall around it near Ojo Caliente, 1886. Photograph by Cosmos or Victor Mindeleff, courtesy the Smithsonian Institution, National Anthropological Archives (Neg. No. 2320).

be seen at Zuni Pueblo and the outlying farming villages.

Traditionally, the Zunis kept a two-year supply of food on hand, in case of drought or insect infestation. Cord upon cord of corn was sealed in rodent-proof storage rooms in case of famine. Vegetables were dried and prepared in myriad ways for consumption during the winter months. Fruit was also dried in the sunshine in the autumn, to be savored in the colder part of the year. It was the diversified agriculture of the Zunis, more than anything else, that allowed them to develop a sedentary society with a rich culture. Within this culture water was sacred, and agricultural lands were zealously guarded, from the most distant floodwater fields to the waffle gardens along the Zuni River.

The development of Blackrock Dam in the early twentieth century, along with federal programs to "modernize" Zuni agriculture, led to the disruption of traditional farming methods. With the development of an economy based on wage labor, subsistence agriculture has become less important. Today Zuni farming consists largely of the production of alfalfa and other livestock forage. Although many people still supplement their diet with corn, squash, and melons from small gardens, few people are dependent on agriculture for their livelihood. Many of the traditional cultigens continue to be grown in small quantities, however, by or for religious leaders for ceremonial use. These traditional cultigens represent an important genetic seed bank of economically useful plants well adapted to the semi-arid climate of the Zuni region.

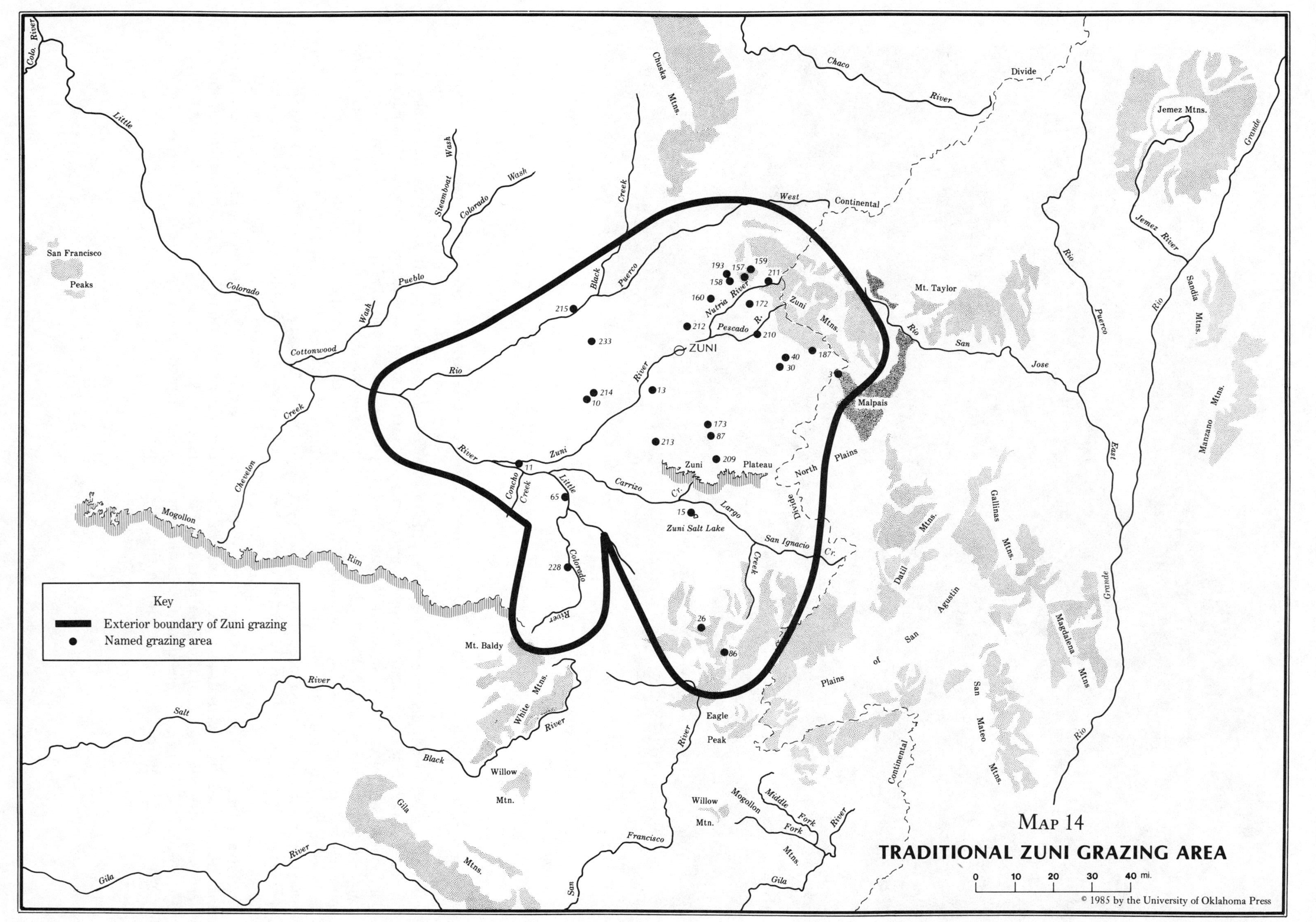

Map 14
TRADITIONAL ZUNI GRAZING AREA

14. TRADITIONAL ZUNI GRAZING AREA

Before contact with Europeans, Zunis tended extensive flocks of turkeys. According to Zuni tradition, they "herded" these flocks over large areas of their territory, using the feathers for clothing and ritual adornment and eating the birds themselves in times of need. The only other domesticated animal kept by the Zunis was the dog.

The Zunis developed a livestock industry with animals introduced into the Southwest by the Spaniards. There is no record that Coronado left any livestock at Zuni in 1540, and it is probable that the Zunis did not obtain their own livestock until after the Catholic missions were established in 1630. By 1692 the Zunis had horses, which they rode out to Pescado to meet the Spaniards returning to Zuni for the first time after the Pueblo Revolt. The first documentary evidence of Zuni ownership of sheep dates to 1721, but archaeological evidence indicates that the Zunis began to graze sheep in the preceding century. Burros, goats, and a few cattle were also kept by the Zunis, but by far the most important Zuni grazing animal was the sheep. By the mid-eighteenth century the tribe had more than fifteen thousand sheep, and wool had become an important source of raw material for clothing and blankets. Before they obtained sheep, the Zunis had woven clothing from yucca, cotton, feathers, and other vegetal and animal materials, hence they soon became expert at weaving wool into a type of Zuni dress called *mantas,* as well as into blankets. Zuni blankets had simple designs and were often black, or white with black and brown stripes. Zuni weaving was known as some of the best among all of the pueblos.

Sheep quickly became an important supply of meat. Many thousands of lambs and sheep were slaughtered each year to provide food for the feasts that are a part of the Zunis' annual *Shalako* celebration, as well as for the traditional ceremonies at the summer solstice and other times of the year. Although the large herds of sheep provided an important source of meat, the Zunis continued to hunt wild animals to supplement their diet. The strategy of Zuni stockmen whenever possible was to build up their wool-producing herds rather than consume them.

During the summer, several large herds of sheep were driven as far as seventy miles from the central pueblos. Several families of Zunis might band their herds together and groups of Zunis would shepherd those herds communally. Tradition determined "use rights" on certain grazing areas. The finest, grassiest areas near the village were saved for the lambing period in the spring, or for times when an Apache or Navajo raid was expected. After lambing, the Zuni herders would range their flocks far from the pueblo, avoiding "floodwater fields" of corn. In the fall, after the crops were harvested at the farming villages, the sheep would be brought in to graze on the stubble of the farm fields and, occasionally, on fields of grain or forage planted specifically as winter feed for the livestock. A number of types of structures were utilized by the Zuni sheepherders while they moved about with their flocks: conical and circular brush shelters or lodges for temporary quarters, cave shelters, rock houses and pens near the lambing areas, watchtowers, fortified sheep camps, and corrals.

Sheep were the most efficient users of the available grazing lands, so only nominal numbers of cattle were maintained. Horses were used for war and for long-distance travel, but most travel was accomplished on foot. Burros did make agricultural production easier at greater distances, for crops could be brought in on the animals instead of carried by individual Zunis, and the burro facilitated trade of heavier goods.

By the nineteenth century, the number of Zuni sheep had grown to at least thirty thousand. By 1900, that number had risen to fifty or sixty thousand. The Zunis had to use good judgment in order not to overgraze the dry grasslands away from the major water sources, rotating the pastures they used in order to conserve the rangeland. When the tribe was forced to pull their herds in and contain them on their small reservation, much of the rangeland on the reservation became severely overgrazed, and the federal government introduced stock reduction programs. Today the Zunis have assigned all available rangeland on the reservation to tribal members for use (See Grazing Units on the Zuni Reservation, Map 37). In addition to ninety-five sheep ranches, there are also two cattle associations. The Zunis have constructed many permanent sheep camps and other facilities to service their modern livestock industry on the reservation.

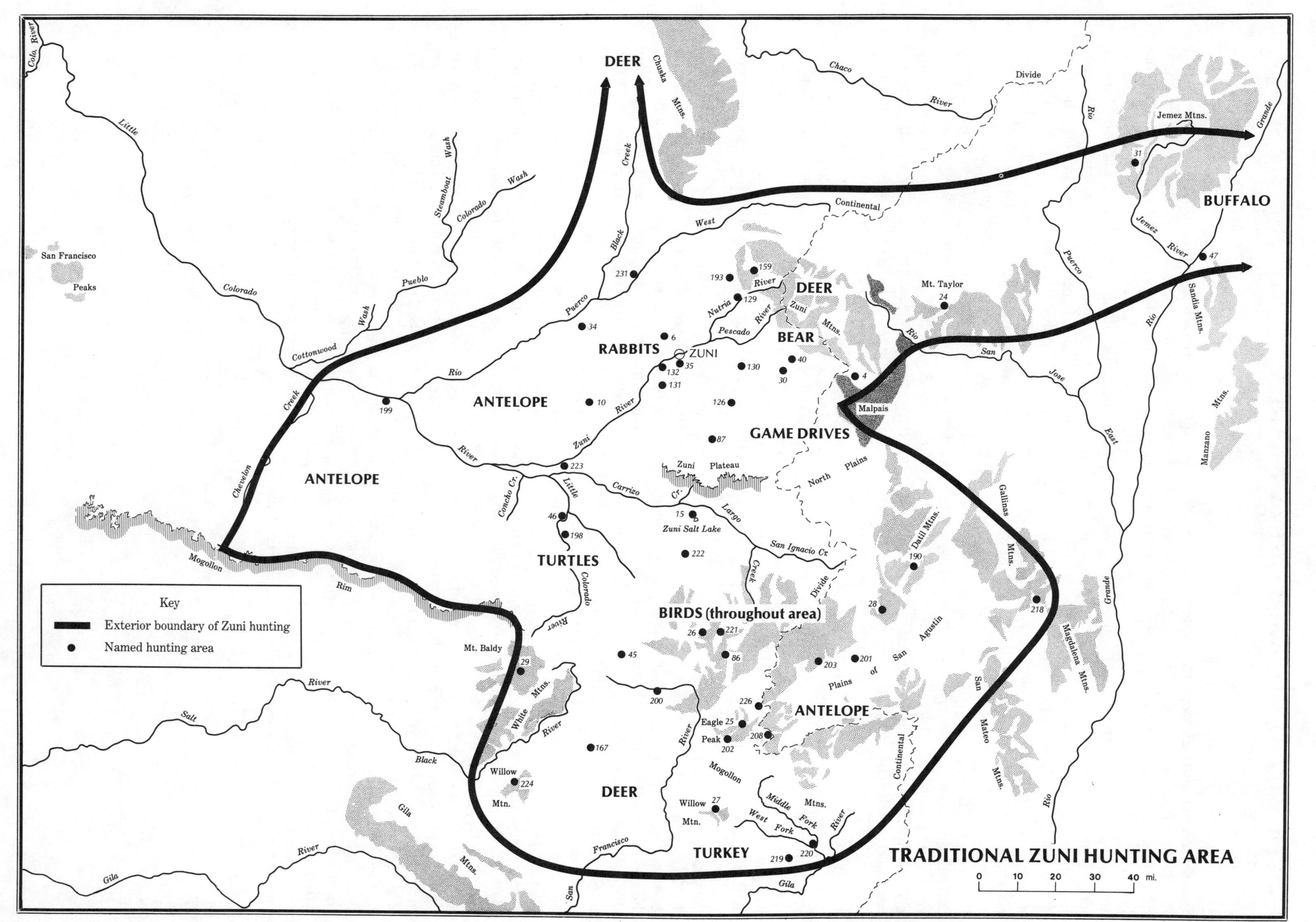

TRADITIONAL ZUNI HUNTING AREA
0 10 20 30 40 mi.
Key
Exterior boundary of Zuni hunting
Named hunting area
DEER
BUFFALO
DEER
BEAR
RABBITS
ANTELOPE
GAME DRIVES
ANTELOPE
TURTLES
BIRDS (throughout area)
ANTELOPE
DEER
TURKEY
ZUNI
Chuska Mtns.
Jemez Mtns.
Sandia Mtns.
Manzano Mtns.
Mt. Taylor
Zuni Mtns.
Malpais
Zuni Plateau
North Plains
Zuni Salt Lake
Datil Mtns.
Gallinas Mtns.
Magdalena Mtns.
San Mateo Mtns.
Plains of San Agustin
Continental Divide
Mt. Baldy
White Mtns.
Eagle Peak
Mogollon Mtns.
Willow Mtn.
Gila Mtns.
Mogollon Rim
San Francisco Peaks
Colo. River
Little Colorado
Steamboat Wash
Colorado Wash
Pueblo Wash
Cottonwood Wash
Chevelon Creek
Black Creek
Rio Puerco
West
Nutria River
Pescado River
Zuni River
Concho Cr.
Carrizo Cr.
Largo Creek
San Ignacio Cr.
Chaco River
Rio Puerco
Rio San Jose
Puerco East
Rio Grande
Jemez River
Colorado River
Salt River
Black River
White River
San Francisco River
Middle Fork
West Fork
Gila River

15. TRADITIONAL ZUNI HUNTING AREA

From the highest mountains to the dryest deserts within their area, the Zunis hunted, trapped, and snared scores upon scores of animals and birds. Among the big game animals that were hunted were bobcats, deer, coyotes, bears, elk, moose, antelope, mountain sheep, wild pigs, foxes, and mountain lions. The largest game animal hunted by the Zunis was the buffalo. Small game was equally important in terms of diet and source of raw materials, and included badgers, porcupines, rabbits, ground squirrels, beavers, and ground hogs. About seventy species of birds have been identified as being used by the Zunis in recent times, including eagles, ducks, wild turkeys, hawks, jays, finches, woodpeckers, owls, crows, and blue birds. In the past, it is safe to assume that nearly every species of bird and animal that could be found in their area was used by the Zuni people, though a small number of species of birds were taboo and not used for any purpose.

All hunting activities had associated religious practices. Some hunting was prompted entirely by religious motives. Most birds were snared in order to obtain feathers for use in the construction of "prayer sticks" —different feathers attached to prepared sticks and used as offerings, along with cornmeal and turquoise, for many esoteric religious activities. Some birds, such as eagles, were kept in cages at the pueblos, fed ceremonial rabbit food, and treated with great veneration, all in order that periodically they might have their feathers plucked for religious use. Game animals were regarded and treated as living relatives by the Zuni people. Hunting was always a sacred activity, with prayers, offerings, and ceremonies to accompany each task. After the killing of a deer, a Zuni hunter was expected to draw the animal's last breath out of its nostrils while himself breathing in the same breath, in order to ensure that the deer would live again. According to Zuni tradition, after slaying a deer a hunter should take the carcass home to "lie in state" in the hunter's household, adorned with fine Zuni blankets and jewelry.

Prayers and offerings were made at hunting shrines along trails that led to hunting grounds. Fetishes, which helped ensure successful hunts, were kept in special jars and "fed" offerings of turquoise and cornmeal. On hunting expeditions that traveled over long distances, such as to the plains east of the Rio Grande where buffalo were hunted, complex and powerful ceremonies accompanied each action of the hunters. Even common hunts, near to the central pueblos, required religious observations.

Considering the expansive territory, the wide range of altitudes and climates therein, and the great variety of animals hunted, it is no surprise that an extensive body of traditional knowledge was maintained among the Zunis in order to harvest the game within their territory. Specialized technologies, intricate rituals, and development of the ability to precisely predict movements of game were memorized and passed down through the generations in kivas, clans, and societies.

Delicate snares were constructed to capture birds—with designs appropriate to each species. Other birds and some large game, such as bears, were hunted with the use of blinds. Solitary hunters and small groups of hunters prepared special, light foods to carry with them and walked or rode to distant locations where deer, antelope, buffalo, moose, and other big game could be found.

Some of the most important hunting was carried out communally, by large but tightly organized groups of Zunis—sometimes numbering in the hundreds. Close to the pueblos, Zuni groups, using boomerang-like "rabbit sticks," rounded up and killed rabbits. In other areas of their territory Zunis constructed and utilized fences, or "drive lanes," in communal hunts. One such fence, probably used to help capture antelope, was reported to be seventy-five miles long. Pits were also used to capture deer, and were dug along drive lanes on existing game trails at appropriate spots.

Hunting not only provided the Zunis with a crucial supply of their meat, but also with hides for clothing and other manufactured articles. Bones, sinew, fur, feathers, and almost every other part of hunted animals were used, providing resources essential for the Zunis' long-term survival. Each part of the Zuni territory provided a crop of different animals over the years, though in some years one area might not be used. In practice, the Zunis traditionally conserved the wildlife in their territory, harvesting only what was necessary for their survival and religious well-being.

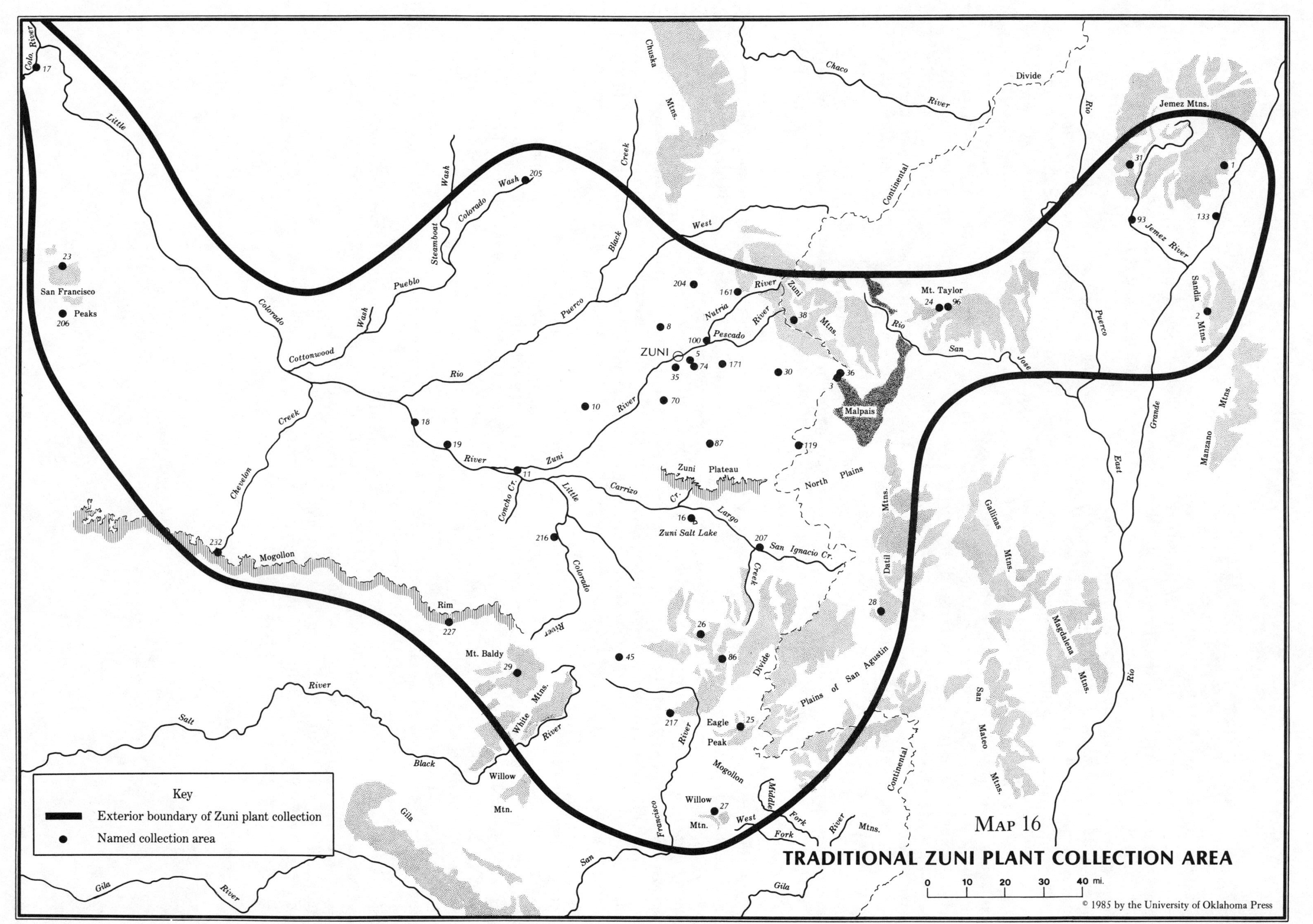

Map 16

TRADITIONAL ZUNI PLANT COLLECTION AREA

16. TRADITIONAL ZUNI PLANT COLLECTION AREA

For centuries the Zunis' ancestors studied the country around them, learning all they could about the properties of each plant that grew within range of their travel. Probably no people will ever know the plant kingdom of that area like the traditional Zuni people knew it. The Zunis respected and cared for the plants, treating them as living beings and even speaking to them, and praying and making offerings for them. At every level of their collective consciousness the Zuni people were aware of their interaction with the land around them. By gathering plants from every corner of the region that they occupied, the Zuni people were able to fill their larders and storage bins with an abundant array of foods, medicines, ceremonial materials, basketry materials, and toiletries. In the hundreds of years during which the Zunis occupied their traditional territory before 1880, there is no evidence that their gathering practices in any way depleted any of their resources. The Zunis had developed a way of life that would sustain them indefinitely in their territory, using the resources from every biotic community within that territory in ways that sustained the resources as well. Much of the traditional knowledge of this great Zuni achievement, the harmonious interaction with the landscape, has continued to be passed down at Zuni to the present day (although much has been lost, as well).

The use of gathered materials for medicinal purposes necessitated visiting an area from the Sandia Mountains in the east, to the San Francisco Peaks in the west. Medicines for every type of ailment were prepared and used, from insect repellent to anaesthetic. Zuni native doctors used such substances as pine gum, gourds, cedar bark, willowroot, pollen, and opiate derivatives in treating illnesses and accidents. Burn ointments, pain killers (with different drugs for headaches, toothaches, or sore throats), and eye ointments were prepared from plants gathered throughout the region. There were depilatory preparations, narcotics, drugs to assist women with childbirth, drugs to induce vomiting, to help in the removal of bullets or arrows, and preparations that helped cause the healing of puncture wounds.

The collection, preparation, and application of specific medicines was always accompanied by religious ceremony. Some medicines were regarded as having properties that could help cure spiritual as well as material afflictions, and some drugs were used to help

"Drying the Heh-li-ewa," a traditional Zuni food, ca. 1890. Photograph by Ben Wittick, courtesy the Museum of New Mexico (Neg. No. 16061).

Zuni doctors cure social disorders, or to identify the source of "witchcraft." One such plant has been written about by anthropologists for a century. This is the plant named *Tenatsali* by the Zunis, which is believed to have colors for all of the six directions (north, south, east, west, nadir, and zenith) on its different petals. This plant is used for special purposes such as divination by those initiated into the secrets of its preparation.

The most common and widespread use of native plants was for food. Gathered foods were used to supplement those grown in fields and gardens, and were also an important reserve resource in case of serious drought or insect infestation. Many gathering practices were based on very old knowledge, perhaps dating to pre-agricultural times, when the Zunis' ancestors relied to a far greater extent on gathering for subsistence. In times when rainfall was slight for a number of years, the Zunis knew how to identify native plants that could be gathered and eaten. There were dozens of edible foods within the Zuni region: pine nuts, water cress, yucca, soapweed, cactus, juniper berries, sunflowers, grasses (including one intriguingly called "father-in-law of corn"), wild rice, wild peas and beans, and puffball fungus. Food products were obtained from tumbleweed, wormwood, milkweed, water parsnips, cocklebur thistle, and nightshade. Milkweed was used to make a kind of chewing gum. The wild potato was one plant used in times of severe drought. Even today some Zuni elders recall the times of drought when potential starvation prompted Zunis to gather the wild potato and eat it along with a special kind of clay in order to make it a little more palatable.

Plants were used to construct all manner of clothes, baskets, and other utilitarian devices. Rabbit brush was used to make baskets. Drop-seed grass was woven into bunches and then fastened together in order to make mats for covering the doorways of pueblo houses and rooms, and was also woven into shelters for temporary protection in the fields at some distance from home. Long-leaf yucca was used to weave winnowing baskets. Milkweed cotton and yucca in pre-contact times provided materials for native textiles that were superbly fashioned and decorated. Dyes were elaborate and varied. Thistle and rabbit weed were used to prepare yellow dye. Red-brown dye was manufactured from coreopsis flowers. Black dye came from the sumac root, and was used to dye the now rare all-black Zuni blankets. Beeweed was used as a base for black and brown paints made to decorate pottery.

Many other plants were used in the construction of costumes, altars, fetishes, and other ceremonial paraphernalia, including body paint, teas, ceremonial offerings, and poisons. Miscellaneous plants provided rouge, perfume, and at least three kinds of soap. Other plants were used in the construction of houses. Even more plants were used in pre-contact and historic times to weave not only clothing, but also rope and dyed decorations. All of this is probably but a fraction of the knowledge about plants that existed among the Zuni people before 1900, knowledge based in their intense, yet measured, use of the landscape around them for plant collection.

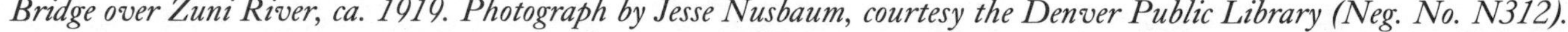

Bridge over Zuni River, ca. 1919. Photograph by Jesse Nusbaum, courtesy the Denver Public Library (Neg. No. N312).

Pottery vessels, with corn in stack and piles in the background, 1879. Photograph by John K. Hillers, courtesy the Smithsonian Institution, National Anthropological Archives (Neg. No. 2268-A).

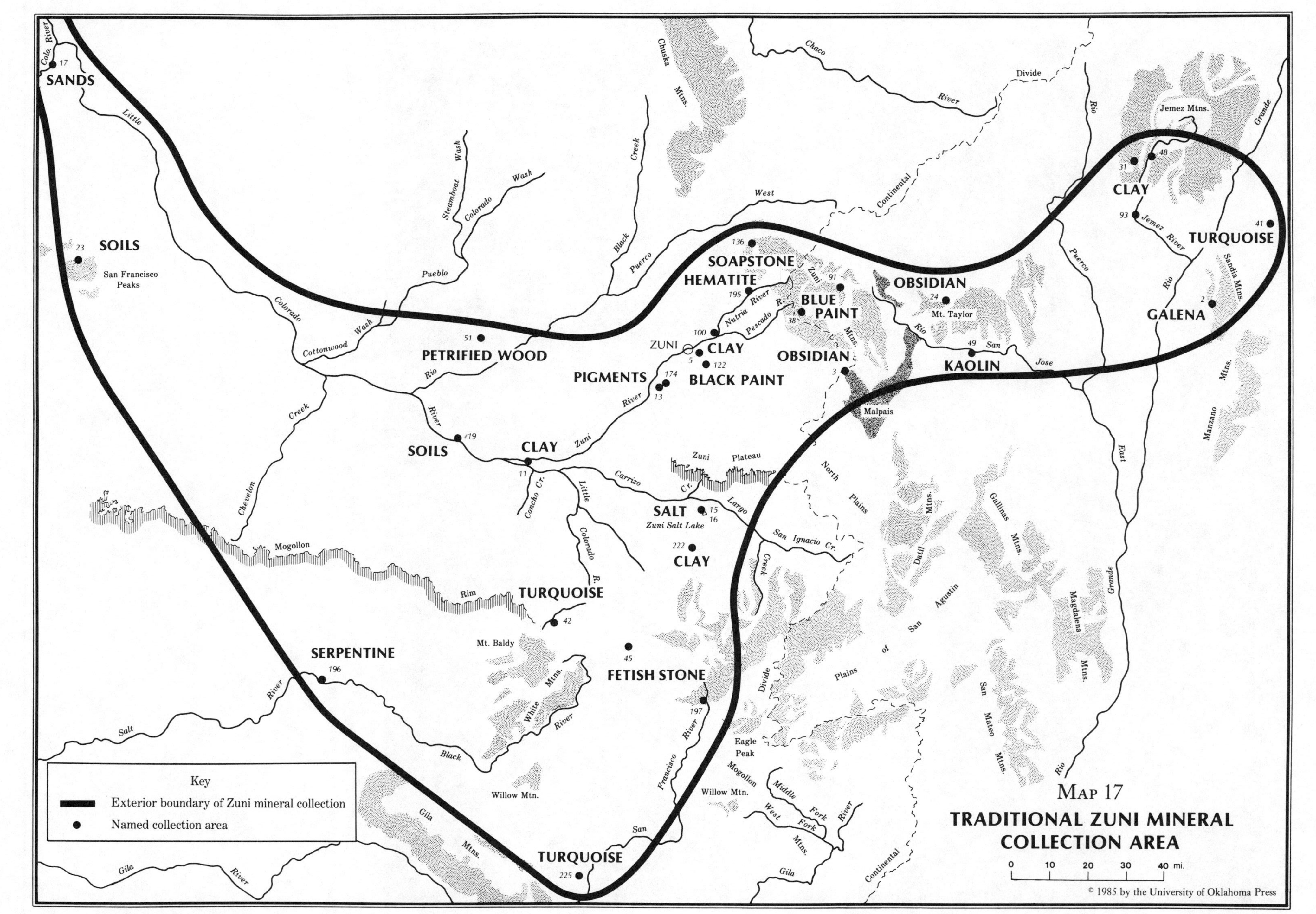

Map 17
TRADITIONAL ZUNI MINERAL COLLECTION AREA

17. TRADITIONAL ZUNI MINERAL COLLECTION AREA

TRADITIONALLY, the Zunis did not differentiate between organic and inorganic materials, but considered all things to be living—the earth and all stones, streams, and materials upon the earth (the distinction here between organic and inorganic is the authors' distinction). All types of inorganic materials were gathered within the boundaries of the Zuni domain: minerals, clays, soils, samples of water, and types of rocks. Salt from the Zuni Salt Lake provided an essential seasoning and preservative, as well as an important trade item. In addition to gathering materials from the surface of the earth, Zunis also quarried and mined various minerals. Obsidian was collected and manufactured into points for arrows and for razor-sharp knives used for both common utilitarian purposes and specialized purposes such as surgery. A certain type of clay that worked like an astringent was used to pack abcesses. Rocks containing sulphates of iron, aluminum, and magnesium were used in the manufacture of dyes, as was a native alum used as a fixing agent. Materials for fetishes were gathered in diverse locations throughout the Zuni territory. The Zunis also gathered materials from the Petrified Forest, the Malpais, the Grand Canyon, the Gallo and Mogollon mountains, and every other corner of their country. From today's vantage point, the Zunis' knowledge of the resources around them, their grasp of the availability of those resources, and their systematic use of the beneficial properties of those resources is very impressive.

A number of different clays and minerals were gathered for use in pottery making. Red, blue, yellow, and white clays were collected from different locations. Ocher, jasper, hematite, iron ore, kaolin and shale were used to make pigments. The clays were gathered at *Kołuwala:wa*, Pescado, Ojo Caliente, and Dowa Yalanne as well as from many other areas in the Zuni region. Broken pottery was gathered from ruins in the region for use as temper, which was mixed with clay to strengthen the ceramic vessals produced. Clays and other materials are still gathered for pottery manufacture at Zuni. Traditionally, Zuni women took great care to return the surface of the ground to its former condition after digging for clay, a practice that may have begun in Spanish times as a method of preventing detection of Zuni resources, but which also helped to prevent erosion.

The Zunis took special care to prevent detection of their mines. There are many historical references to Zuni mining and quarrying of ores, stones, gems, pigments and paints. The blue pigment, or paint, of the Zunis, sometimes described as being taken from silver ore, was well known in the Spanish period. There is also considerable evidence that the Zunis mined copper ore and produced some primitive copper objects. The Zunis, along with other Pueblo tribes, worked the mines in the Cerrillos area. At those workings there were tunnels as deep as two hundred feet, and pits more than three hundred feet wide. The Zunis also had diggings for copper and turquoise in the Zuni Mountains, diggings described in 1879 as including many recent and ancient excavations. The Zunis used native-made spades, wooden digging sticks, and stone tools to excavate the copper ore. In pre-contact times the Zunis probably used a kind of *zurron*, a bag that was attached to the head via a tumpline, to transport ores.

A Zuni man drilling turquoise beads, 1899. Photograph by Adam Clark Vroman, courtesy the Smithsonian Institution, National Anthropological Archives (Neg. No. 2263-B).

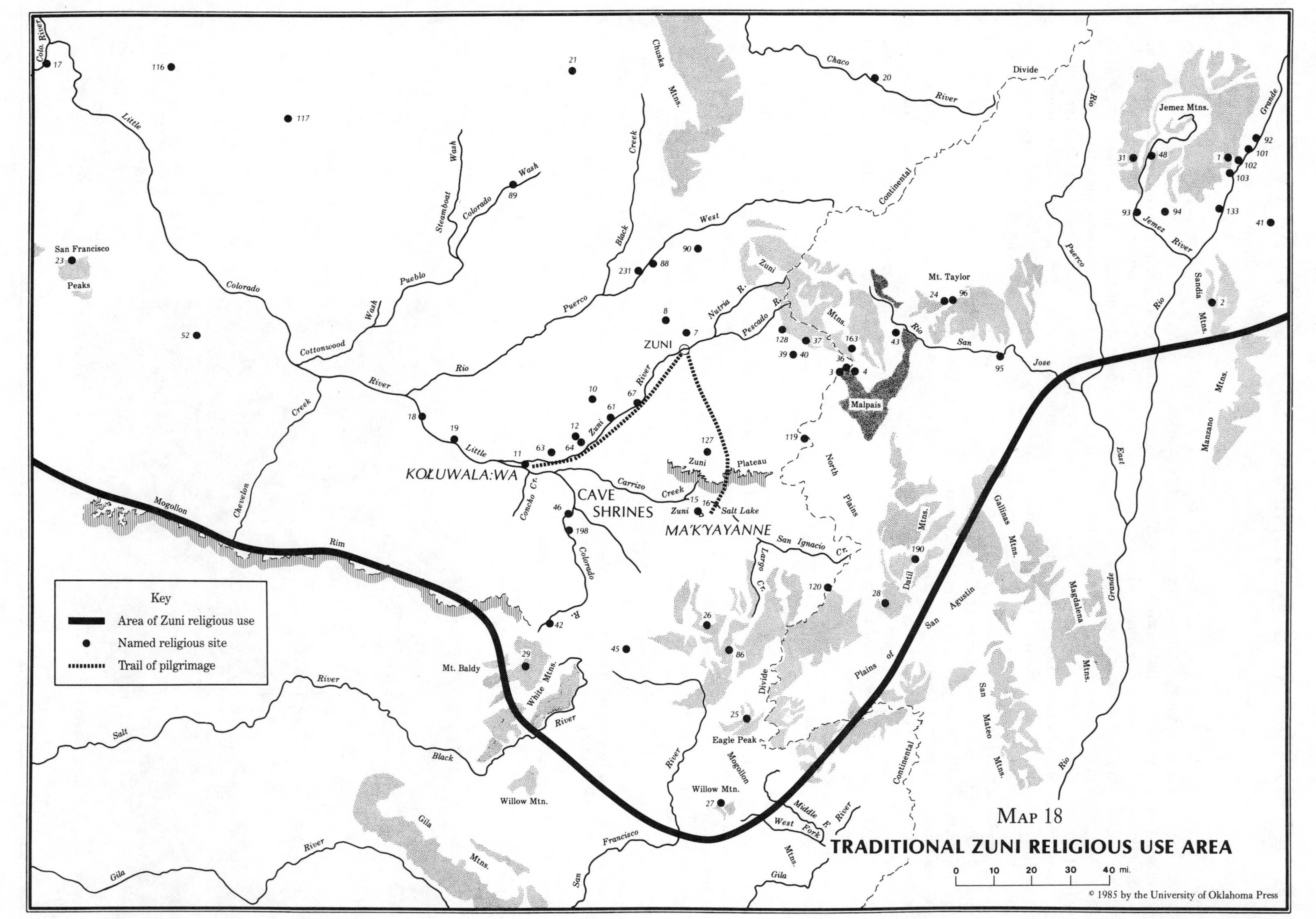

MAP 18
TRADITIONAL ZUNI RELIGIOUS USE AREA

18. ZUNI RELIGIOUS USE AREA

THE Zuni people had, and continue to have, extraordinary knowledge of, affinity with, and empathy for the landscape about them. To the Zunis, the landscape is considered a spiritual relative and thus is cared for with reverence, because it provides the physical setting within which Zuni religion is grounded. Although traditional Zuni thought did not conceptualize environment in a scientific manner, in effect, because of religious belief, the Zunis conserved their natural resources. The Zunis want other people to understand the depth of feeling they have for the landscape, and to understand that they have treated the environment with the same kind of respect that they have for their friends and relatives. This relationship permeates their religious use of the landscape, and, by extension, their utilitarian and political use as well.

Zuni people often use a metaphor to try to express to non-Zunis how they feel about the land. They say, "The landscape is our church, a cathedral. It is like a sacred building to us." Although the entire building (that is, all of the landscape) is sacred to the Zuni people, certain portions of it are especially hallowed—particularly buttes, geological formations, lakes, mud ponds, ruins, and religious trails. In this pervasive folk metaphor, a mesa may be an altar, or a spring a sacred alcove. All these places are remembered in prayers, and offerings are regularly left at many of them. All water is considered sacred in this semi-arid climate, and springs are considered to be the most precious things on earth.

In a traditional religious sense, the outside boundaries of Zuni land are a series of mountains and geographical regions, all held especially sacred to the Zuni people. These are: the Sandia Mountains, near the present city of Albuquerque, New Mexico; Mount Taylor, at the northeast end of the Zuni Mountains; Sierra Abajo, or Blue Mountain, to the north near Monticello, Utah; the Mohave Desert and the Grand Canyon area to the northwest; the San Francisco Peaks, near Flagstaff, in the west; and the Mogollon, Gallo, and Tularosa mountains to the southwest and south. Inside these general boundaries are innumerable springs, ruins, cliffs, waterways, trails, mesas, buttes, and other places of unique religious significance. Regions, as well, may take on important and singular religious values.

The Zuni people believe that after they came into the world from a spot variously located in the Mohave Desert or the Grand Canyon, they searched for many years, across what is now Arizona and New Mexico, for the "middle place" (See Zuni Origin and Migration, Map 8). The spot that they eventually found is very near the heart of Zuni Pueblo, and is believed to be the center of all six directions: north, west, south, east, zenith and nadir. Each of these directions is closely associated with a color, and with plants, seasons, animals, and clans, as well as with religious organizations in existence at Zuni Pueblo. Indeed, the entire culture and being of the Zuni people are tied inextricably to the landscape about them.

There are many specific shrines or sacred places within the Zuni region. Many places along the trail in the migration tradition of the Zunis are held sacred by the Zuni people. Many stories and legends tell of the religious value associated with shrines and sacred places across the Zuni landscape. In the western part of Zuni territory *Detso'ya:wa* (the Painted Desert), *Denatsal Im'a*, and *Wanu/attin* (Jacob's Well) are spoken of in tales and have religious significance. Each waterway in Zuni territory is of religious importance, and two streams west of Zuni Pueblo are *K/awannal-hann/a* (Rio Puerco of the West) and *Sunha:kin K'yawa:na Lhana* (the Little Colorado River). The length of the entire Zuni River has been held sacred, from its headwaters at Nutria Springs, Pescado, and Ojo Caliente, to its confluence with the Little Colorado River. The Zuni River is used as a sacred pathway for pilgrimages to *Kołuwala:wa*, a place at the confluence of the Zuni and Little Colorado rivers where the spirits of the Zunis go after death. North of it is *K'ya:dul Łana*, an archaeological site, which, like many others, is used ceremonially and religiously by the Zuni people.

To the south is the Zuni Salt Lake, also visited on religious pilgrimages, the Zuni Plateau, the Rito Quemado area, Broken Pottery Mountain, and Eagle Peak, all places where Zunis make religious offerings. To the east are shrines in the Zuni Mountains, Agua Fria, El Morro, Mount Taylor, and other important sites even farther east. To the north are Zuni Buttes, Bear Springs, Jacob's Well, Houck, Chaco Canyon, and Blue Mountain. These are but a fraction of the many shrines and sacred places used by the Zunis for centuries past.

Religious pilgrimages and use of religious areas helped the Zunis keep abreast of what plant, animal, and mineral resources were available for beneficial use, and have provided the foundation for Zuni life, past and present. Many of the religious sites throughout the area continue to be used to support Zuni religious activities, although, with increasing non-Zuni development in the area, access to many of them is growing more difficult.

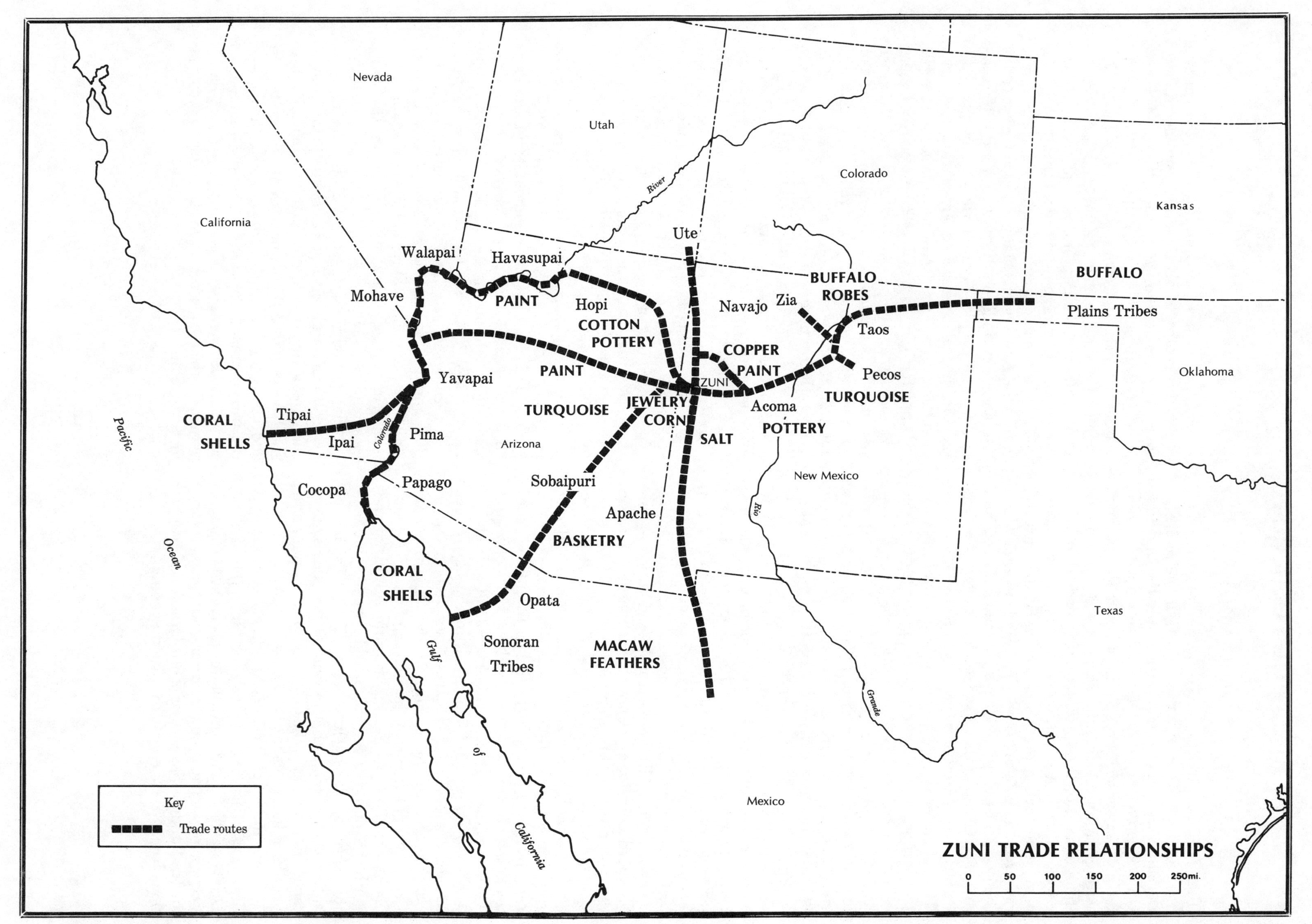
Nevada
Utah
Colorado
Kansas
California
Ute
Walapai
Havasupai
BUFFALO
ROBES
BUFFALO
Mohave
PAINT
Hopi
Navajo
Zia
Plains Tribes
COTTON
POTTERY
Taos
COPPER
PAINT
Oklahoma
PAINT
Pecos
Yavapai
ZUNI
JEWELRY
CORN
Acoma
TURQUOISE
TURQUOISE
CORAL
SHELLS
Tipai
Pacific
Ipai
Colorado
Pima
Arizona
SALT
POTTERY
Papago
New Mexico
Cocopa
Sobaipuri
Apache
Rio
BASKETRY
Ocean
CORAL
SHELLS
Opata
Texas
Gulf
Sonoran
Tribes
MACAW
FEATHERS
Grande
of
Mexico
Key
Trade routes
ZUNI TRADE RELATIONSHIPS
0 50 100 150 200 250mi.
California

19. ZUNI TRADE RELATIONSHIPS

For the past five centuries, trade has been an important activity for the Zuni people. For centuries before that, the ancestors of the Zunis were developing trade routes and relationships over a wide area. Ancestors of the modern Zunis had developed trade with peoples in the Gulf of California and the Mogollon area between A.D. 600 and 900. These trade relations were expanded over the next three centuries, during which time the Zuni villages were part of the impressive Chaco complex. When the Chaco complex disintegrated, the Zuni area became a nexus in a realigned trade network, and by A.D. 1250 had become an important hub in Southwestern regional trade. From then until the arrival of the Spaniards in the sixteenth century, the Zunis were involved in trading goods between the Southwest and Mesoamerica, the Great Plains, and the Pacific Coast, using regular trade routes running both north to south and east to west.

The number of tribes and the different kinds of goods involved in Zuni trade relations are impressive. Zuni trade relations during pre-contact times have been documented with the ancestors of the Pimas; Yumas; Mojaves; Yavapais; Hualapais; Cocopas; the Rio Grande Pueblos, particularly with Pecos; the Havasupai; the California Indians of the tribes of Tipais and Ipais; and with the Indians of the province of what is now Sonora, Mexico. Strong ties were maintained in pre-contact times with the Opata and Sobaipuris of southern Arizona and northern Sonora.

Dressing a skin, ca. 1921–23. Photograph by D. A. Cadzow, courtesy the Museum of the American Indian, Heye Foundation (Neg. No. 13110).

Trade items included a wide variety of materials. In pre-contact times, three important items the Zunis had to offer to distant tribes were salt, turquoise, and buffalo robes. Zunis obtained turquoise from the mines at Cerrillos, to the east, and from locations within their own domain. Buffalo skins and turquoise were considered highly valuable by many tribes and were traded at great distances. Buffalo robes passed from Zuni hands to the Opata and on into Sonora, while macaw feathers reached Zuni as payment from the Opatas. Zuni hunters brought in buffalo robes, and traders from the eastern pueblos, especially Pecos, also traded skins with the Zunis. Salt was obtained at the Zuni Salt Lake, the enchanted home of the Salt Mother. Several other tribes also collected salt at the Zuni Salt Lake, submitting to the conditions of the Zunis in doing so—sometimes tribes paid for the privilege, but usually the Zunis only required the proper religious observation and that visiting parties stay on trails and at designated camping places.

Other trade goods that the Zunis bartered with near and distant tribes included: peridot (a green gem), blankets, cloth or cotton, jewelry, wicker baskets, ceramics, paint pigments, plants, animals and animal parts, jet, seashells, ceremonial and dance accoutrements, and leather clothing such as moccasins. The importance of certain pigments, paints, and stones should not be underestimated. The blue paint of Zuni was famous, and several of their other pigments were particularly well known.

Thus, when the first Spaniards reached the Zuni villages in the mid-sixteenth century, they found the area, especially Hawikku, to be the hub of a large regional trade network, where macaw feathers were traded for turquoise and blue paint; shells for corn; coral for pigment; cotton, cotton thread, and cloth for buffalo hides, and jewelry for blankets. Zunis visited, and were visited by, tribes in what are now California and Mexico, and literally dozens of tribes in between. In the seventeenth century one Spaniard observed that ten different languages were spoken along the trail from Zuni to the coast of California.

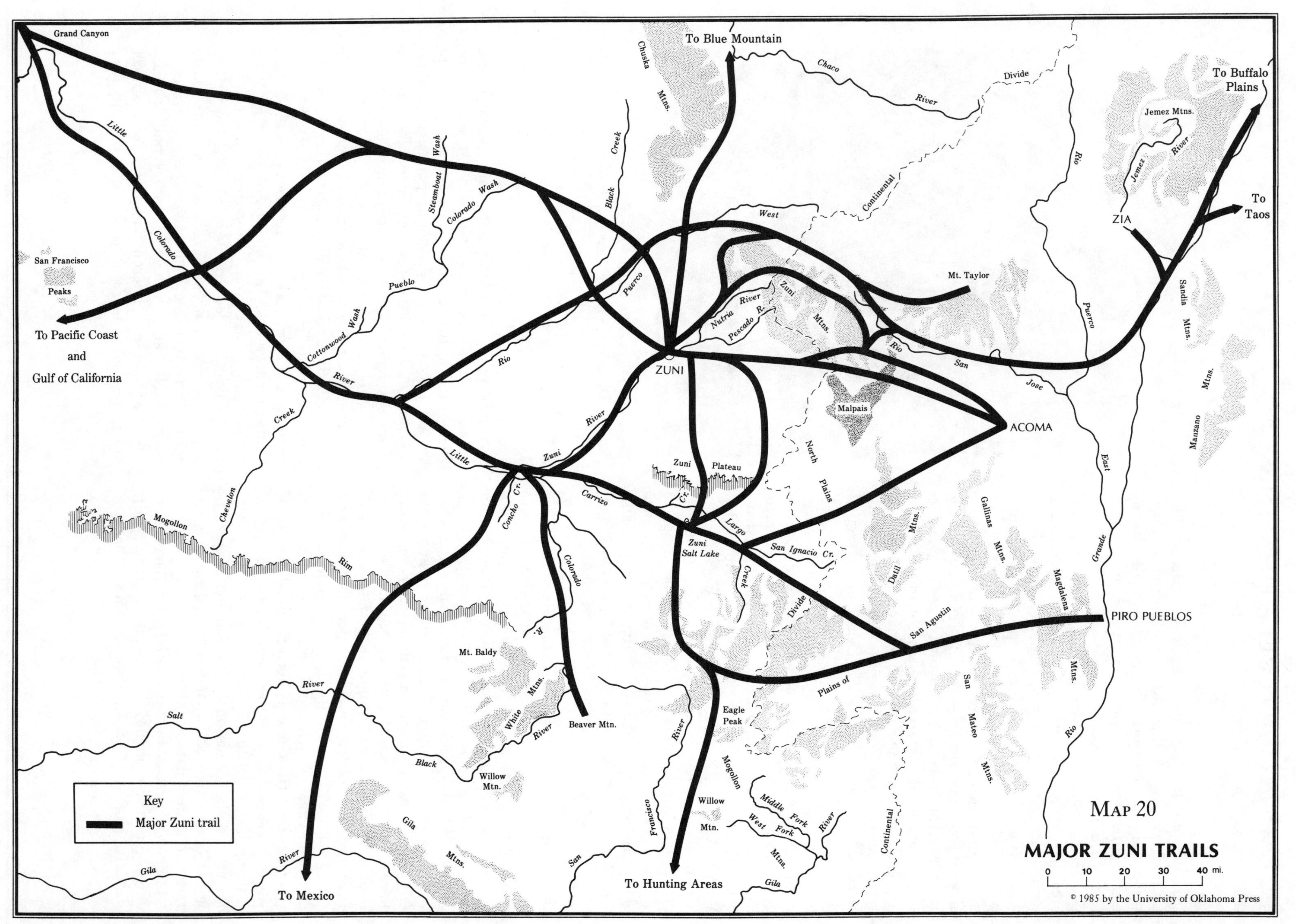

Grand Canyon
To Blue Mountain
To Buffalo Plains
To Taos
Jemez Mtns.
Jemez River
ZIA
Sandia Mtns.
Manzano Mtns.
Chuska Mtns.
Chaco River
Divide
Continental
Rio Puerco
West
Black Creek
Steamboat Wash
Colorado Wash
Little Colorado
San Francisco Peaks
To Pacific Coast and Gulf of California
Pueblo
Cottonwood Wash
Puerco
Rio
River
Mt. Taylor
Zuni Mtns.
Nutria River
Pescado R.
Rio San Jose
ZUNI
Malpais
ACOMA
East
Grande
North Plains
Creek
Chevelon
Little
Zuni River
Zuni Plateau
Cr.
Gallinas Mtns.
Datil Mtns.
Magdalena Mtns.
Concho Cr.
Carrizo
Mogollon Rim
Colorado R.
Largo Creek
Zuni Salt Lake
San Ignacio Cr.
Divide
San Agustin
PIRO PUEBLOS
Plains of
Mt. Baldy
White Mtns.
River
Beaver Mtn.
Salt River
Black
Willow Mtn.
Eagle Peak
San Mateo Mtns.
Rio
Key
Major Zuni trail
Gila Mtns.
Gila River
To Mexico
San Francisco River
To Hunting Areas
Mogollon Mtns.
Willow Mtn.
Middle Fork
West Fork
Gila
Continental
Map 20
MAJOR ZUNI TRAILS
0 10 20 30 40 mi.

20. MAJOR ZUNI TRAILS

TRADE continued to be an important part of the Zuni economy after the arrival of the Spaniards in the sixteenth century. The Zuni tribe had trails that stretched out for hundreds of miles in every direction, connecting them with trading partners in dozens of tribes spread over thousands of square miles. To keep these networks open, to maintain connections, and to protect the trails and keep them safe was an activity of high priority with the Zuni government. Zuni War Chiefs would act against any party restricting or endangering Zuni trails, just as they would respond to encroachments on their territory. Before the 1860s, Zuni was nearly always spoken of as a very safe place to travel to and visit.

The Zunis not only allowed many and diverse groups to travel within their territory in order to carry out trading operations, they *encouraged* such trade and travel. Many groups of people traveled the Zuni roads to reach the trading center of Zuni Pueblo. Many groups of Zunis, as well as individuals, also traveled out across the roads to trade with other tribes. Before 1846, Zuni trading parties were more likely to be communal affairs involving groups of Zunis.

In pre-contact times, Zuni traders established a vast network of contacts and traded a diverse and rich selection of goods with various peoples. Worn, well-marked trails went out from Zuni like the hub of a wheel. One trail led to the Rio Grande pueblos, with branches to Zia, Pecos, and Taos, and then led on past the eastern pueblos to the buffalo plains. Two branching trails went to the northwest to the Hopi villages and then on to the Grand Canyon and farther down the Colorado River, where the Havasupai and other tribes were located. To the south, a trail led to the Gila River country and on into Sonora.

The Zunis used collections of water from streams, springs, rivers, and the ocean for religious purposes. A sample of water from the great ocean helped to attract clouds to the Zunis' periodically parched land. So it was that Zunis made pilgrimages to the Pacific Ocean, not only to trade for shells, coral, and other exotic goods, but also to obtain water from the shores of the great sea, samples of which were sealed in vessels and taken back to Zuni Pueblo.

The arrival of the Spaniards in the Southwest disrupted some of the distant trade of the Zunis, but they continued to participate in an extensive regional trade network with other indigenous peoples in the Southwest during the sixteenth, seventeenth, and eighteenth centuries. The Zunis also began a brisk trade with the Spaniards, who early recognized the value and quality of the Zunis' blue paint. As the Navajos and Apaches moved closer to Zuni land, the Zunis began to increase trade with them as well. Much of the trade with the Navajos and Apaches was considered illegal by the Spanish and Mexican authorities, who considered these tribes to be enemies. Zuni was far from the seat of Spanish and Mexican colonial governments in Santa Fe, however, and the sovereignty of Zuni with respect to free trade was seldom tested by the colonial authorities.

During the early years of the Mexican period the Zunis encountered their first United States citizens, trappers who came out across the trails to Zuni in order to outfit themselves at the last outpost of civilization before going into what were to them unknown lands. The Zunis welcomed these trappers and encouraged their activities in order to promote trade. The Zunis also welcomed the first official United States representatives in 1846, and subsequently supplied the United States Army forts in the area with a large sale of feed corn. Those who wrote of Zuni trade in the nineteenth century gave a uniform picture of a people who were sharp but honest dealers, whose trails and roads were kept open to anyone who might have commercial business to take up, and were protected, as best they could be, from bandits or warring tribes.

Many of the engineering expeditions sponsored by the United States government to explore routes for wagon roads and transcontinental railroads traveled and mapped major Zuni trails and roads. When the railroad was finally constructed in the 1880s, it was built at the edge of Zuni territory along the Rio Puerco of the West. Today several New Mexico State Highways follow what were originally Zuni trails. New Mexico State Highway 53 from the Zuni Indian Reservation through the Zuni Mountains to the Malpais near Grants, New Mexico, is officially recognized as "the Ancient Way," and was once one of the main trails from Zuni to Acoma. Map 20 projects the locations of some of the many Zuni trails.

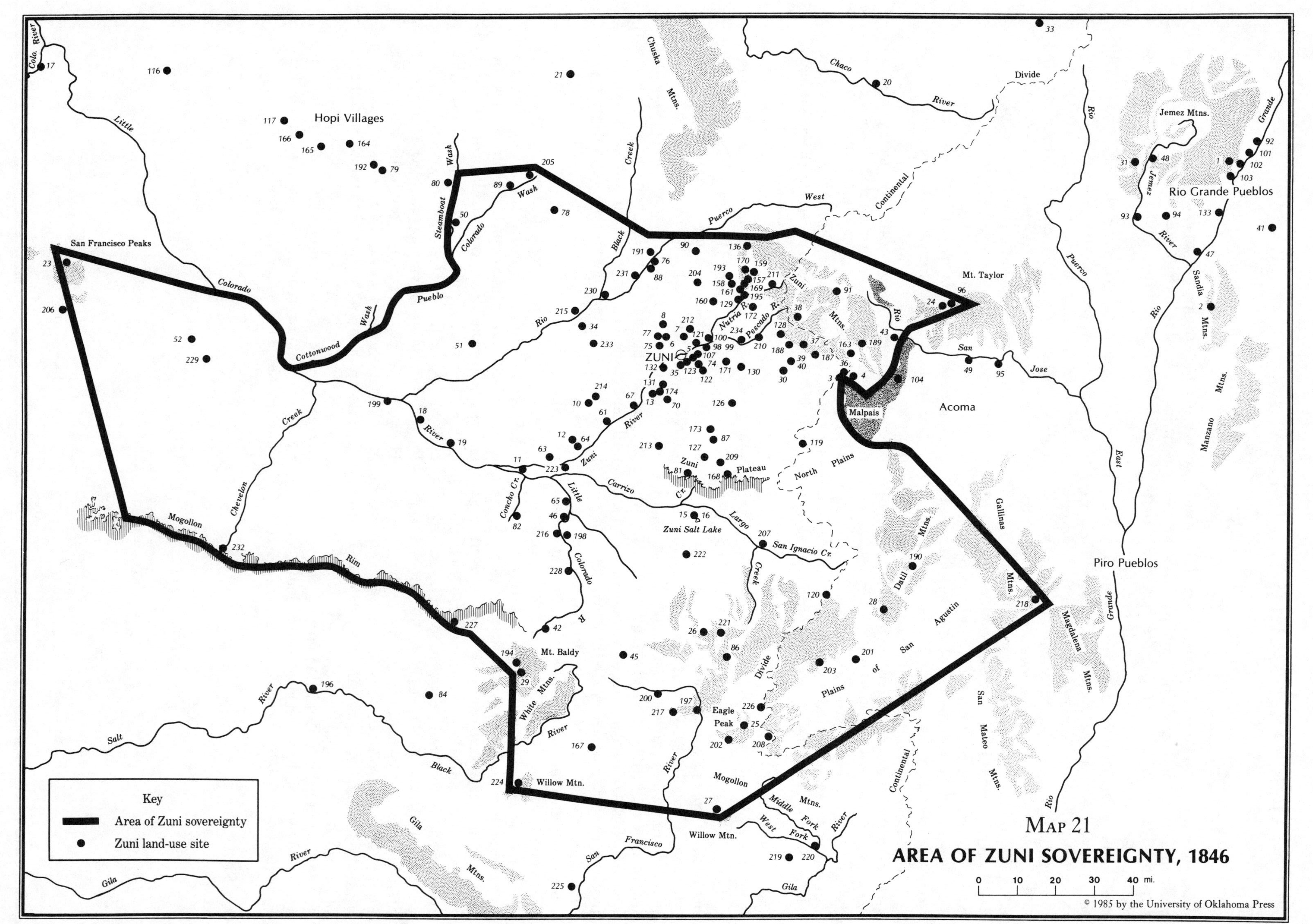

Map 21
AREA OF ZUNI SOVEREIGNTY, 1846

21. AREA OF ZUNI SOVEREIGNTY, 1846

THE Zunis' vast accumulation of knowledge about the environment around them was compartmentalized into the social, religious, medicinal and political institutions that structured the Zuni tribe. The organization of the tribe's priesthoods, kivas, clans, curing societies, and politics has itself defied description by outsiders, and within these institutions a vast and intricate body of traditional knowledge was passed on orally and learned by rote, word for word, action for action, by each new generation.

The sophisticated technology necessary to move the desert waters and grow crops of corn, wheat, and vegetables was learned by each generation. Communal and solitary hunts continued, decade after decade. The flocks of sheep herded by clans and families grew and were guarded against human and animal predators. In bad years, gathering practices helped the Zunis to survive, even when drought left their farms parched. In good years, luxuries of all kinds could be found among the hills and plains. A profitable trade pushed traders in and out along the trails that radiated from the "mid-most point" of Zuni Pueblo. Accompanying all of the Zuni activities were elaborate religious ceremonies—prayers, rituals, and offerings at shrines throughout the Zuni area.

By using all aspects of their environment, and yet not depleting that environment, the Zunis were able to maintain a territory that could sustain them on a very long-term basis. In fact, there is no reason to believe that they could not have used their traditional practices to live in that territory *indefinitely* had not the Europeans arrived on the scene.

The traditional boundaries of the Zunis were known and understood by members of the tribe (and by members of other, neighboring tribes). The political organization of the Zunis was led by the Governor, the Lieutenant Governor, and their *Tenientes,* or representatives to the tribal council. These officers were traditionally appointed by a Council of High Priests. The enforcement of tribal policy was carried out by the Priesthood of the Bow. The traditional political organization of the Zuni tribe was theocratic in nature, and European titles for its executive officers were acquired only after contact with the Spaniards.

The governor and his council dealt with all non-Zuni political contacts. These officials encouraged and developed trade relations with outside peoples. They formed alliances and determined policy towards aggressors or potential aggressors (all under the watchful eye of the highest priests, who were not supposed to directly involve themselves in secular affairs or disputes). The Priesthood of the Bow enforced the laws of the tribe to protect the Zuni people from internal and external threats, and also guarded the trails and kept them safe for travel by friendly people. The Bow Priests protected the tribe's borders from the encroachment of non-Zunis by establishing War God shrines at important boundaries and along trails. The War Gods protected Zunis and non-Zunis alike, as long as the Zunis lived within the established order, and the War Gods helped to keep the world as a whole at peace. When war did have to be waged, the Zunis were superb fighters. Historically, however, their main political weapons were organization, alliance, policy, statesmenship and good faith—all of which led to the healthy respect in which they were held by all their neighbors.

In 1846, General Stephen Watts Kearny's Army of the West exerted United States sovereignty over what is now New Mexico. When one of Kearny's officers, Alexander W. Doniphan, visited Zuni territory and established the first official peaceful relations with the Zuni tribe, the Zunis were maintaining a large territory in the manner described above. The Zunis had held this territory for centuries, against many aggressors, including the Spaniards. The Treaty of Guadalupe Hidalgo, signed in 1848, officially transferred the New Mexico territory, including the Zuni area, from the political control of Mexico to the United States. This treaty obligated the United States to respect and protect the property and rights of all Mexican citizens within the lands transferred, including the Zuni Indians. The full extent of Zuni land and property rights was not adequately recorded in the archives of Santa Fe, however, and over the next hundred years 90 percent of the Zunis' land was lost as the Americans spread into the area. The Zuni people have been left with only the heart of the living cathedral within which their ancestors traditionally lived and worshipped.

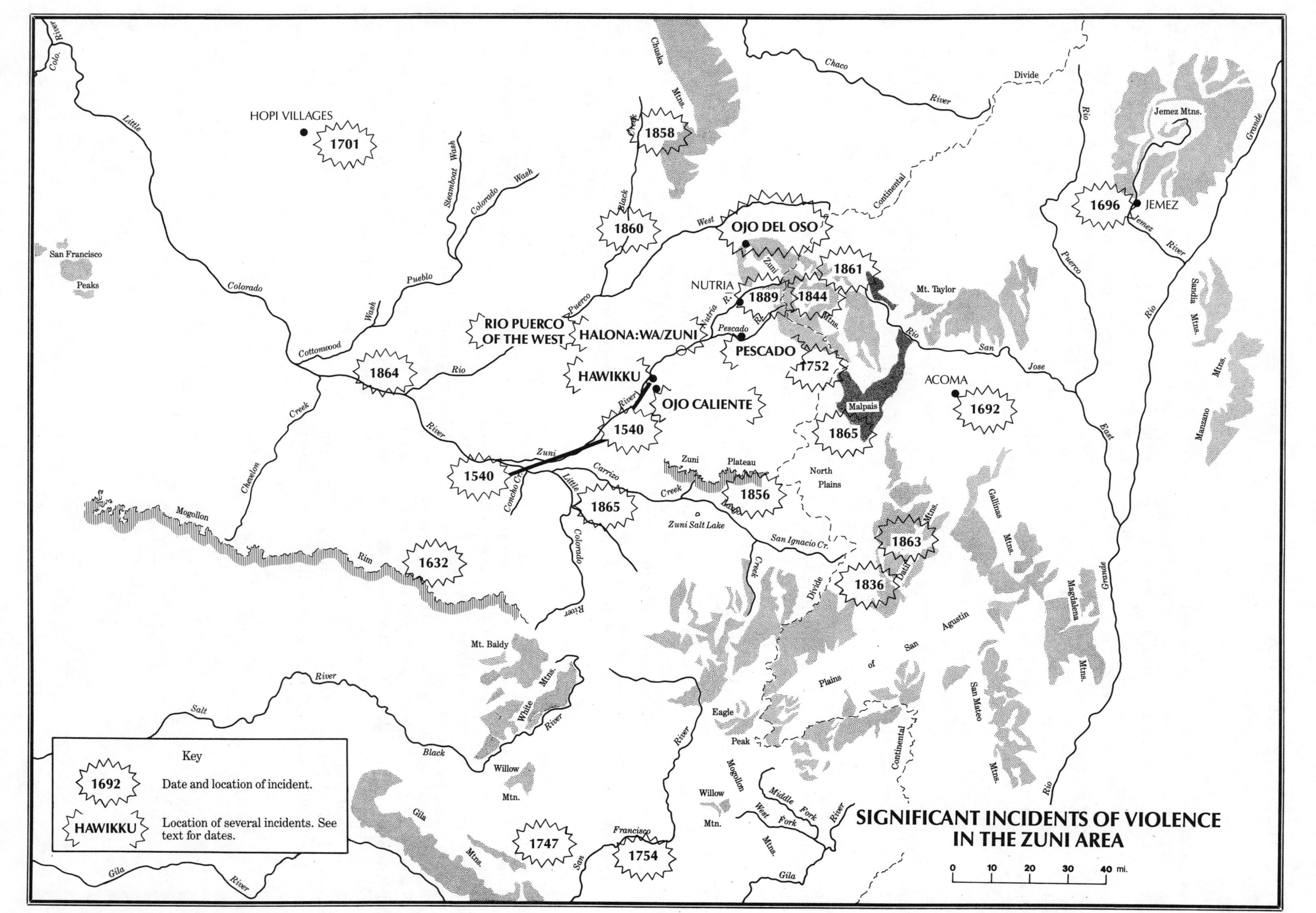
SIGNIFICANT INCIDENTS OF VIOLENCE IN THE ZUNI AREA
Key
1692 Date and location of incident.
HAWIKKU Location of several incidents. See text for dates.
0 10 20 30 40 mi.
HOPI VILLAGES
1701
1858
1860
1864
1540
1540
1865
1632
1747
1754
OJO DEL OSO
1861
1844
1889
NUTRIA
PESCADO
1752
HALONA:WA/ZUNI
RIO PUERCO OF THE WEST
HAWIKKU
OJO CALIENTE
1865
Malpais
1856
1863
1836
ACOMA
1692
1696
JEMEZ
Jemez Mtns.
Mt. Taylor
Chuska Mtns.
Zuni Mtns.
Zuni Plateau
North Plains
Zuni Salt Lake
Plains of San Agustin
Gallinas Mtns.
Magdalena Mtns.
San Mateo Mtns.
Sandia Mtns.
Manzano Mtns.
Datil Mtns.
Mogollon Rim
Mt. Baldy
White Mtns.
Willow Mtn.
Eagle Peak
Mogollon Mtns.
Gila Mtns.
San Francisco Peaks
Continental Divide
Little Colorado River
Chaco River
Rio Puerco
Rio Grande
Rio San Jose
Jemez River
Zuni River
Black Creek
Pescado
Nutria R.
Carrizo Creek
Concho Cr.
Cottonwood Wash
Chevelon Creek
Pueblo Wash
Steamboat Wash
Colorado Wash
Salt River
Black River
White River
San Francisco River
Gila River
Middle Fork
West Fork
San Ignacio Cr.
Colo. River

22. SIGNIFICANT INCIDENTS OF VIOLENCE IN THE ZUNI AREA

WHENEVER possible, the Zunis avoided violence and warfare in their political relations with other groups. They fought only in defense of their territory and people—there is no record of the Zunis ever acting as aggressors in a war. But when they fought, the Zunis were well organized, highly motivated warriors. When they fought to protect their sacred land, they fought with zeal and precision. In battle, the Zunis were led by their Bow Priests, also called War Chiefs. The scalps taken from slain enemies were revered and kept in a shrine near Zuni Pueblo. Like all aspects of traditional Zuni life, the organization and structure of warfare was integrated into the Zuni religion.

The Zunis occasionally entered into political alliances that required their participation in military action. The earliest historic example of such a political alliance is the Pueblo Revolt of 1680, in which the Zunis joined with all of the other pueblos in New Mexico to drive the Spaniards out of their territory. In the eighteenth and nineteenth centuries, the Zunis provided military auxiliaries for Spanish, Mexican, and American campaigns against the Navajos and Apaches who were encroaching on their land. The following list of incidents of violence gives dates and places and provides brief descriptions of the major conflicts, skirmishes, and battles historically documented in the Zuni area.

INCIDENTS OF VIOLENCE IN THE ZUNI AREA: 1539—1889

1539 Hawikku

A black Moor, Esteban, led a party into Zuni territory looking for the fabled "Seven Cities of Cibola." The Zunis killed Esteban and a number of the Indians accompanying him when Esteban made excessive demands of the Zuni people and attempted to take Zuni women for his use. The remaining Indians in Esteban's party fled back to the south, where they joined Friar Marcos de Niza, who had been following Esteban to Zuni, and together they all retreated to the Spanish settlements in Mexico. The Zunis sent word to their neighbors that the Spaniards were mortal and could be killed. Most historians have identified the site of Esteban's death as Hawikku, but there is a strong tribal tradition that the execution took place at Kyaki:ma, one of the largest of the Zuni villages at that time.

1540 Little Colorado River and Hawikku

Responding to stories told by Friar Marcos de Niza, Coronado led a party of Spanish conquistadores into Zuni territory. This party consisted of approximately 230 mounted Spaniards, 70 foot soldiers, several Catholic priests, several hundred Mexican Indians, and large herds of cattle and sheep. The Zunis monitored the progress of the invading army and finally attacked in a narrow canyon near the juncture of the Zuni and Little Colorado rivers. Guerrilla tactics were used by the Zunis against the conquistadores until they reached the area in the plains south of the village of Hawikku. Here as many as six hundred Zunis battled the well-armed Spanish cavalry and foot soldiers. The Zunis' well-organized battle tactics, which included the use of a horn and smoke signals to direct operations, allowed them to repulse the first Spanish attack on Hawikku. But when the Spaniards retreated to regroup, the Zunis abandoned their positions in Hawikku, and left for their other villages with a great number of wounded and about twenty dead. This was the only major military confrontation between Zunis and Europeans, and was followed by an arranged peace between the Zunis and Spaniards.

1632 Hawikku and along the trail to the Opata

Soon after Catholic missions were established at the Zuni villages, the Zunis rebelled against Spanish authority by killing Friar Francisco Letrado at Hawikku and Friar Martin de Arvide and his two soldier escorts along a trail that probably led to the Opata, who were then allies of the Zunis. The Catholic missions were burned at this time.

1672 Hawikku

Friar Pedro de Avila y Ayala was killed by Apaches at Hawikku. There is some evidence to suggest that there was complicity on the part of the Zunis.

1680 Hawikku and Halona:wa

During the Pueblo Revolt the Zunis took control of the Catholic missions in their villages and may have killed one priest, though Zuni tradition records that they saved and adopted a priest, named "Juan Gray-Robed-Father-of-Us-All."

1692 Acoma

De Vargas reported that the Zunis were at war with Acoma.

1696 Jemez

The Zunis were reported to have sent eight warriors to fight as allies with Jemez Pueblo in its uprising against the Spaniards in 1696.

1701 Hopi Villages

A joint Zuni-Spanish force made an ineffectual attack on the Hopi villages. One Zuni Bow Priest was killed.

1703 Halona:wa

At Halona:wa, Zunis killed three Spaniards who had engaged in notorious and immoral behavior at the pueblo.

1705 Halona:wa

Zunis joined a Spanish expedition against marauding Navajos.

1705 Halona:wa

Apaches killed three Zunis during an attack on Halona:wa.

1706 Halona:wa

Hopis killed three Zunis during an attack on Halona:wa.

1708 Halona:wa

Apaches killed twelve Zunis in several raids.

1709 Halona:wa

Zunis killed four Spaniards at Halona:wa.

1728 Halona:wa

Apaches caused two deaths at Halona:wa.

1747 Gila River drainage

A Zuni-Spanish expedition attacked Apaches south of the Zuni Salt Lake and in the drainage of the Gila River.

1752 El Morro

Apaches killed three Zunis near El Morro on the trail to Acoma.

1754 San Francisco River

A Zuni-Spanish expedition attacked Apaches along the San Francisco River.

1755 Hawikku

A Zuni sheepherder was killed by Apaches beyond Hawikku.

1771 Halona:wa

Fifty Apaches attacked Halona:wa and killed six Zunis.

1786 Not given

A joint Spanish-Zuni expedition was carried out against Apaches.

1805 Canyon de Chelly

Zuni guides led the Spaniard Lt. Antonio Narbona on a raid against Navajos at Canyon de Chelly. Zuni war parties attacked Navajos during the same period.

1807 Halona:wa

Three hundred Apaches attacked Zuni and fought almost all of one day. One Zuni was killed, twelve wounded. Six hundred sheep were stolen by retreating Apaches.

1809 Halona:wa

Twenty Apaches killed five Zunis during a raid on Zuni Pueblo.

1815 Halona:wa

One hundred Mogollone Apaches attacked Zuni herders, killing three Zuni men and one woman.

1821 Bear Springs

Several Navajos were killed by a Spanish military expedition at Ojo del Oso (Bear Springs).

1822 Bear Springs

Navajos were attacked by Mexican troops at Ojo del Oso.

1836 Silver Mountains and Datil Mountains

Mexican troops carried out a campaign against the Navajos hiding in the Silver and Datil mountains.

1836 Halona:wa and Bear Springs

Navajos were killed in the Ojo del Oso area, and two were turned over to Mexicans at Zuni Pueblo.

1837 Halona:wa

Three Navajos were killed by Zunis near Zuni Pueblo.

1844 Zuni Mountains

Navajos were reported in the Bluewater region. Zunis were reported to have killed Navajo women who were attempting to collect pine nuts in the mountains.

1846 Not given

Zuni was reported to have joined with the United States Army in a war against the Navajo.

1846 Halona:wa and Pescado

A large force of Navajos attacked the Zunis' ranches near Pescado. When Zuni warriors went out to meet the attack, a second and larger Navajo force attacked Zuni Pueblo. However, the remaining people in the village, mostly women and children, successfully defended the pueblo until the Zuni warriors returned home at nightfall.

1849 Halona:wa

Zunis reported that Navajos were harassing them. Two Zuni women were kidnapped by Navajos during a winter raid.

1850 Halona:wa

In July and August, Navajos committed two raids against Zuni Pueblo. During the first, two Zunis were killed when fifty Navajos attacked. During the second, the Zuni Lieutenant Governor was killed when one hundred Navajos attacked. After obtaining permission from United States authorities to counterattack, Zuni warriors killed thirty Navajos in September. Then in October, while Zuni men were helping to provide an escort for the visiting Bishop of Durango, a very large body of Navajos attacked Zuni Pueblo, held it in siege for sixteen days, and stole much of that year's corn crop. In response, the United States eventually sent relief ammunition supplies to the Zunis.

1851 Halona:wa

More Navajo raids were reported against Zuni.

1856 Halona:wa

In October, a raid by Coyotero Apaches took place. Zuni sent a war party in pursuit, which killed one Apache.

1856 Zuni Plateau

In November a large raiding party of Coyotero and Mogollone Apaches killed the United States Indian Agent for the Navajos, Henry Dodge, near the base of the Zuni Plateau.

1856 Halona:wa

In December at least ten Zunis were killed by Coyotero and Mogollone Apaches, who also stole twelve hundred sheep.

1857 Halona:wa

In the fall, one Navajo woman was killed by Zunis during a Navajo raid on Zuni cornfields.

1858 Near Fort Defiance

One hundred and sixty Zunis, fighting in alliance with United States troops under Colonel Dixon S. Miles, attacked Navajos in the Fort Defiance area. On October 17, the Zunis rescued twenty-five United States troops from three hundred attacking Navajos. Three Navajos and one United States soldier were killed, but no Zuni casualties were reported. Later, during skirmishes in the Pueblo Colorado Wash area, two Zunis were wounded and Navajo stock was captured by the Zunis.

1859 Halona:wa

One Navajo was killed in raids against Zuni Pueblo, during which some Zuni cattle were stolen.

1860 South of Fort Defiance

United States troops attacked Navajos south of Fort Defiance.

1861 Bear Springs

United States troops attacked Navajos at Ojo del Oso. During the period between 1858 and 1868, United States troops pursued Navajos into the mountainous regions around the borders of Zuni territory.

1861 Bluewater

Zunis killed three Navajos hiding near Bluewater.

1863 Saint Johns, Arizona

United States troops attacked Navajos in the upper Little Colorado drainage near Saint Johns.

1863 Halona:wa

Zunis killed Navajos near Zuni Pueblo and left the bodies in the field.

1863 Datil Mountains

A large force of three hundred Pueblo Indians killed Navajos where they were found hiding in the Datil Mountains. Zunis took part and later performed a scalp dance.

1864 Little Colorado

United States troops attacked Navajos along the Little Colorado River.

1865 Halona:wa

Zunis and United States troops under Antonio Mejicano killed twenty-one Navajos within nine miles of Zuni.

1865 Pescado

Zunis killed one Navajo at Pescado.

1865 Malpais

Citizen bands attacked Navajos in the lava beds east of Zuni Pueblo.

1865 Rio Puerco

Zunis report they killed three Navajos encountered on the Rio Puerco.

1865 Ojo Caliente

Zunis killed two Navajos near the Zuni farming village of Ojo Caliente.

1866 Escondido Mountains

Zunis attacked Navajos in Escudilla (Escondido) Mountains.

1871 Not Given

Two Zunis were killed by Navajos, and in retaliation, Zunis killed two Navajos.

1873 Rio Puerco

Zunis fought Navajos on the Rio Puerco of the West. In the battle, thirty Navajos and fifteen Zunis were reported killed.

1889 Box "S" Canyon

Four Zunis were killed in a battle with non-Indian cattle rustlers in the Nutria area. The story of this incident is still well known to most Zunis today.

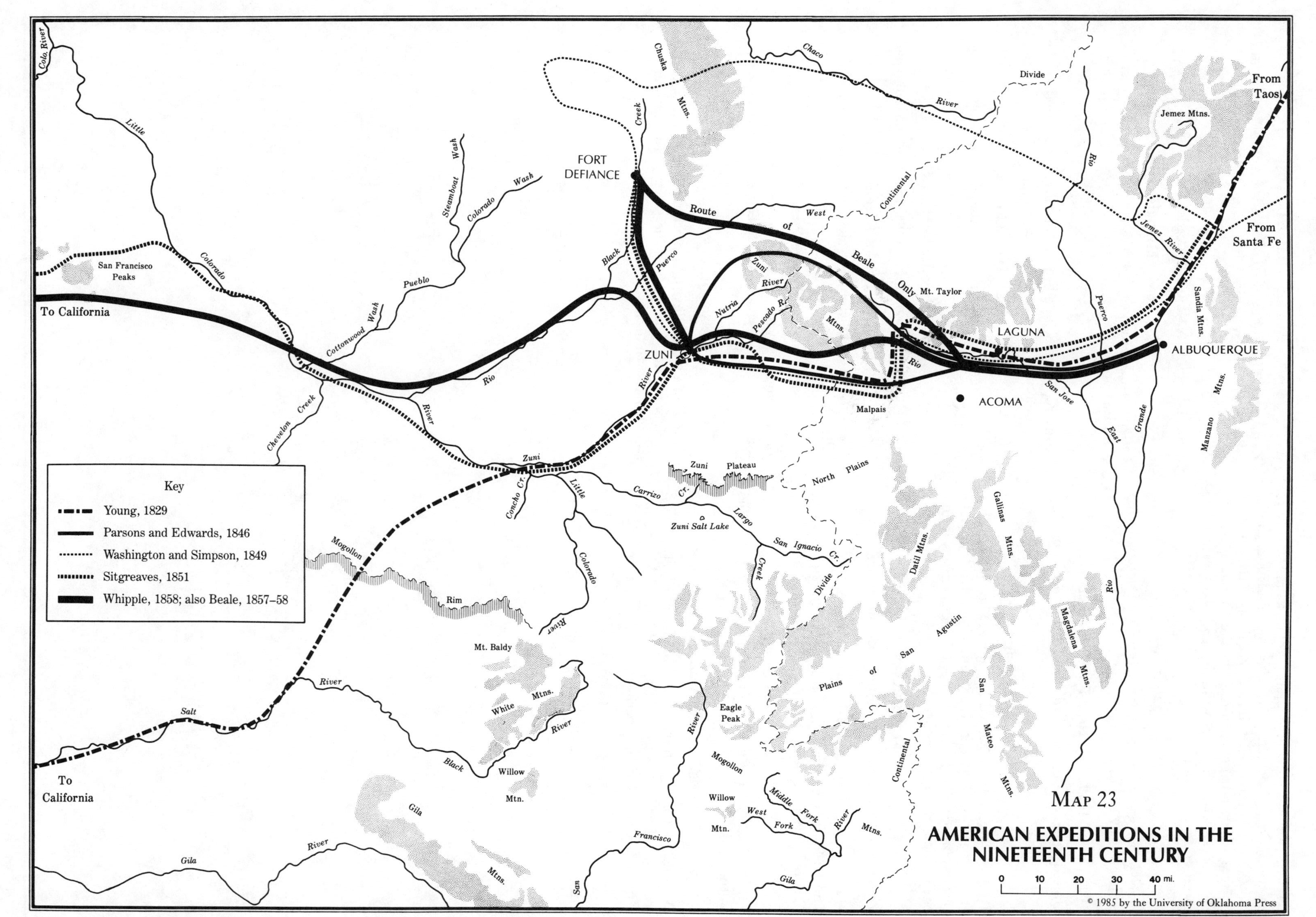

Map 23
AMERICAN EXPEDITIONS IN THE NINETEENTH CENTURY

23. AMERICAN EXPEDITIONS IN THE NINETEENTH CENTURY

THE FIRST CITIZENS of the United States to make contact with Zuni did so shortly after the beginning of the Mexican period. Initial contacts were made by trapping parties who outfitted themselves through trade at the Pueblo, and some of whom trapped in parts of Zuni territory. The first trapper to reach Zuni was William Sherley ("Old Bill") Williams, who was befriended by the Zunis in 1826. He was followed by Richard Campbell in 1827 and Ewing Young in 1829. These American trapping companies were officially illegal under Mexican law, but Zuni welcomed the trade and contact and allowed some trapping to take place within its borders. There was some trapping by Americans in Zuni territory in the 1830s, but contact between Zuni and the United States disappeared between 1835 and 1846.

With the outbreak of the Mexican War, Zuni contact with official United States parties began. From the beginning, Zuni allied itself with the United States by feeding, housing, and fighting alongside United States troops. The first official parties to reach Zuni came in 1846, when Stephen Watts Kearny's Army of the West took possession of New Mexico. When Navajo problems arose, Kearny ordered Colonel Alexander W. Doniphan to march into Navajo country and either scare the tribe into submission or force them into peace. Three parties under Doniphan made contact with the Zunis: a party under Captain John H. Reid, another under Captain Monroe M. Parsons, and the main column under Doniphan himself. The march culminated in the signing of the Treaty of Bear Springs by the United States, Zuni, and representatives of several Navajo bands. This treaty was never ratified by the United States Congress.

The United States authorities vastly underestimated the military capacity of the Navajos and bungled policy toward its Indian allies, including Zuni. The Navajos ignored the series of treaties that were signed in the 1840s and the 1850s and gradually grew more and more powerful and devastating in their raids against both Indian and non-Indian settlements. In 1849, the territorial governor and military commander, John M. Washington, ordered an expedition against the Navajos. Along with Washington went Lieutenant James Hervey Simpson of the Corps of Topographical Engineers, to plot the way and keep a journal of the trip. Although the expedition was unsuccessful in quelling Navajo depredations, the United States, through Simpson's work, began mapping Zuni country. A series of expeditions in the 1850s and 1860s mapped and plotted Zuni country.

In 1851 another topographical engineering party passed through Zuni, with the mission of determining if the Zuni River was navigable. This party, under Captain Lorenzo Sitgreaves, mapped the Zuni River to its juncture with the Little Colorado and then went on to California. In 1853, Lieutenant A. W. Whipple led another expedition through Zuni, this time with the purpose of determining a practicable route for a railroad line from the Mississippi River to the Pacific Ocean, roughly following the 35th parallel.

By 1857, although quite a number of American parties had passed through Zuni on their way to California, the parties had not included wagons. In that year, Edward Fitzerald Beale led a road-building expedition along Whipple's old route to make a more passable road to California, as well as to test the twenty-five camels he had with him for use in the Southwestern deserts.

Between 1858 and 1868, military operations against the Navajos dominated United States activities in Zuni territory, but it was not until after the subjugation of the Navajos and their return from Fort Sumner in 1868 that a complete mapping of the Zuni area was attempted. In 1873 the Topographical Engineers, under George M. Wheeler, began a systematic mapping of the entire Zuni region. By 1879, travel through Zuni was common and the newly formed Bureau of Ethnology (later known as the Bureau of American Ethnology) sent an expedition to Zuni to collect artifacts. Thousands of pots and other items were collected and taken back to Washington, where they still are in the collections of the Smithsonian Institution. One member of that expedition was Frank Hamilton Cushing, a young ethnologist who stayed on at the Pueblo after the others left, and who was eventually adopted into the tribe and the Bow Priesthood—experiences he wrote about in important early ethnographic accounts about the Zuni Tribe.

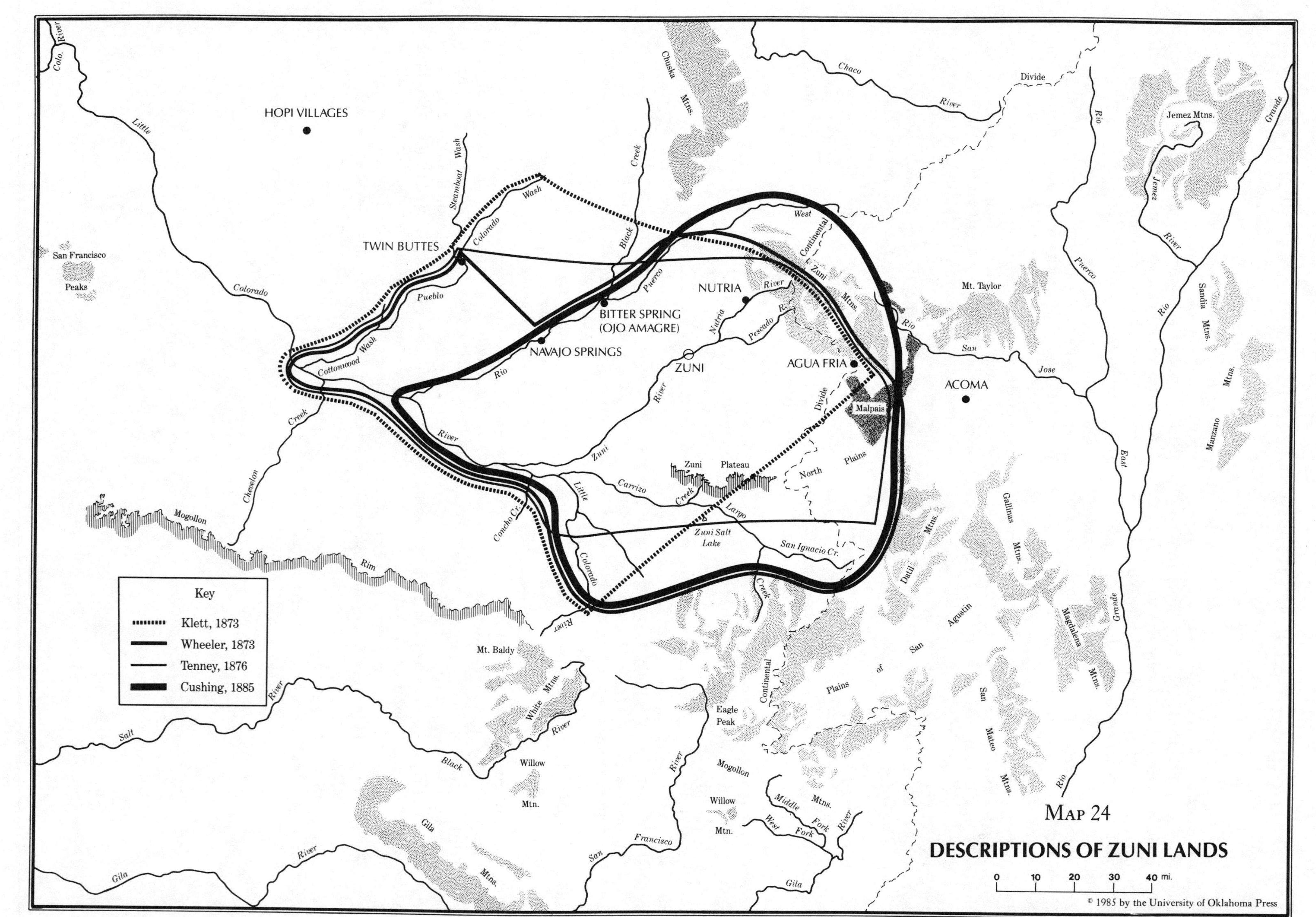

Map 24
DESCRIPTIONS OF ZUNI LANDS

24. DESCRIPTIONS OF ZUNI LANDS

By 1873, when George M. Wheeler's Topographical Engineers were mapping the Zuni area, the Zunis had already lost a considerable amount of land. Although agreements had been reached with the United States which guaranteed the Zunis rights to their land, encroachments were increasing rather than decreasing, as more and more Americans came into the area. The governor of Zuni, Pedro Pino, made sure to tell Wheeler of his people's grievances. Both Wheeler and one of his survey party leaders reported conversations with Pedro Pino (or Lai-iu-ah-tsai-lu) about the then-current extent of Zuni lands and of encroachments that were taking place.

Frances Klett, leading one of Wheeler's surveying parties, arrived at Zuni on July 22, 1873. Pino described Zuni land for him:

> . . . the country between the Neutrias and the Colorado Chiquito, some sixty miles, and Aqua Fria and the Moquis Settlements, about one hundred miles.

Wheeler himself was at Zuni in August, 1873. Pino told him that the tribe's land had been guaranteed by a grant from the Mexican government (the United States was obliged to honor all such grants under the terms of the Treaty of Guadalupe Hidalgo). Wheeler wrote:

> The grant from the Spaniards, or rather the Mexicans as asserted by Pedro Pino, covers the following area: bounded on the north by the dividing ridge between Zuni River and the Puerco, on the east by the summit of the Zuni Mountains, on the south by an east west line through the Salt Lake, and on the West by the Little Colorado.

A third description of Zuni lands was provided by Mormon missionary Ammon Tenney. In his journal of 1876, Tenney described the Mormon's early efforts to baptize Zunis and ended with a description of Zuni territory, as Governor Pino gave it to him:

> This Pelo [*sic*] Pino sais [*sic*] he was at Santa Fe at the time that each delegation was called & got the understanding that Zuni territory was from Agua Fria—dos cieros—salina—Rio Colorado—dos Mesa redondo—Ojo Navajo—Oho a Magre—Rio Puerco—Ciera da Zuni to the place of commencement.

The most precise description of Zuni land was provided by Frank Hamilton Cushing in the late nineteenth century, who, after his work at Zuni gave the following account:

> . . . today [1885], with a sneer of impatience, a gesture of injured deprecation of the narrowness of his present possession, any middle-aged Zuni will define minutely its [the province of the Zuni] boundaries.
>
> These were to the eastward, the plains at the foot of the Gallo above Agua Fria; to the northward the Trans-serranian Valley of the Rio Puerco, from the longitude of Mount Taylor to the Colorado Chiquito; on the west, in Arizona the latter river nearly to its sources; on the south, after the conquest of Marata, the valleys of the Salt Lake and Rio Quemado, which lie along the bases of the Sierra Datila and Sierra Ladrone. Thus the Cibolan dominion had, from west to east, an extent of one hundred and fifty miles, from north to south, of seventy-five or eighty.

All four of these descriptions of Zuni land represent what Zuni boundaries were in the 1870s or 1880s, at a time when the tribe had already lost a great portion of what they had dominated under the Spanish and Mexican governments.

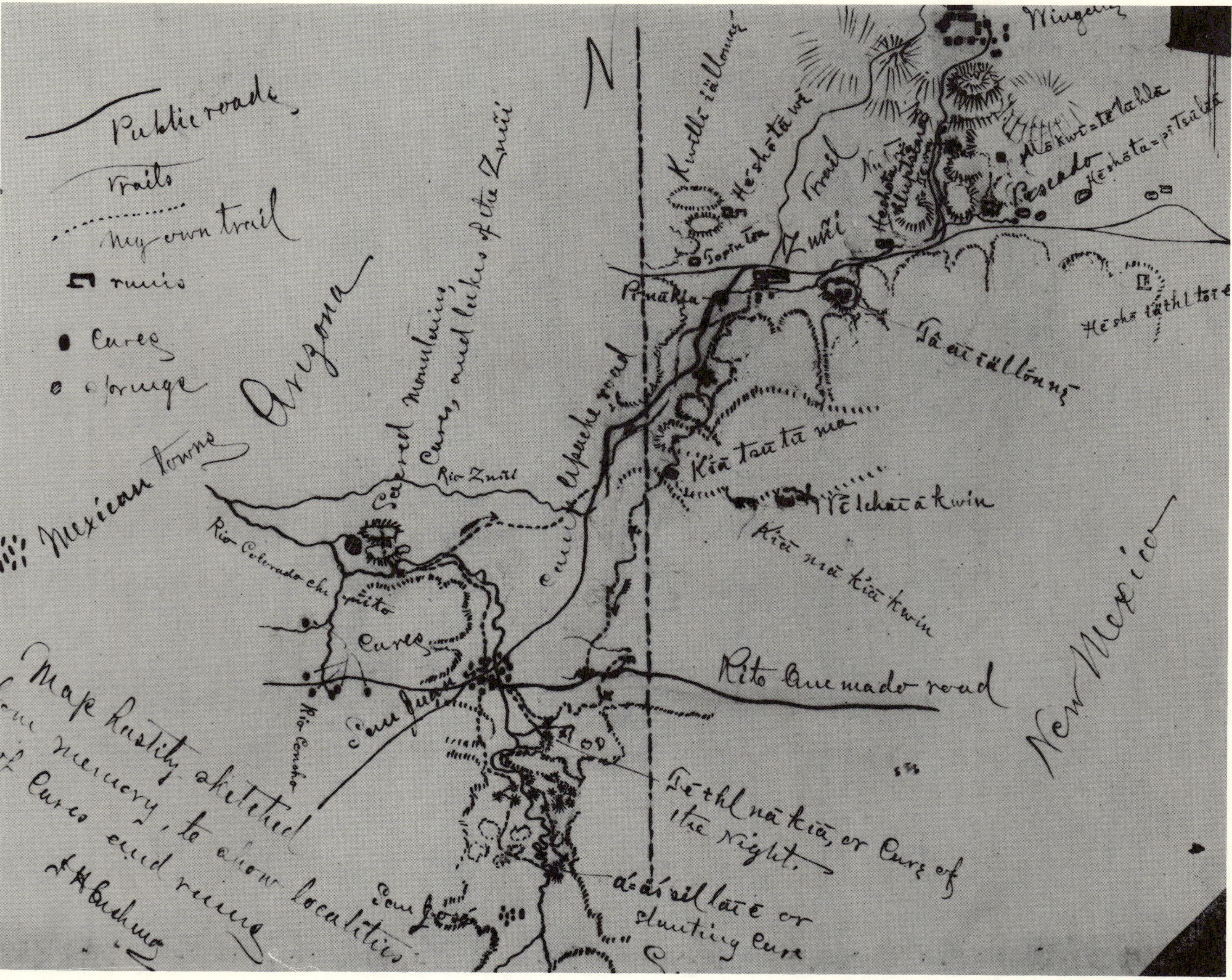

MAP 25. "Map Hastily Sketched from Memory, to Show Localities of Caves and Ruins," by F. H. Cushing, courtesy National Anthropological Archives, Smithsonian Institution.

25. "MAP HASTILY SKETCHED FROM MEMORY, TO SHOW LOCALITIES OF CAVES AND RUINS," by F. H. Cushing

ALTHOUGH stories of the Province of Cibola had prompted the movement of Coronado's army over thousands of miles of uncharted land, and although rumors of the Seven Cities of Cibola had prompted the opening of the Southwest to Europeans and an entire episode of Southwestern history, by the time of the United States invasion into New Mexico the location and identification of the Cibolan pueblos had long been forgotten. Gradually, as military exploration reached the area of Zuni and as historians and ethnologists speculated about the history of the region, Americans realized that Zuni and Cibola were one and the same and that Zuni had a rich and fascinating history that was centuries old.

At the same time, travelers and explorers began to praise the hospitality of the Zuni people and to impressionistically describe the depth of the Zunis' religious beliefs and the complexity of their culture. By the 1870s, the tribe was internationally renowned, even though they were in one of the most remote areas of the United States. At the same time, John Wesley Powell, who believed that Indians and their cultures were sure to disappear as "civilization" advanced, was instrumental in founding the Bureau of Ethnology. The Bureau of Ethnology, which was eventually absorbed into the Smithsonian Institution, had as one goal the investigation of American Indian cultures.

With little formal training, but obvious youthful brilliance, Frank Hamilton Cushing secured a position with the Bureau of Ethnology. In 1879, when Colonel James Stevenson led an expedition of army and Bureau personnel to Zuni Pueblo to collect artifacts, Cushing obtained permission to go with the party. When the expedition left Zuni Pueblo, Cushing stayed behind, pleading poverty to the Zunis. With their typical hospitality, the Zunis took the young Anglo in, clothed him, fed him, and sheltered him, and eventually adopted him as a member of the tribe, giving him the Zuni name Tenatsali (Medicine Flower). All of this was according to Cushing's plan, which was to observe and learn about Zuni beliefs and customs by participating in daily life at the pueblo.

Cushing, or "Cushy," as he was popularly called at Zuni, learned the language, which was no easy task; was adopted into a clan; and eventually became a member of the Priesthood of the Bow. All the while, Cushing was writing of what he learned about the Zunis' culture. His writings are remarkable for their time and provide a penetrating look at the inner workings of Zuni religion and society. Partly because of the early foundation of ethnological writing that Cushing laid at Zuni, many of the world's great anthropologists have subsequently visited the pueblo to do field work and write about the tribe in the years since.

In 1881, after learning of a series of sacred Zuni shrines to the south, and despite being warned by Zuni religious leaders not to visit them, Cushing set out to examine the sites. The shrines were plotted on a "hastily drawn" map showing the area between Zuni and the settlement of Saint Johns (San Juan), and described in letters to his superiors at the Bureau of Ethnology. Upon examining the shrines, which were located in caves and cinder cones, Cushing was able to determine that they had been in use over a very long period of time, and that the whole shrine complex was still in use. One of these shrines continues to be used today, and every four years the Zuni religious leaders make a religious pilgrimage to the area.

Cushing removed more than one hundred items from these shrines and returned with them to Zuni Pueblo, intending to send them to the Smithsonian Institution to be added to their already extensive collection of Zuni artifacts. As a result of this sacrilege, Cushing was called to a council of religious leaders, who explained to him the ritual significance of the artifacts, pointing out that many of them were associated with the Bow Priests and the Zuni War Gods. At this council, the Zuni religious leaders decided which of the artifacts were to be kept by them and ritually disposed of, and which Cushing could send to the Smithsonian Institution. Unfortunately, the artifacts sent to the Smithsonian Institution were lost in transit and never arrived.

Cushing's investigations contributed valuable ethnological documentation, but they also, unfortunately, helped lead to the looting of the shrines. Already, by the 1880s, there was a brisk trade in Southwestern Indian religious articles. Within months of Cushing's visit to the shrines, after a local newspaper reported on their discovery, thieves had stolen many of the remaining Zuni offerings and religious relics. In fact, Cushing himself was offered an apparently lucrative deal by a trader if he would point the way to more shrines (an offer Cushing declined). Today, one hundred years later, stiff penalties await those who steal from Zuni shrines on the Zuni Indian Reservation or other federal land. It is illegal to buy, sell, or in some cases even possess items taken from such shrines.

Zuni Pueblo from Cushing's housetop, ca. 1890. Photograph by Ben Wittick, courtesy the Museum of New Mexico (Neg. No. 16053).

Frank Hamilton Cushing in his Zuni garb. Photograph courtesy of the Smithsonian Institution.

Frank Hamilton Cushing, photographed kneeling next to a scalp pole in the Big Plaza of Zuni Pueblo, ca. 1879. Photograph by I. W. Taber, courtesy the Museum of New Mexico (Neg. No. 78724).

26. "GENERAL MAP OF THE PUEBLO REGION . . .," by Victor Mindeleff

THE greater part of the *Eighth Annual Report of the Bureau of Ethnology*, published in 1891, is devoted to "A Study of Pueblo Architecture, Tusayan and Cibola," by Victor Mindeleff. Profusely illustrated with maps, photographs, and architectural plans, the report examines the ruins and contemporary villages of Zuni (Cíbola) and Hopi (Tusayan). Victor Mindeleff had studied the available literature on Zuni. In fact, his brother Cosmos had put together an annotated bibliography on Zuni and Hopi sources that contains worthwhile information but was never published by the BAE. Victor Mindeleff visited Zuni Pueblo in 1881 while Cushing was in residence, and recorded traditions about the architecture, took notes, made measured drawings, and had photographs made of buildings and ruins. He also studied Ojo Caliente, Pescado, and Nutria, the three Zuni farming villages then in intensive use, recorded details of the seasonal occupation there, and noted field structures used in association with herding and farming. Much ethnographic data of interest today can be gleaned from Mindeleff's work.

Mindeleff not only focused on the inhabited villages of the Zunis as they looked in 1881, but also on the principal ruins, including those occupied by the Zunis in 1540 when Coronado arrived, as well as some of the more ancient sites. He noted the resemblance between some of the ruins in the immediate vicinity of the pueblo and such ruins as Kin Tiel, which were of a much earlier date. He saw a connection between the architectural styles of Zuni and Hopi villages in the early 1880s and the ruins in the region, and concluded that the ancestors of the two tribes had occupied the area in times past, a theory that was surprisingly innovative at the time.

The shaded area in the map, although it does not begin to suggest the real limits of Hopi and Zuni aboriginal boundaries, at least indicates that Mindeleff was aware that Hopi and Zuni boundaries abutted and formed a contiguous border. Zuni territory also formed a contiguous border with Acoma lands, though this map does not indicate such. These common boundaries of the western pueblos are important to note, because they helped to keep the Navajos in check to the north and the Apaches restricted to the mountainous territory to the south, a situation that had been maintained under Spanish and Mexican rule. In the four decades before the drafting of this map, the United States had driven the Navajos out of the north and into Hopi and Zuni territory, a situation that disrupted the stable political relationships in the region and destabilized the boundaries of all the tribes involved.

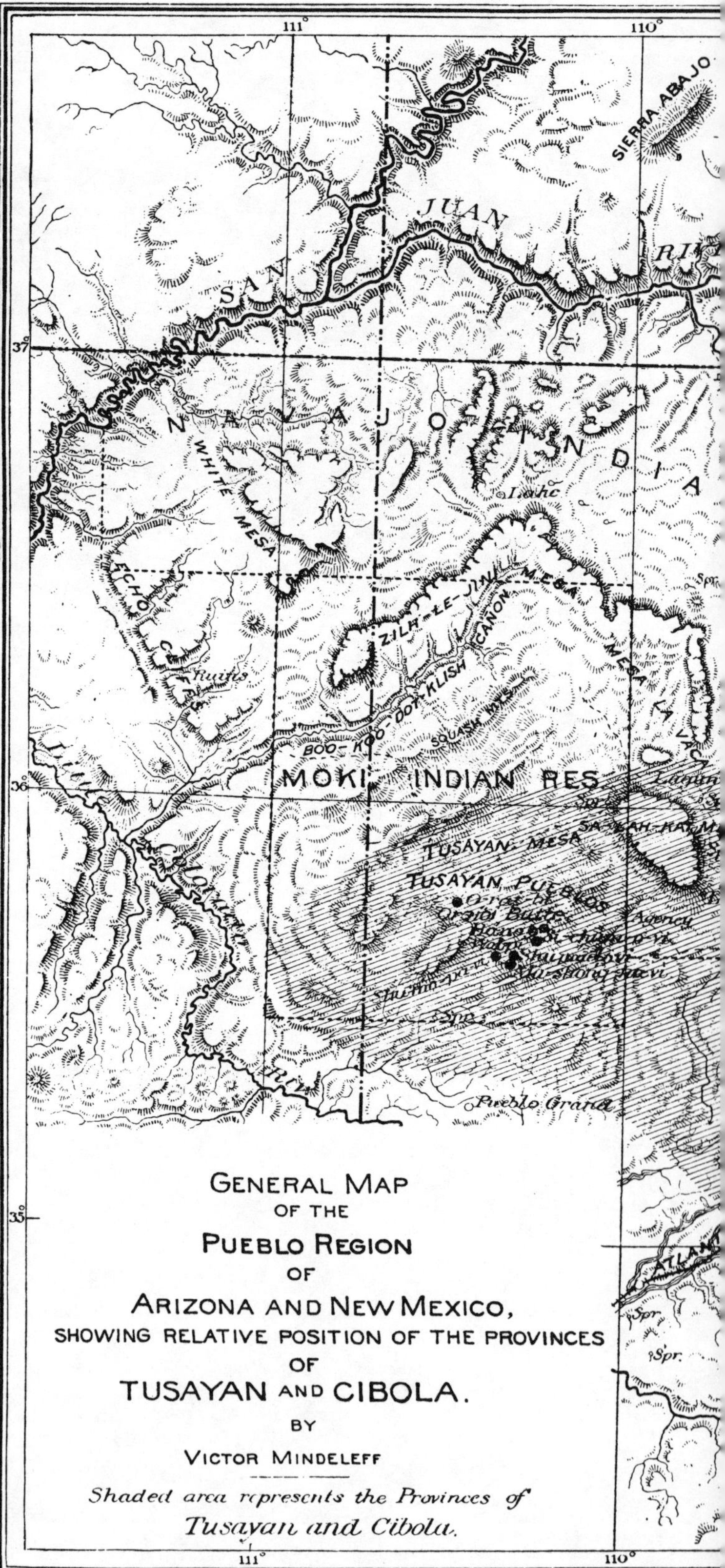

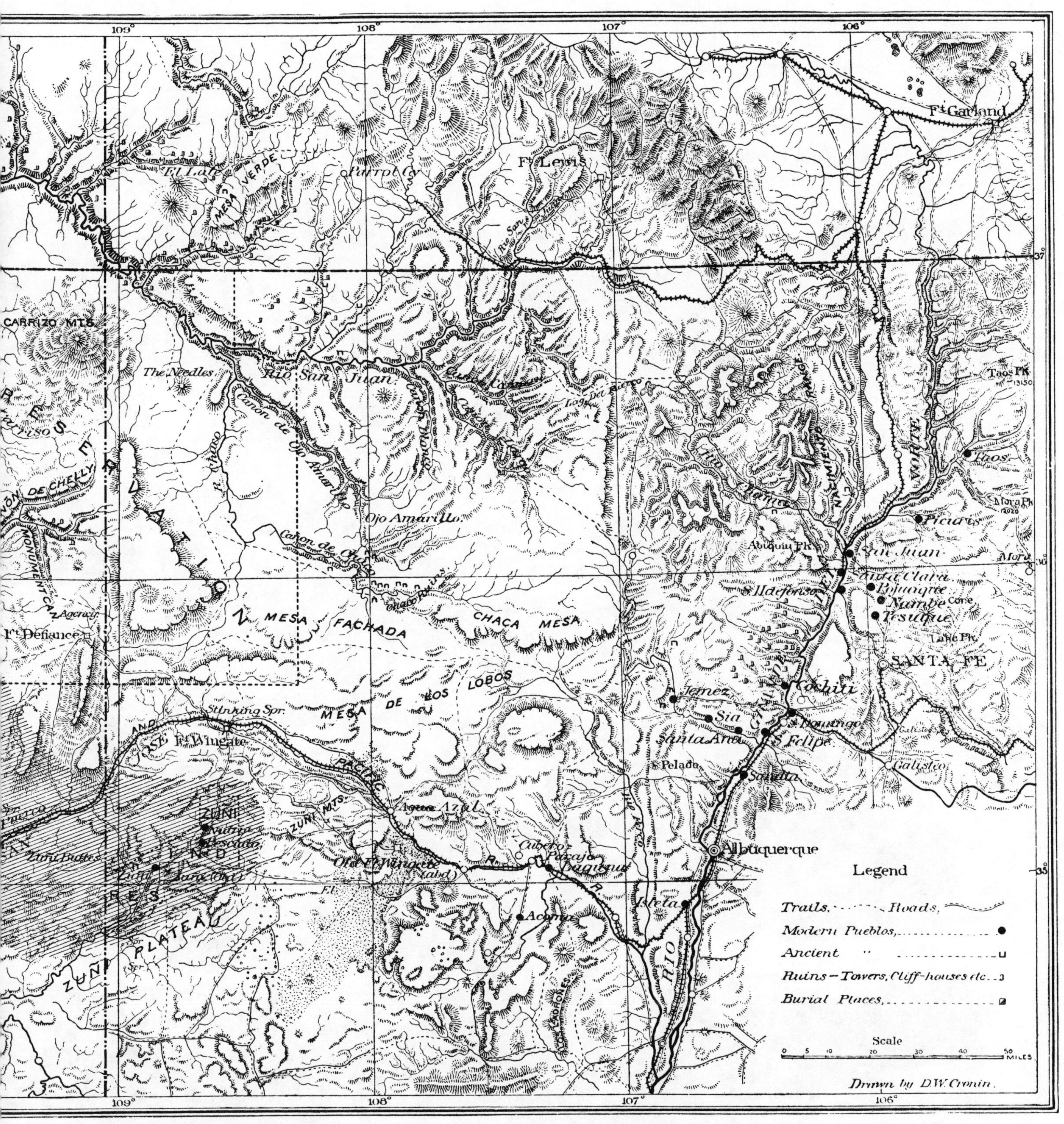

MAP 26. "General Map of the Pueblo Region . . ." (1891), by Victor Mindeleff. From "A Study of Pueblo Architecture: Tusayan and Cibola," *Eighth Annual Report of the Bureau of Ethnology*, Washington, 1891.

Map 27. "Plan of Zuni Pueblo," by Victor Mindeleff. From "A Study of Pueblo Architecture: Tusayan and Cibola," *Eighth Annual Report of the Bureau of Ethnology*, Washington, 1891.

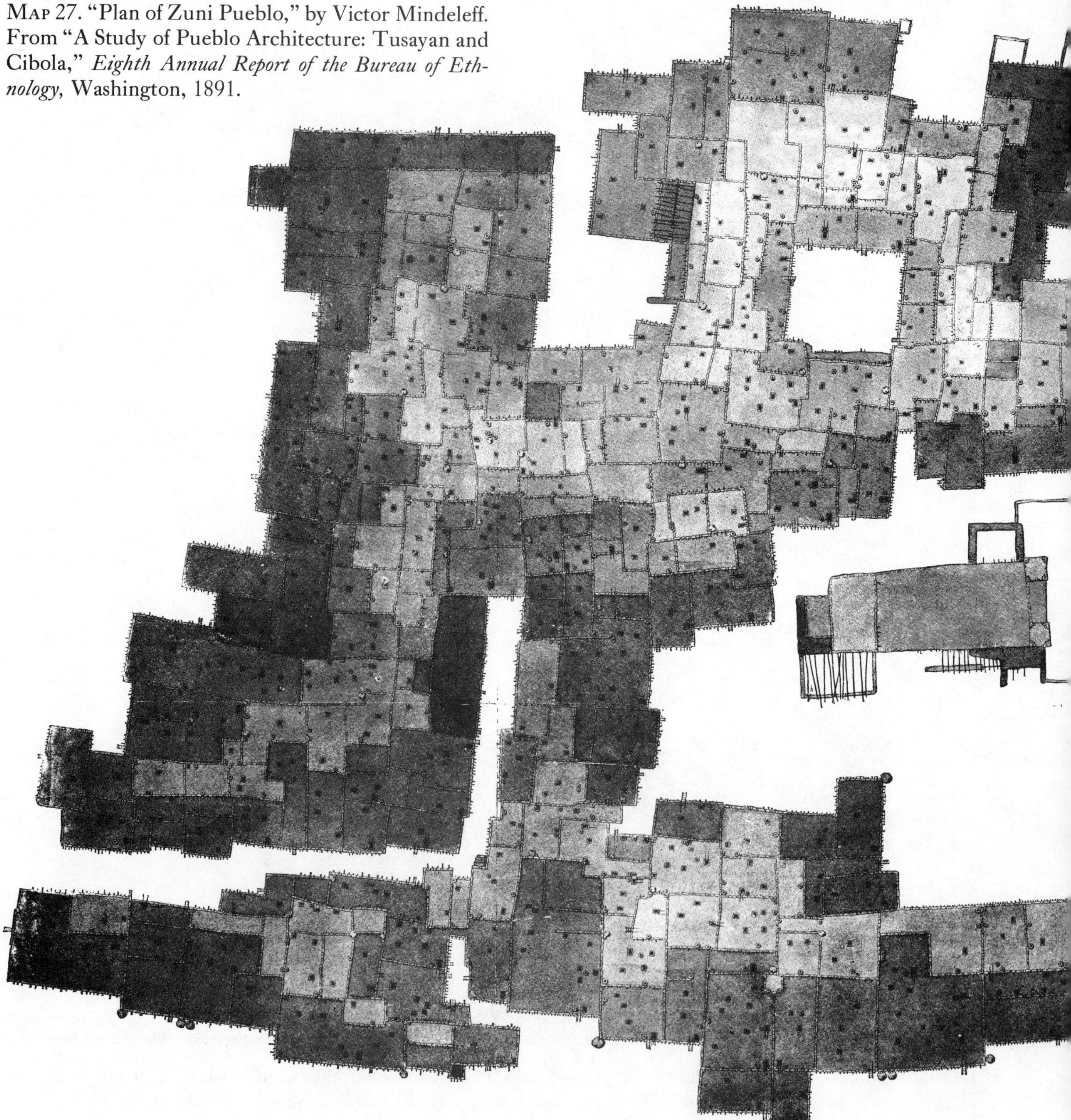

27. "PLAN OF ZUNI PUEBLO, 1881," by Victor Mindeleff

ONE of the most interesting maps produced by Victor Mindeleff in "A Study of Pueblo Architecture, Tusayan and Cibola" is the plan view of Zuni Pueblo in 1881. Carefully mapped with a compass and tape, Mindeleff's plan of Zuni Pueblo provides a scale drawing of the village at its most architecturally compact phase, before the extensive architectural change the pueblo has undergone in the twentieth century. At the time Mindeleff mapped Zuni Pueblo, the village consisted of seven large blocks of contiguous houses arranged around a number of streets and plazas. Each multistoried house block contained many individual houses joined together into a single building. In Mindeleff's drawing of the plan, progressively lighter shading is used to indicate successively higher stories. In the center of the largest plaza stood the Catholic mission, which was roofless at the time, having been abandoned by the Catholic church after Mexican independence.

The oldest part of the village was the highest, most densely clustered area around the two small plazas in the northeast corner of the pueblo. This part of the village, situated at the crest of a small knoll, was occupied in 1540 when the Spaniards first arrived in the Zuni area. At that time, Halona:wa, as Zuni Pueblo was then called, was relatively small compared to some of the other Zuni villages then occupied, such as Hawikku and Mats'a:kya. After the Pueblo Revolt of 1680 the whole Zuni tribe consolidated into a single pueblo at Halona:wa, and the village was greatly ex-

The southern roomblocks at Zuni Pueblo, looking west, 1879. Photograph by John K. Hillers, courtesy of the Smithsonian Institution, National Anthropological Archives (Neg. No. 2267-F).

panded. Additional rooms were added to the existing house blocks, and new house blocks were constructed on the slopes of the hill facing the Zuni River. Eventually, three house blocks were constructed on the flatter ground to the east, enclosing the Catholic church, originally constructed in 1629–30 at the edge of the village, within a large plaza. This basic architectural plan persisted throughout the eighteenth and nineteenth centuries.

In the nineteenth century, Zuni Pueblo was often compared to a large anthill or beehive because of the compact shape of the massive, multistoried house blocks that faced inward toward the plazas. In part, the architecture of Zuni Pueblo was defensive, designed to keep unwanted intruders outside of the village. The openings into the interior of the pueblo were narrow and constricted, and there were few doors or windows in the ground-story walls. Access into house interiors was via ladders that led to roof entryways. Hundreds of the roof entryways can be seen on Mindeleff's map, along with the small, dome-shaped ovens or *hornos* used to bake Zuni bread. By pulling up the ladders that led into the pueblo interior, the Zunis could protect themselves from hostile raids by the Navajos and Apaches.

A prominent feature of the nineteenth-century architecture of Zuni Pueblo was the use of rooftops as areas for outdoor activity. In most of the village the relatively flat rooftops formed terraces, the roof of one room or set of rooms providing an open area for the rooms above. The rooftop terraces were used for many activities, including food preparation, hide tanning, storage, ceramic production, and for sleeping in the summer. The rooftop terraces were also used for access around the pueblo, and many people gathered on the rooftops to observe the dances and ceremonies conducted in the plazas. The terraces formed by rooftops were generally oriented to face east or

View of Zuni, looking northeast, 1879. Photograph by John K. Hillers, courtesy the Smithsonian Institution, National Anthropological Archives (Neg. No. 2267-J).

south, providing exposures that took maximum advantage of passive solar heating and were protected from the prevailing westerly winds by the high walls of the westernmost house blocks.

The compact architectural complex of nineteenth-century Zuni Pueblo provided ample space for the domestic and religious activities of the Zuni people. Situated at the crest of a small hill, the pueblo also commanded a majestic view of the red- and white-cliffed mesas that border the Zuni River valley. An architectural transition between the massive house blocks of the pueblo and the open landscape was provided by the many corrals and gardens. Although not indicated on Mindeleff's plan of Zuni Pueblo, corrals of upright wooden stakes for penning the livestock so important in the Zuni economy surrounded the house blocks, and "waffle gardens" used to grow chiles, onions, and herbs were located on the banks of the Zuni River. Beyond the rectangular enclosures of the corrals and gardens were the more open corn fields and rangeland that provided a sharp contrast to the densely constructed architecture of Zuni Pueblo.

28. "MAP SHOWING THE POSITION OF THE MORE IMPORTANT RUINS NEAR ZUNI," by Jesse Walter Fewkes

THE ZUNI REGION has one of the greatest concentrations of archaeological sites in North America. The Zunis and their ancestors have left hundreds, indeed thousands of ruins across the landscape in the Zuni area. One of the first archaeologists to locate and map some of these ruins was Jesse Walter Fewkes (1850–1930). Trained in natural history, Fewkes became interested in anthropology and in 1889 took over the leadership of the Hemenway Archaeological Expedition from Frank Hamilton Cushing, who had floun-

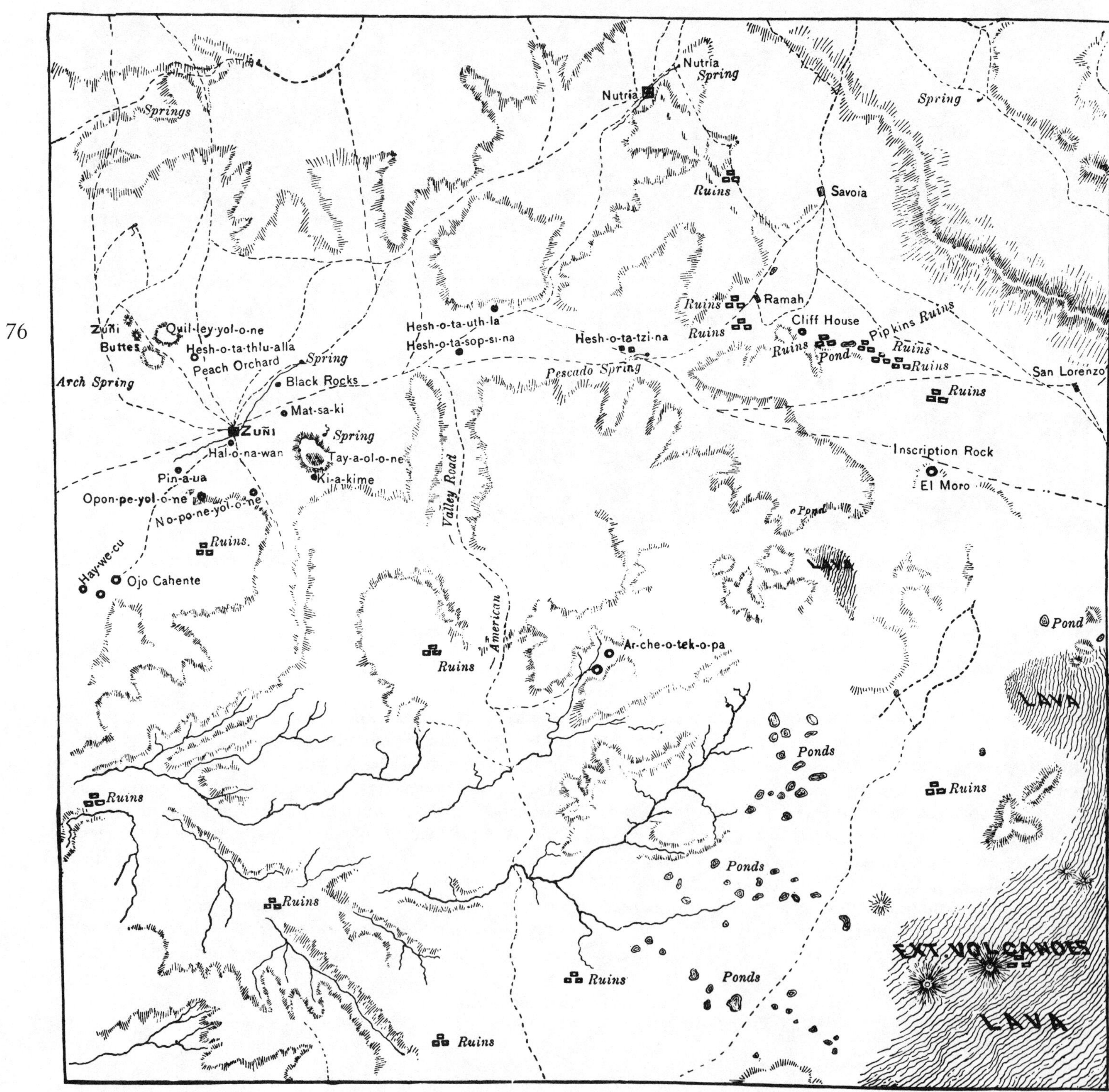

MAP 28. "Map Showing the Position of the More Important Ruins Near Zuni" (1892), by Jesse Walter Fewkes. From *A Journal of American Ethnology and Archaeology*, vol. 1, pt. 3 (1891).

Log ladder at Nutria, 1885. Photograph by Cosmos or Victor Mindeleff, courtesy the Smithsonian Institution, National Anthropological Archives (Neg. No. 79-4268).

dered in his attempts at bookkeeping. The publications of Fewkes's early archaeological research in the Zuni area are built upon Cushing's research and provided a base of knowledge that was expanded by many more archaeological reports over the next century, including work by scholars such as Frederick Webb Hodge, Victor Mindeleff, Adolf Bandelier, A. L. Kroeber, Leslie Spier, Frank H. H. Roberts, Jr., and Richard Woodbury. The research conducted in the Zuni area has had an important influence on the overall view of Southwestern archaeology, prehistory, and history.

Today, the value of Fewkes's archaeological research lies in his description of prominent ruins as they existed in the late nineteenth century. The "Map Showing the Position of the More Important Ruins Near Zuni," taken from Fewkes's "Reconnaissance of Ruins in or Near the Zuni Reservation," published in the *Journal of American Ethnology and Archaeology* in 1891, identifies some of the larger and better-known ruins in the upper drainage of the Zuni River. Many of the large ruins described by Fewkes had walls that were standing two or three stories high when he visited them in the summer of 1890. Today these same ruins have almost all been reduced to low mounds of rubble, obscuring architectural detail. The descriptions and sketches of these sites by Fewkes thus provide valuable architectural information no longer available elsewhere. Fewkes's brief description of the Hemenway Expedition excavations at Halona and Heshotauthla, directed by F. H. Cushing and F. W. Hodge, provides one of the few published accounts of the work conducted at these important sites. Fewkes visited only a few of the larger and most easily accessible archaeological sites near Zuni, and subsequent archaeological research has revealed the presence of hundreds of additional ruins.

In addition to providing important information about Zuni archaeology, Fewkes's "Map Showing the Position of the More Important Ruins near Zuni" is valuable because it shows the organization of the landscape around Zuni in 1890. Zuni trails are plotted, as well as the "American Valley Road," which led to an early Anglo ranch and to the Zuni Salt Lake. Fewkes shows the location of the peach orchards north of Zuni Pueblo, which were planted during the Spanish period and which were still in production in 1890. Remnants of these peach orchards are still visible today. Several important springs are also shown on Fewkes's map.

Fewkes was interested in ethnology as well as archaeology. Although Fewkes is better known for his ethnological work at Hopi, he also recorded valuable ethnographic data at Zuni. He interviewed Zunis about various ruins he recorded, attempted to interpret the Zunis' comments as they applied to the archaeology, and published descriptions of the Zuni religious ceremonies that he observed in 1890. Using wax cylinders, he was the first anthropologist to make recordings of Zuni songs and music.

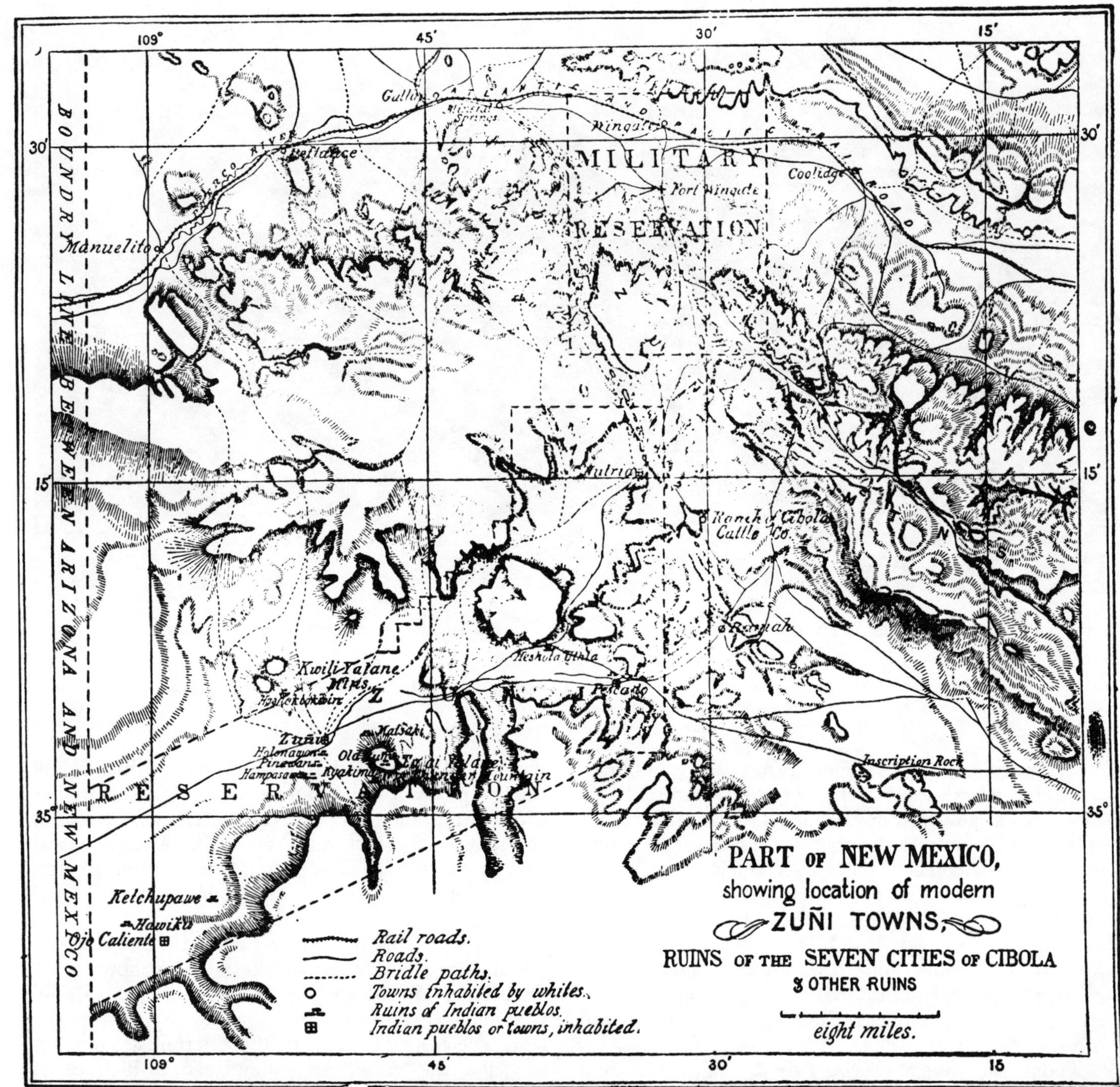

Map 29. "Part of New Mexico, Showing Location of Modern Zuni Towns, Ruins of Seven Cities of Cibola and Other Ruins," by Washington Matthews, 1893.

29. "PART OF NEW MEXICO, SHOWING THE LOCATION OF MODERN ZUNI TOWNS, RUINS OF THE SEVEN CITIES OF CIBOLA & OTHER RUINS," by Washington Matthews, 1893

In December, 1886, Frank Hamilton Cushing led the Hemenway Southwestern Archaeological Expedition into the field. Named for Mrs. Mary Hemenway, who financed the operations, the expedition was designed to study the Pueblo Indians and their ancestors through archaeological, ethnographic, historical, and biological investigations. On the basis of traditions that he had previously learned from the Zunis, Cushing believed that he could prove certain theories regarding prehistoric Pueblo migration by excavating ruins in the Salt and Gila river valleys near the town of Tempe, Arizona. To avoid working at Zuni during the cold and snowy winter, Cushing commenced the work of the expedition in southern Arizona after a brief visit to Zuni. While working in the Salt River Valley in 1887, the expedition discovered evidence of an extensive canal irrigation system that had been used by the prehistoric Hohokam Indian. A wealth of archaeological features and artifacts were exposed by excavation, despite competition and pressure from commercial relic hunters who blatantly looted the site, sometimes in broad daylight.

From June, 1888, through July, 1889, the Hemenway Expedition returned to Zuni to focus its energies on the ruins in that area. To accommodate the Hemenway Expedition, Cushing expanded the house on the south bank of the Zuni River that he had built during his previous residence in the pueblo, exposing in the new foundations the thirteenth-century village of Halona:wa. Additional excavations were conducted at other important sites, including the ruins on top of El Morro and Heshotauthla. During this period Cushing's frail health worsened, and his management of the Hemenway Expedition came under criticism. He was eventually replaced by Jesse Walter Fewkes.

Cushing's archaeological investigations in both the Salt-Gila and the Zuni areas unearthed numerous human burials. Dr. Washington Matthews, a surgeon in the United States Army stationed at Fort Wingate, was asked to join the Hemenway Expedition to oversee the preservation of the bones that had been collected, and to analyze the scientific information they represented. In his report, "The Human Bones of the Hemenway Collection in the United States Army Medical Museum," Matthews included a map of "Part of New Mexico, Showing Location of Modern Zuni Towns, Ruins of the Seven Cities of Cibola & Other Ruins."

In locating the Seven Cities of Cibola on his map, Matthews relied on documentary materials accumulated by Adolf F. Bandelier and on traditional Zuni history collected by Cushing. While this information showed without a doubt that the sixteenth-century Zuni pueblos were the Cities of Cibola, it did not reveal the exact locations of these sites. Subsequent research has shown that several of the ruins marked as the "Seven Cities" on Matthews's maps were not occupied when the Spaniards first arrived in the Southwest. Today, with more information available, the actual locations of the Zuni villages in 1540 are known (see Sixteenth-Century Zuni Villages and Spanish Entradas, Map 10).

Matthews's map is interesting in part because it shows the development of transportation networks in the Zuni area in the late nineteenth century. It indicates a portion of the system of native trails and roads used by the Zunis, suggesting how extensive the entire native system actually was. The impact of the railroad's entry into the region is illustrated in Matthews's map in the development of roads in the timber-rich Zuni Mountains east of the Fort Wingate Military Reservation. The railroad was also responsible for the establishment of the town of Gallup, north of the Zuni Reservation. When the track reached Gallup, cattle ranching became a profitable business on the newly accessible rangelands.

The Cibola Cattle Company, whose ranch is shown on Matthews's map just to the east of the Zuni Reservation, was operated by officers from Fort Wingate. Matthews himself served as president of the Cibola Cattle Company for a period. The army officers who owned the company were in a very advantageous position, since they could use the railroad, which ran through the northern portion of the Fort Wingate Military Reservation, to market their cattle. Evidently some of the officers involved also used their influence to purchase, at a fraction of its market value, railroad "checkerboard" sections of land adjoining Fort Wingate, even though some of the land had been homesteaded years before by Mormon missionaries. This gave the Cibola Cattle Company additional grazing property at a fraction of what anyone else would have to pay for it. In addition, since the United States Army was entrusted with the job of enforcing property rights in the area and preventing trespass on government and Indian lands, the army officers who owned the Cibola Cattle Company were able to trespass with impunity on Zuni range.

30. "ZUNI HOUSES AND CLANS, 1916," by A. L. Kroeber

In 1917, A. L. Kroeber published a study entitled "Zuni Kin and Clan," in the *Anthropological Papers of the American Museum of Natural History.* Based on two summers of fieldwork at Zuni Pueblo in 1915 and 1916, this masterful study analyzed the importance of families and clans in Zuni society. As a part of his fieldwork, Kroeber decided to plot every house in Zuni Pueblo and record the clan affiliation of the occupants. In order to do this, he found it was necessary to produce a new plan view of the pueblo, for it had changed substantially since Mindeleff had mapped it in 1881.

Kroeber hired a surveyor from Gallup to help him map the village, and together they prepared a plan view of the village in 1915. A transit and stadia were used to measure the angles and distances from the highest point of the pueblo to the corners of the house blocks in order to establish their outlines. Once the outlines of the house blocks were established, the individual houses within them were mapped by using a

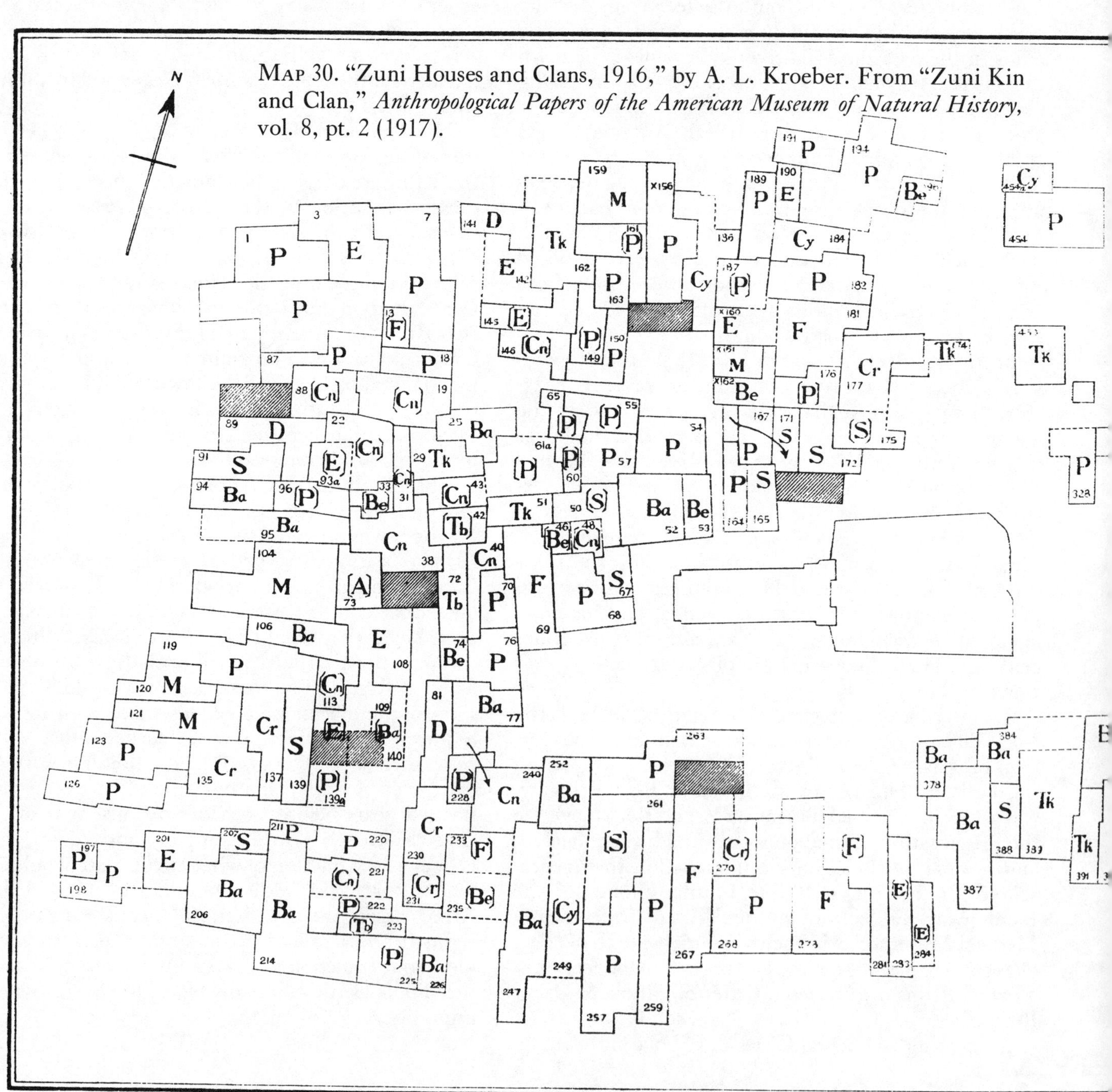

Map 30. "Zuni Houses and Clans, 1916," by A. L. Kroeber. From "Zuni Kin and Clan," *Anthropological Papers of the American Museum of Natural History,* vol. 8, pt. 2 (1917).

measuring chain. An effort was made to plot the new plan of Zuni Pueblo at the same scale as Mindeleff's map, forty-three feet to the inch, so that comparisons between Zuni Pueblo in 1881 and in 1915 would be easier.

After completing the mapping, Kroeber concluded that while the outlines of the house blocks in Zuni in 1915 bore a remarkable similarity to the plan of Zuni in 1881, actually almost every house in the pueblo had been reconstructed. New houses had been built along the lines of old ones, but generally with larger rooms and higher ceilings. By 1915 the uppermost rooftop terraces had been dismantled, for it had become preferable to live at ground level rather than on the upper stories.

Kroeber used the plan view of Zuni Pueblo he produced as a base on which to display the distribution of various types of social groups in the village. The map of "Zuni Houses and Clans" is only one of many maps Kroeber used to illustrate "Zuni Kin and Clan." It depicts the distribution of the fifteen clans present in Zuni Pueblo in 1916, and, in addition, indicates the location of the six kivas with hachuring. The fifty-two houses on the map with clan symbols in parentheses were abandoned at the time Kroeber conducted his study.

In the early twentieth century, Zuni Pueblo was undergoing a radical architectural transition as houses were abandoned in the old pueblo and a substantial portion of the Zuni population resettled in newly con-

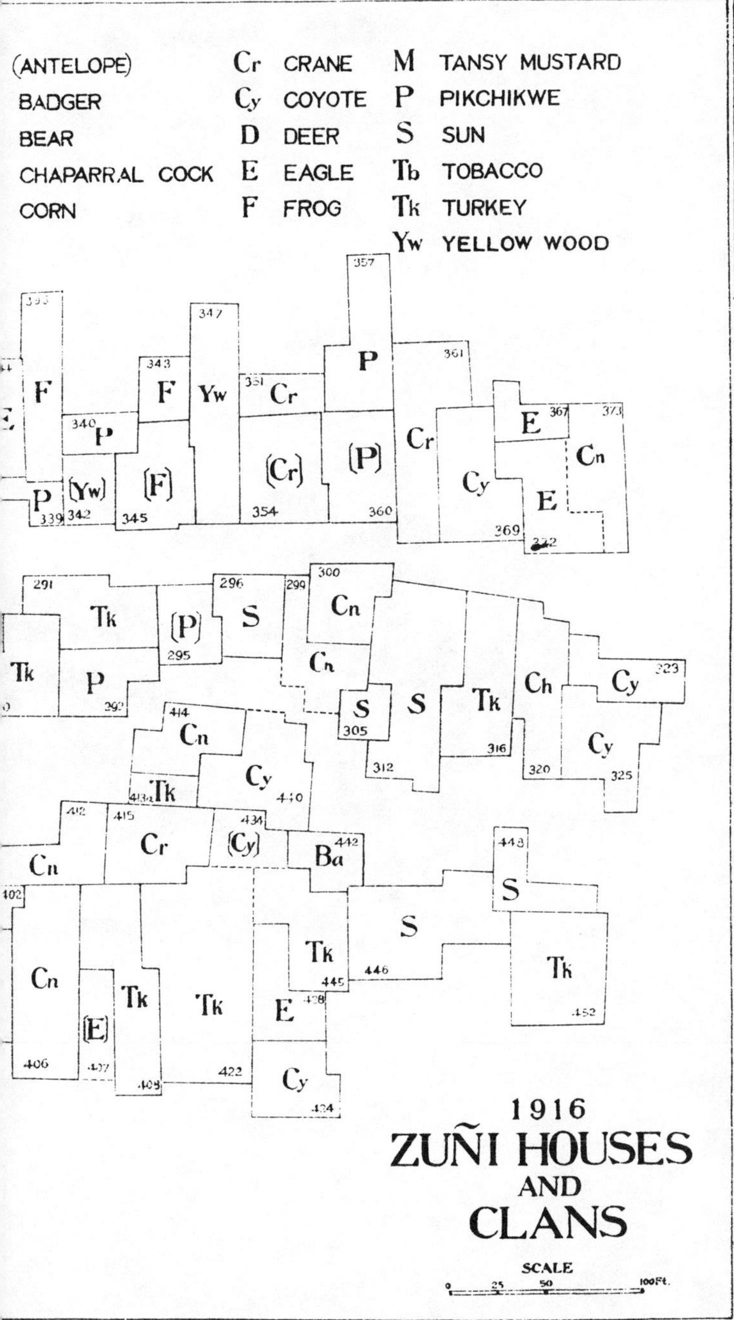

Lalio, a Zuni leader, ready for a stick race near Hawikku, 1919. Photograph courtesy the Museum of the American Indian, Heye Foundation (Neg. No. 7419).

FIGURE 2. *Zuni Pueblo and expansions, 1915.*

structed suburbs. This process had begun in the late nineteenth century after Athabaskan raiding ceased, and greatly accelerated after the turn of the century. Out of the 220 families that occupied Zuni Pueblo in 1916, eighty-one of them, almost 37 percent, resided in the suburbs. The population of the tribe numbered 1,164 people at the time.

Kroeber also mapped the suburban expansion of Zuni Pueblo which had extended to encompass both the north and south sides of the Zuni River (figure 2). On the south side of the river were two stores (one of which had been originally constructed by Frank H. Cushing and remodeled to serve as the Hemenway Expedition house), a mission operated by the Christian Reformed church, and several Zuni houses. Many more Zuni houses were located outside the old pueblo on the north side of the river. At the northern edge of the suburban expansion was the newly constructed government day school.

N

Aerial view of Zuni, 1948. Photograph by Cutter-Carr Flying Service, (for Stanley Stubbs), courtesy the Museum of New Mexico (Neg. No. 5049).

A celebration of Ojo Caliente in 1919 honoring the Hendricks-Hodge Expedition excavation of Hawikku. Photograph by F. W. Hodge, courtesy the Museum of the American Indian, Heye Foundation (Neg. No. 51346).

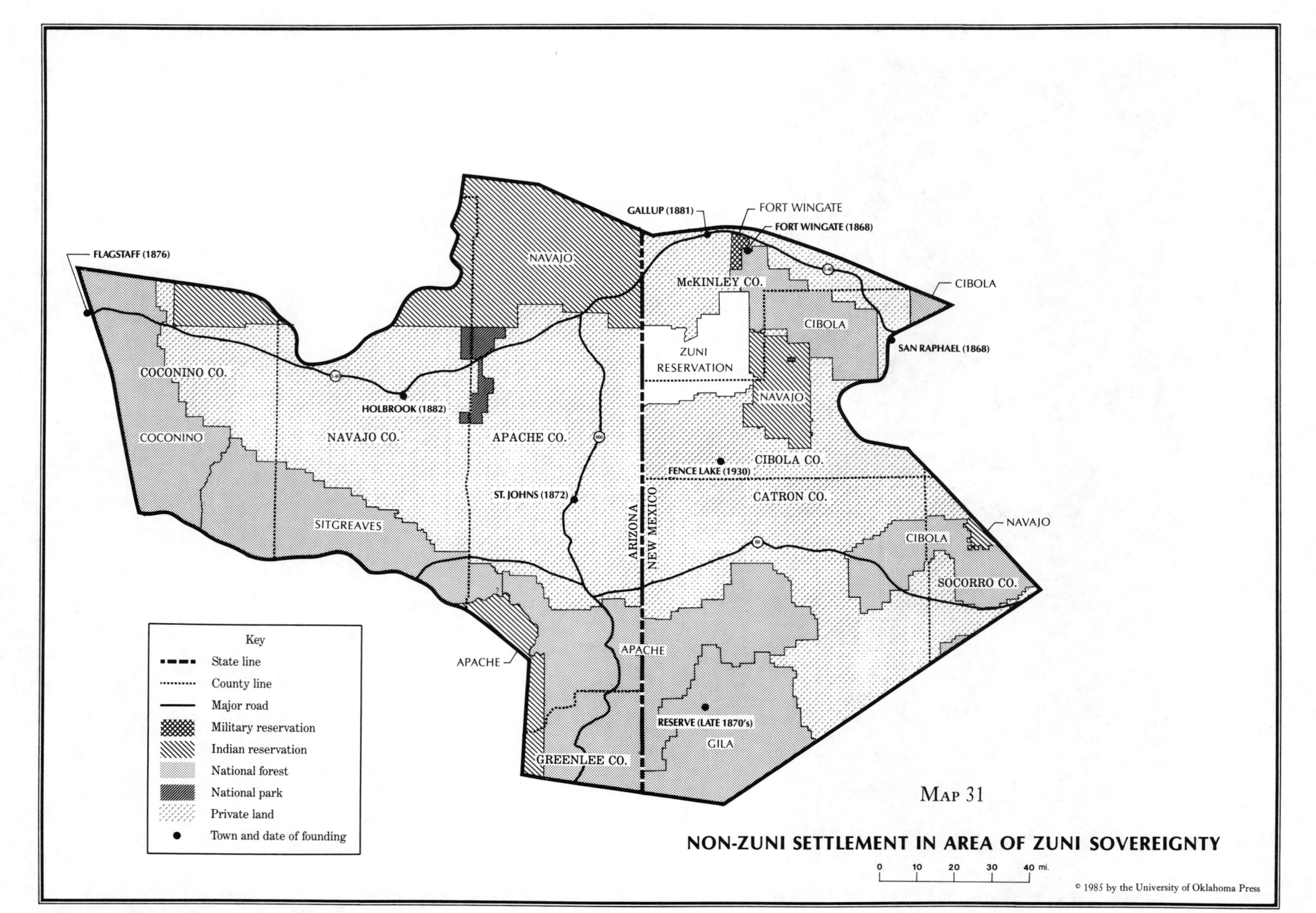

Map 31

NON-ZUNI SETTLEMENT IN AREA OF ZUNI SOVEREIGNTY

31. NON-ZUNI SETTLEMENT AREA OF ZUNI SOVEREIGNTY

A CONTEMPORARY MAP of the original area of Zuni sovereignty reveals a mosaic of settlements, private land, federal reserves, and Indian reservations in two states, crisscrossed with county lines, roads, and railroads. Much of the private land in the area contains federal checkerboard sections too small and numerous to map. The whole area officially became territory of the United States in 1848, with the signing of the Treaty of Guadalupe Hildago with Mexico.

Between 1858 and 1868, some erosion of Zuni land took place as Apaches and Navajos fled into Zuni territory, pursued by United States troops intent on stopping the Athapaskan raiding that had made American settlement of the area difficult. Apaches pushed into the far western and southwestern portion of Zuni land, as well as to the south. In 1871 a reservation was established for the Apaches that included the White Mountains at the southwestern edge of Zuni territory. Navajos found refuge from military pressure in the remote mountainous areas throughout the Zuni region, especially along the southern boundaries of Zuni territory. Navajos also pressed down from the north to the Rio Puerco river basin. In 1868, after the failure of the forced Navajo relocation to Fort Sumner, the Navajos were provided a reservation north of Zuni, part of which was taken from what were Zuni aboriginal lands. At this time some Navajos also returned to the Zuni Mountains, where the Zunis permitted several families to settle. In the mid-twentieth century, this area of Navajo settlement was eventually made into the Ramah Navajo Indian Reservation.

The first non-Indian settlements in the Zuni area were military forts associated with the Navajo and Apache campaigns of the United States Army. In 1860 the United States Army established a fort at Bear Springs, north of the Zuni farming village of Nutria. A second fort was established in 1862 at the eastern end of the Zuni Mountains, close to where the small Hispanic community of San Rafael was established six years later. In 1868 these two forts were consolidated into a single fort at Bear Springs and named Fort Wingate. Today, the 64,000 acres of the Fort Wingate Military Reservation are used for the storage of explosives and ammunition.

The first civilian non-Indian settlements were established in the Zuni area only after cessation of Navajo and Apache hostilities. In the south, mining activities prompted settlements in the Reserve area in the 1870s. At the same time, in the west, Mormon expansion and missionary activities led to the establishment of ranching and farming communities along the Little Colorado River drainage, including Saint Johns. Hispanic and Anglo sheep and cattle operations began in a limited way in scattered parts of the Zuni region during the same decade. These early non-Indian settlements encroached on the water resources vital to the Zunis' use of their traditional territory.

The arrival of the railroad in Zuni country in 1882 brought with it a string of communities along the tracks, where they wound down the Rio Puerco of the West, through New Mexico and Arizona. Towns such as Gallup and Holbrook had early reputations for attracting lawless and rough crowds. But a more important impact on Zuni lands came from the fact that the railroad opened up the possibility for grazing large herds of cattle on the open ranges and then marketing them by rail. Such herds were established west of Zuni during the 1880s, and cattle ranching competed with Zuni sheepherding in areas to the east and south of Zuni Pueblo, as well. In fact, military officers at Fort Wingate took up ranching and competed for Zuni land and water. Gradually the non-Indians fenced the countryside, further restricting Zuni access to traditional grazing, hunting, gathering, and sacred areas.

The railroad also made possible the exploitation of timber and other materials within the region. Limited lumber operations began in the Zuni Mountain area in the 1880s, and in the 1890s, massive clear-cutting of the forest began. In excess of 2 billion feet of merchantable sawtimber were cut in the Zuni Mountains between 1890 and the early 1900s. After the clear-cutting, private concerns overgrazed the area with cattle and sheep, causing such extreme damage to the Zuni watershed that the area has never completely recovered.

As the Zunis were finally driven back onto their reservation, some non-Indian communities were established in the Zuni grazing lands to the south, such as the one at Fence Lake, where Texan emigrants attempted to establish bean farms in the economically depressed 1930s. These bean farms failed, but some of the homesteaders were able to establish small ranches and run livestock in the area.

Today, much of the land that was part of the Zuni area of sovereignty is sparsely populated and exploited primarily for ranching purposes. Nonetheless, some resources, such as water, are being depleted to a dangerous extent. It is impossible to project long-term human habitation at today's levels within the area as a whole. In contrast, under the long period of Zuni control it can be said that the exploitation of resources in the area was undertaken in a non-depleting manner. In fact, the Zunis treated the area with great reverence at the same time that they used its resources to sustain life.

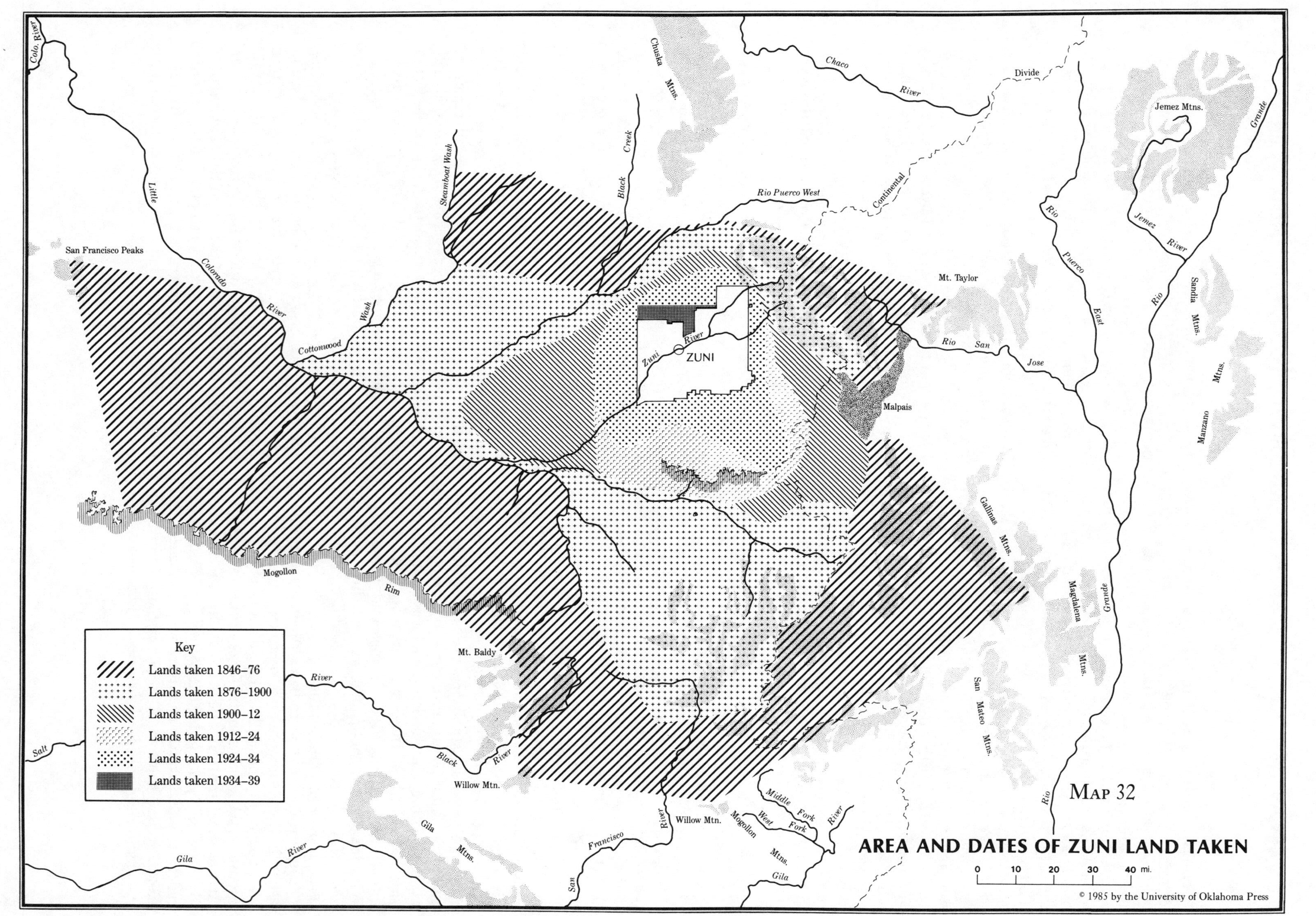

MAP 32

AREA AND DATES OF ZUNI LAND TAKEN

32. AREA AND DATES OF ZUNI LAND TAKEN

The Zuni people exercised sovereignty over their territory for many centuries before the arrival of United States military forces in 1846. Under the Spaniards, from 1540 to 1821, the Zunis had maintained all of their lands and had resisted any encroachment by non-Zunis. Similarly, during the Mexican period, from 1821 to 1846, the Zunis fought off, sometimes with the help of Mexican troops, any attempts by non-Zunis —Apaches, Navajos or Mexicans—to settle within Zuni boundaries.

The boundaries of Zuni territory were well known to tribal leaders. With their complex religious, social, and political organization, Zuni people kept track of their resources. All of the resources necessary for survival over a long period were guarded by the tribe —game, minerals, farming and grazing land, and religious sites. The Bow Priests kept shrines and made offerings to War Gods at important points along trails and on peaks that marked common boundaries between Zuni and other tribes. Common boundaries existed between Zuni and Hopi, and between Zuni and the Acomas. The Zunis also maintained boundaries between the Navajos to the north and the Apaches to the south. At times the Zuni tribe permitted members of other tribes to use Zuni resources, if the supply was adequate. For instance, many tribes were permitted to gather salt at the Zuni Salt Lake, as long as they submitted to the conditions imposed by the Zunis. Often those conditions consisted of staying on the prescribed trails, camping at known campsites, and paying respect to the shrines and religious areas of the Zunis. But the Zunis occasionally obtained payment for use of the Zuni Salt Lake, and in time of war would kill or capture any member of an adversary tribe whom they caught in the region around the lake. The lake itself and its immediate vicinity were very sacred, and battles or violence were never contemplated there.

Thus the Zunis maintained their boundaries, even through three hundred years of European colonization of the Southwest. But with the arrival of the United States military forces in the Arizona-New Mexico area, the pattern began to change. The Zunis were able to maintain their boundaries under United States rule until the subjugation of the warring Navajos in the late 1860s. They had enjoyed a healthy trade with the United States military posts until that time, and had fought as allies against the Apaches and Navajos. But when those tribes were forced into peace, the government abandoned its alliance with the Zunis and began to allow, in fact encourage, non-Zuni settlement on the Zunis' lands. Between 1868 and 1876, use of a large portion of Zuni territory was quickly lost to the tribe. Mormon emigrants settled along the Little Colorado River and its tributaries. Navajos pushed down out of the reservation established for them north of Zuni, and Hispanic settlers and herders pushed into the eastern limits of Zuni lands.

United States troops stationed at Zuni in 1897. Photograph courtesy of Elaine Thomas.

Between 1876 and 1900, especially after the construction of the railroad in 1882, another very large portion of the Zunis' aboriginal territory was lost to non-Indian settlement. Large cattle companies, mostly financed from overseas, dumped carloads of cattle onto the plains to the west, and the establishment of the railroad led to settlements along the Rio Puerco of the West. To the south, mining, ranching, and some farming prompted Anglo and Hispanic settlements. To offset the loss of other resources, the Zunis began to place more and more reliance on their herds of sheep for subsistence, and the tribe's lands can best be measured in the ensuing years by the limits of Zuni grazing.

Between 1900 and 1934 the Zunis' grazing lands were gradually reduced as Anglo farmers and ranchers pushed into the area. Bit by bit the Zunis were pushed back towards the boundaries of their reservation, until, in 1934, they were actually restricted to it. In that year, as part of the Indian Civilian Conservation project, the boundaries of the reservation were fenced for the first time, and Zuni herders were forced onto the reserve, causing severe erosion of reservation lands, reduction of Zuni herds, and economic privation among tribal members. Zuni herders were still allowed to use what came to be called the "Zuni North" and "South Purchase areas," land eventually purchased and held in Trust by the United States government under a New Deal program. But even the use of a large portion of these lands was lost to the Zuni tribe in 1939. Though the Navajos had been provided a large reservation, they continued to push southward, encroaching on more and more Zuni land. Commissioner of Indian Affairs John Collier had attempted in the 1930s to establish a permanent boundary between the Navajos and the Zunis at the northernmost edge of the Zuni North Purchase area, and had ordered Navajos not to move south of that line. But by 1939, Navajos had pushed into the North Purchase area, and the northern portion of that tract of land was taken from the Zunis and opened to non-Zuni settlement.

Within a hundred years of the arrival of the United States military in the Southwest, the Zunis were left with but a tiny fraction of their original territory. Although they had allied with the United States, fought with and fed their troops, and welcomed the expected freedoms that they had heard democracy would bring, the Zunis lost access to and use of most of their traditional land base. Today, despite this history, the Zuni people and their democratic tribal government are staunch supporters of United States constitutional government. The Zunis diligently exercise their rights of citizenship in this nation, while strenuously guarding their tribal religion, society, and culture.

"The summer Pueblita on the Nutria & the Stonewall," ca. 1890. Photograph by Ben Wittick, courtesy the Southwest Museum (Neg. No. 20,951).

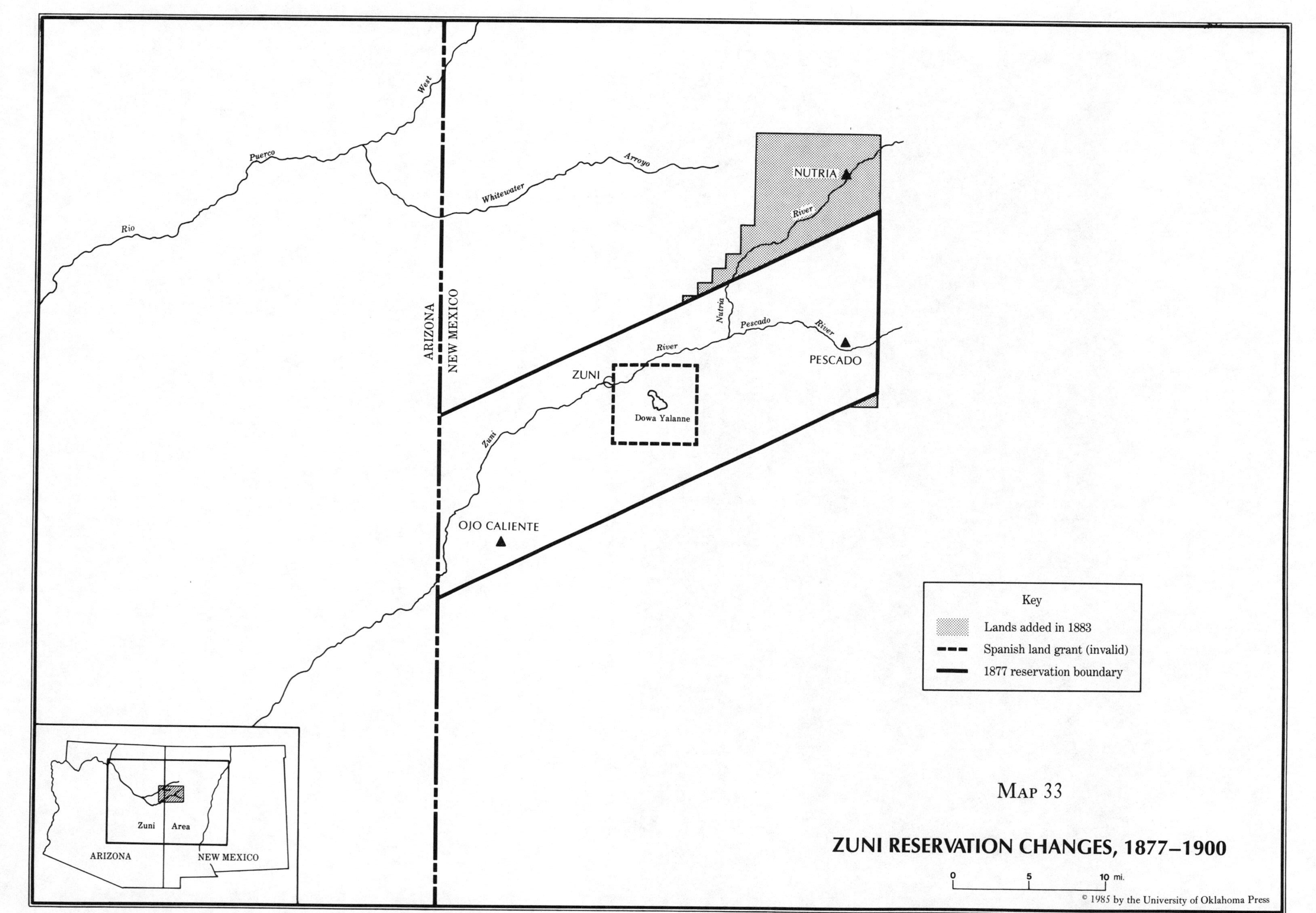

MAP 33

ZUNI RESERVATION CHANGES, 1877–1900

33. ZUNI RESERVATION CHANGES, 1877-1900

By 1867 the warring Navajos had been subjugated and Zuni territory became much more attractive to non-Zunis. Although United States officials had promised to protect Zuni lands from encroachments in a series of treaties and agreements, after Navajo hostilities were suppressed, the government's officials in New Mexico and Arizona virtually ignored Zuni land and water rights.

In 1868, Hispanos settled the town of San Rafael at the east end of the Zuni mountains. By 1873, the prospects for cattle and sheep ranching in the Zuni area were being explored by non-Indians and a few of them had settled within Zuni's borders. The Zunis complained to government officials, and fully expected that the government would live up to its agreements, but by 1875, when the boundary line between the territories of New Mexico and Arizona was surveyed, officials seemed totally unaware of any property rights of the Zunis. Still, the Zunis supplied the surveyors with food and forage and provided them with guides, not knowing that the line that was being marked would someday become the western limit of their lands.

In the early 1870s, Anglo and Hispanic settlers began to sift into Zuni country, especially along the Little Colorado River drainage. Competition was greatest for lands with water. Although the United States Army, situated at Fort Wingate on the old Bear Springs site, was mandated to protect Indian property and rights, the cattle company mentioned earlier that was formed by some of the officers there and some political allies in Washington, D.C., grazed their stock on both government and Indian land. Not owning any land themselves, they soon decided to try to get title to the land surrounding the springs at Nutria, one of the Zuni's outlying farming areas.

With pressures against Zuni land mounting, in 1877 the Indian agent to the Pueblos recommended a reservation for the Zunis, and by executive order President Rutherford B. Hayes set aside a tract of land in the tribe's name. The original reservation was but a tiny fraction of the tribe's aboriginal homeland, and was inadequate to supply the Zunis with the grazing land, hunting ranges, gathering areas, and cultivated fields necessary to support themselves. Worst of all, the reservation did not even include the Zunis' farming village of Nutria. The springs at Nutria supply a major portion of the Zuni River, and had those waters been lost to the tribe, their ensuing history might well have been a short one.

Fortunately for the Zunis, ethnologist Frank Hamilton Cushing learned of the travesty after he arrived at the pueblo in 1879. During the next four years, as he studied and wrote of Zuni culture, Cushing enlisted the help of several Eastern writers and news reporters and brought national attention to the "land grab attempt." Although his pressure on government leaders eventually led to his removal from Zuni, Cushing and his newspaper friends applied enough pressure to cause the president to enlarge the reservation slightly in 1883 in order to include the springs and village at Nutria, thus thwarting the ranchers among the army officers at Fort Wingate.

In the 1930s, the United States Congress confirmed a Spanish land grant to Zuni of one square league around Dowa Yalanne in the middle of the Zuni Reservation. Subsequently it has been determined that the document this confirmation was based on was a crude forgery, evidently perpetrated in the mid-nineteenth century by a group of non-Indians in Santa Fe who were involved in a scheme to defraud many different pueblos of their lands. Zuni tradition suggests that the Spanish and Mexican governments granted the tribe a much larger tract of land, but no document has survived to verify the claim. However, it is known that the Spanish and Mexican governments honored the Zunis' rights to all of their aboriginal homeland, and used their armies to help defend the tribe's boundaries.

Throughout the period from 1877 to 1900, the Zunis continued to use a much larger area of land than was represented by the reservation boundaries. In 1900, with sixty thousand head of sheep, the Zunis were grazing their herds many miles outside the reservation, which was not fenced or properly surveyed. Neither the Zunis, nor the government Indian agent, nor the Zunis' neighbors knew where the reservation boundaries were until the 1930s.

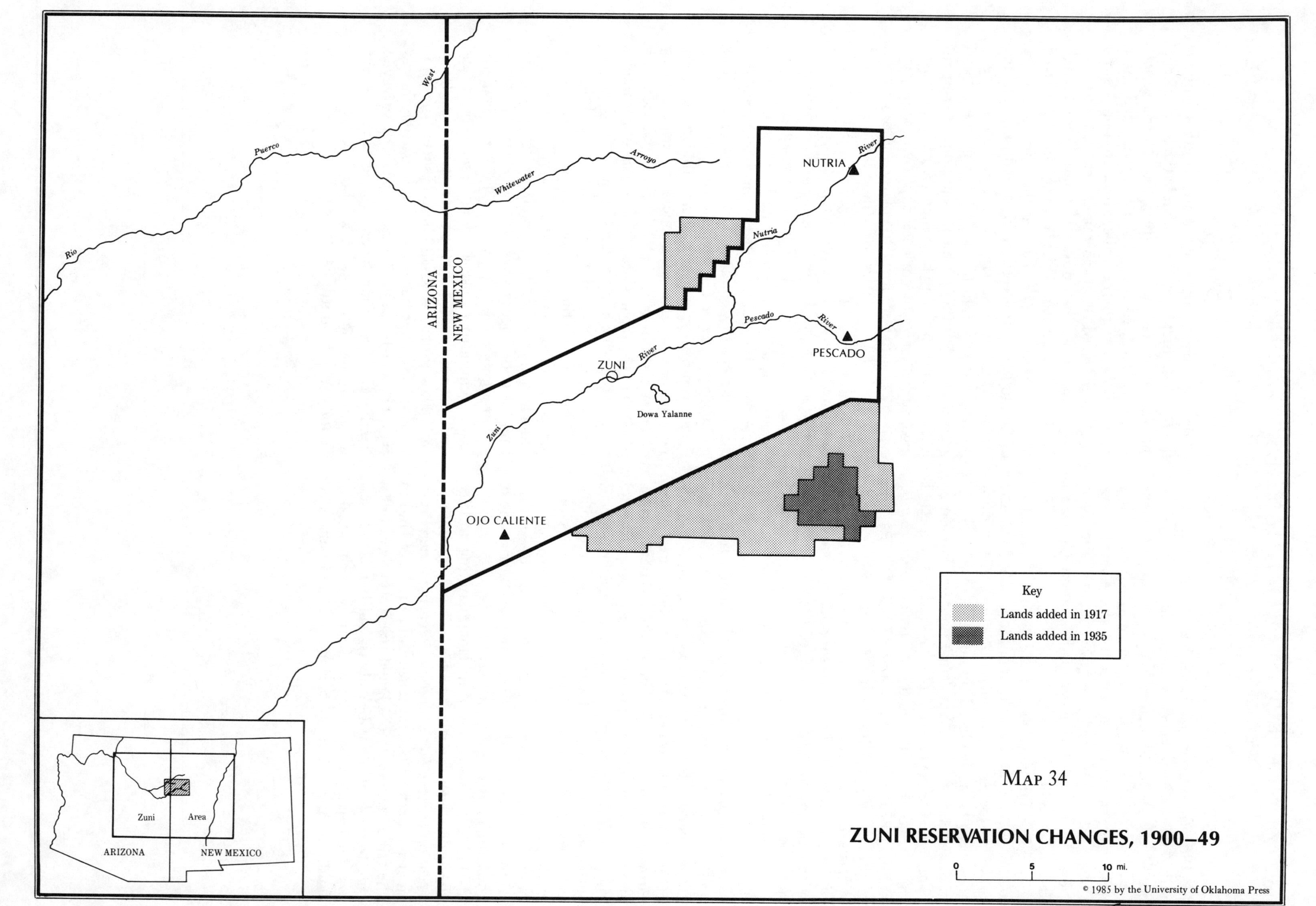

Map 34

ZUNI RESERVATION CHANGES, 1900–49

34. ZUNI RESERVATION CHANGES: 1900–49

Between the years 1900 and 1935, the Zunis were pressured out of their aboriginal grazing territory and into the reservation set aside for them by the government. Between 1880 and 1920, as traditional hunting and gathering areas were lost to the Zunis, grazing and grazing lands became more important. The tribe's herds increased dramatically, from about thirty thousand in 1880 to about sixty-five thousand head of sheep in 1913. As the tribe was pushed into its reservation, Zuni leaders and some Bureau of Indian Affairs officials realized the inadequacy of the Executive Order reservation. The 285,000-acre reservation could support only a fraction of the Zunis' sheep.

Both Zuni leaders and government officials began to petition the President, Congress, and the secretary of the interior to enlarge the reservation to a size that would allow the Zunis to continue to be self-sufficient. Nevertheless, in 1909 and 1910 lands were withdrawn from the Zuni Reservation and added to National Forests in the area. Fortunately, in 1912 President William H. Taft reversed those actions and returned the lands to the Zunis, who had never ceased using the acreage.

In 1917, in response to the numerous protests and petitions from Zunis, another Executive Order was issued by President Woodrow Wilson, adding nearly eighty thousand more acres to the reserve. In the middle of the southern part of the land that was added in 1917 was a large, irregularly shaped piece of land that was temporarily left out of the reservation. This piece of land, known as the Miller Division of the Cibola National Forest, was added to the reservation in 1935 by an act of Congress, and put into trust status. Thus, by 1935 the official reservation had a total of a little over 340,000 acres of land within its exterior boundaries.

In 1934 the Zuni Reservation was fenced, a development that made it easier for the government to restrict Zuni grazing to the reservation. A few Zunis tried to continue using parts of their traditional grazing areas by leasing them from the state or federal government, but by and large the Zunis were forced into their reservation. The rapid concentration of Zuni livestock into a much smaller area in the mid-1930s led to overgrazing. This necessitated a massive reduction of livestock, a government program that caused severe poverty for many Zuni families.

The lands within the 1935 reservation were not all of the lands the Zunis controlled, however. Two "Indian New Deal" statutes allowed the government to purchase lands to be held in trust for the tribes in the United States. Several tracts were purchased for Zuni between 1934 and 1949, and put into trust status in the latter year.

Blackrock Dam under construction in 1906. Photograph courtesy the Museum of the American Indian, Heye Foundation (Neg. No. 26781).

Zunis waiting to get Indian Relief and Rehabilitation work cards at the Nutria Trading Post, 1936. Photograph courtesy the Maxwell Museum (Neg. No. 7-1-36).

A Zuni sheep corral, ca. 1906. Photograph courtesy the Museum of the American Indian, Heye Foundation (Neg. No. 26760).

Zuni baking ovens, 1919. Photograph courtesy the Museum of the American Indian, Heye Foundation (Neg. No. 5607).

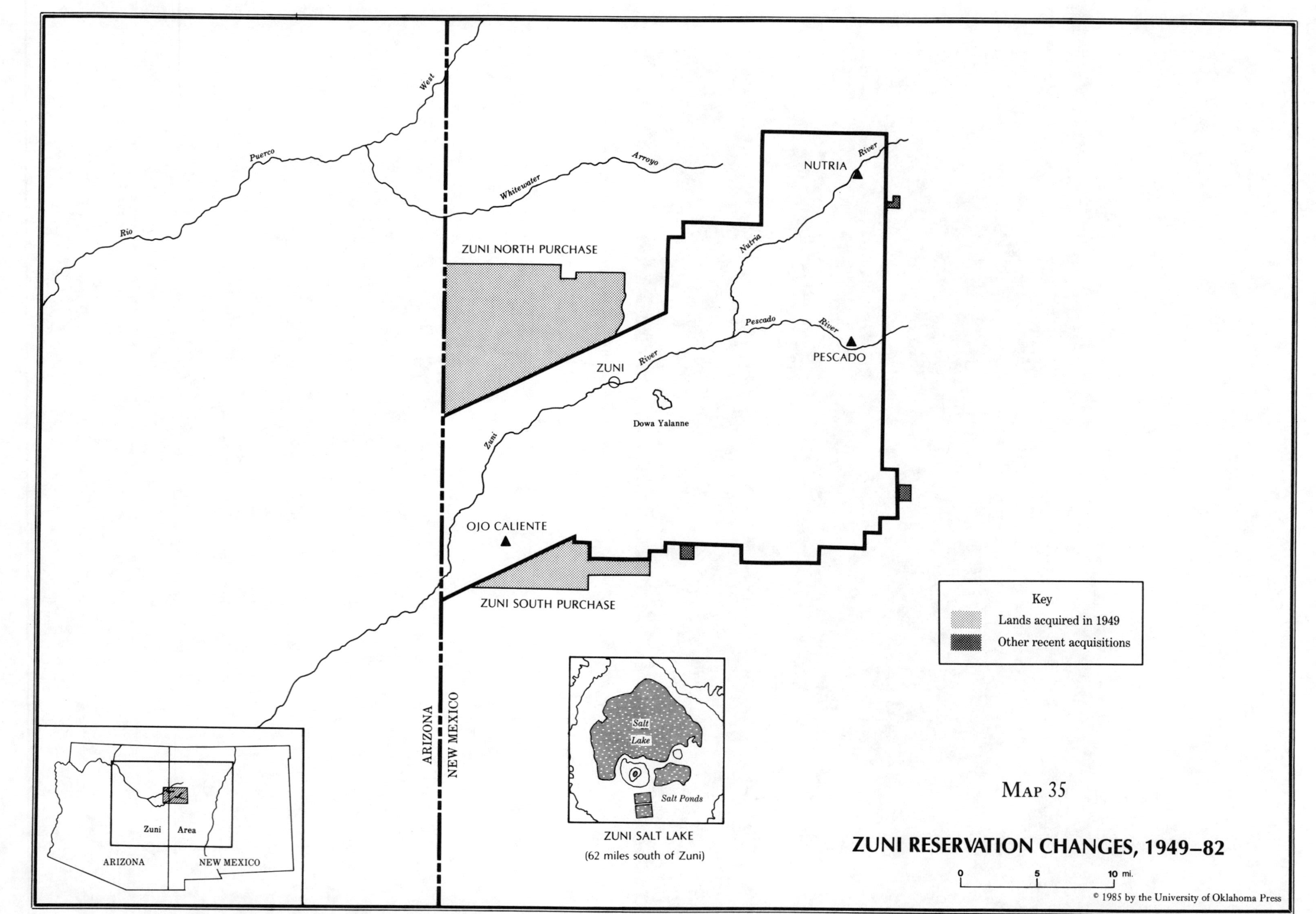

MAP 35

ZUNI RESERVATION CHANGES, 1949–82

35. ZUNI RESERVATION CHANGES: 1949–82

By an act of Congress almost sixty thousand additional acres were added to the Zuni Reservation in 1949 (though almost all of this land had always been used by the tribe). This acreage included what was known as the Zuni North and South Purchase Areas. These pieces of land were purchased by the government under authority of the National Industrial Recovery Act of 1933, as part of what was known as the "Resettlement Administration Purchases" or "Submarginal Lands Acquisitions" program.

Other small additions were made to the reservation in 1962 and 1978, bringing the total land within the exterior boundaries of the Zuni Reservation to 409,134 acres, or 636 square miles.

The following Executive Orders and Congressional Acts provided title to the Zuni lands:

Executive Order, March 16, 1877
Executive Order, May 1, 1883
Executive Order, November 30, 1917
National Industrial Recovery Act of 1933 (48 Stat. 200)
Indian Reorganization Act of 1934 (48 Stat. 984)
Act of June 20, 1935 (Stat. L., Vol. 49, Pt. 1, p. 393)
Act of August 13, 1949 (63 Stat. 604)
Act of March 16, 1962 (76 Stat. 33)

For many decades Zuni leaders pressed United States authorities to provide some recourse for the injustice the tribe had suffered in the loss of their lands without compensation. Finally, by a Congressional Act of May 15, 1978 (P.L. 95-280, 92 Stat. 244), jurisdiction was provided for the Zunis to seek redress in the United States Court of Claims. As a part of the provisions of this same act, the federal government was authorized to acquire the Zuni Salt Lake in a land exchange with the State of New Mexico and add it to the lands held in trust for the Zuni people. The Zuni Salt Lake for centuries has provided the Zunis with salt for trade and for their own consumption, and the lake plays an important role in Zuni religion as well. It has a long documentary history, having been visited and described by early Spanish expeditions and analyzed by scientists in more recent years. At this writing, although the Zunis have assumed control over the lake through a lease, title has not yet been transferred because the State of New Mexico continues to claim the mineral rights to the salt in and surrounding the lake.

Zuni women building an oven near Hawikku in 1919. Photograph by Jesse L. Nusbaum, courtesy the Museum of the American Indian, Heye Foundation (Neg. No. 4717).

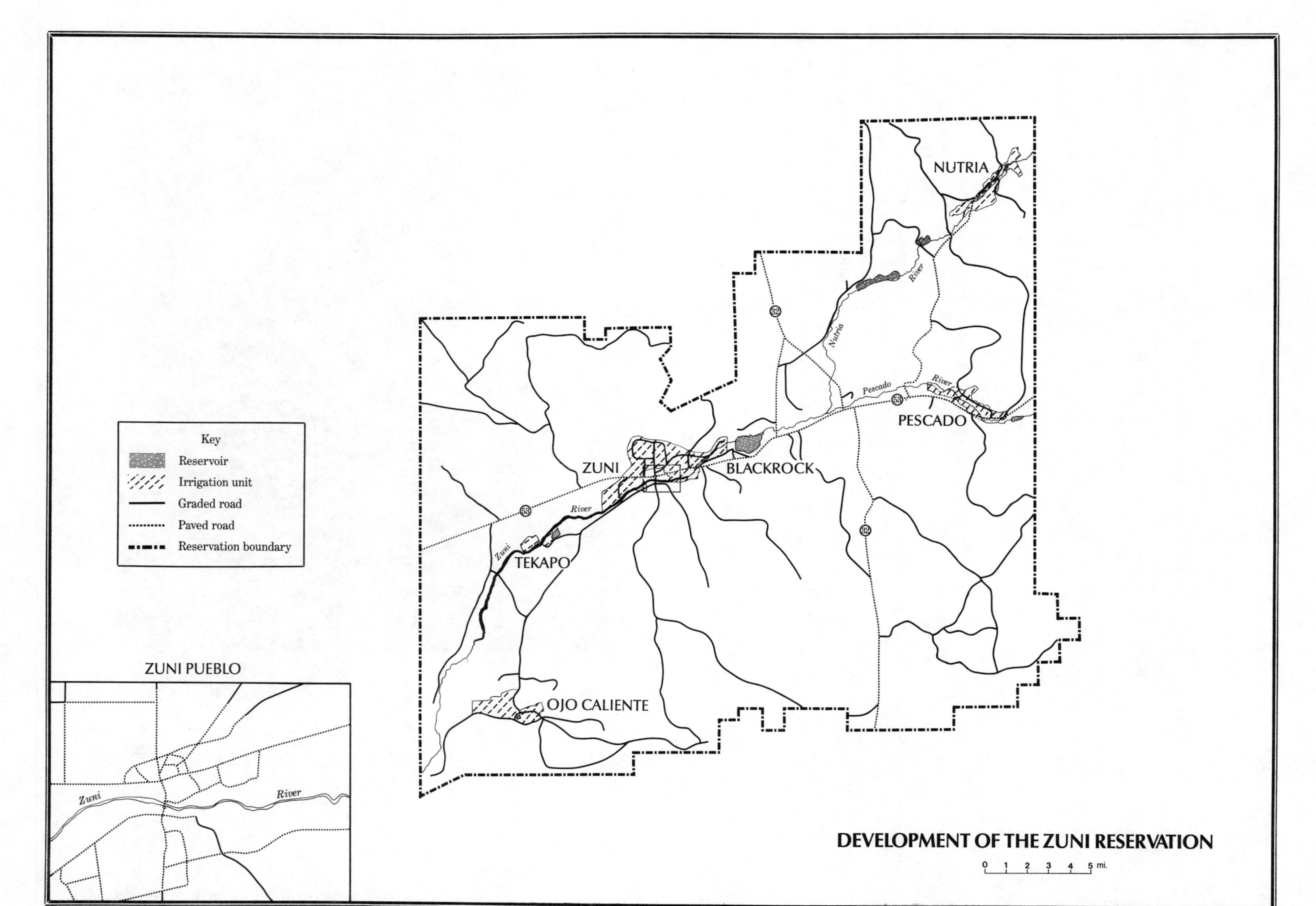

DEVELOPMENT OF THE ZUNI RESERVATION
0 1 2 3 4 5 mi.
NUTRIA
PESCADO
BLACKROCK
ZUNI
TEKAPO
OJO CALIENTE
Nutria River
Pescado River
Zuni River
53
32
Key
Reservoir
Irrigation unit
Graded road
Paved road
Reservation boundary
ZUNI PUEBLO
Zuni River

36. DEVELOPMENT OF THE ZUNI RESERVATION

CROWDED onto a small reservation and forcibly prevented from using most of their traditional lands and resources, Zuni leaders have worked energetically to develop to the fullest extent possible the lands available to them. The tribe has participated in many different state and federal programs to improve the reservation and raise the standard of living of tribal members.

An extensive system of paved and improved dirt roads has been constructed to provide vehicular access to all parts of the reservation, thereby facilitating trade, ranching, and farming, and permitting the reservation back country to be used for recreational purposes such as tourism and fishing. State of New Mexico Highways 32 and 53 connect Zuni Pueblo to off-reservation population centers at Gallup, Quemado, Grants, and Saint Johns, and include approximately 60 miles of paved roads on the reservation. The Bureau of Indian Affairs (BIA) maintains approximately 17 miles of paved road, 2 miles of gravel roads, and 271 miles of dirt roads on the reservation, linking the Pueblo with remote areas of the reservation and requiring the maintenance of eleven bridges totalling 284 linear feet. In addition to the approximately 356 miles of maintained roads on the Zuni Reservation, many miles of unmaintained dirt roads and jeep trails are also used.

Eight major reservoirs have been constructed, and five irrigation units established for farming. The first dam on the reservation was constructed at Blackrock between 1904 and 1908. The Blackrock Dam was intended to provide irrigation water for thousands of acres of farmland in an irrigation unit north of Zuni Pueblo, but in less than twenty years the dam lost over 75 percent of its storage capacity because of sedimentation, and in recent years little or no water has been available for irrigation. A canal from the Blackrock Irrigation Unit feeds a small reservoir and irrigation unit at Tekapo, and a small farming village was founded at Tekapo soon after completion of the dam. In the 1930s, springs were developed and reservoirs were constructed at Pescado, Nutria, and Ojo Caliente. Later, irrigation units with leveled farmland were established around these farming villages. Several other small reservoirs have been constructed on the reservation since the 1930s.

The economic importance of farming at Zuni has decreased in recent years, and today the Zuni economy is based on livestock, jewelry production, and wage labor. The reservoirs have been stocked with fish and developed for recreational use by the tribe. All available rangeland has been assigned to tribal members for grazing of sheep and cattle (see Grazing Units on the Zuni Reservation, Map 37).

The population on the reservation is centered in Zuni Pueblo and Blackrock, the only settlements inhabited year-round. In recent years, more and more houses have been constructed between Zuni and Blackrock, and the two settlements are gradually merging into one. In 1967 the tribe constructed an airstrip at Blackrock, formerly headquarters of the BIA Agency and now the site of a large Public Health Service Hospital, as well as a number of houses and apartment units. A small industrial park was constructed at the same time, and for several years an electronics factory was located there. But the factory eventually moved off the reservation, and the distance from Zuni to markets and major transportation arteries has made it difficult to attract new industry. As a result, recent economic development projects have concentrated on other resources, such as the BIA program to develop timber resources in the southeast quarter of the reservation.

With the assistance of state and federal governments, the Zunis have worked to develop their reservation in order to provide a modern standard of living for tribal members; even so, the small reservation is not adequate to support the self-sustaining economy the Zunis traditionally maintained, an economy dependent on extensive land use. The reduction of the Zuni land base to a small reservation constitutes the basic economic problem the Zunis are working to overcome in the second half of the twentieth century. Future development of the reservation will be largely dependent on the natural resources available on Zuni land, including rangeland, timber, water resources, minerals, and soils.

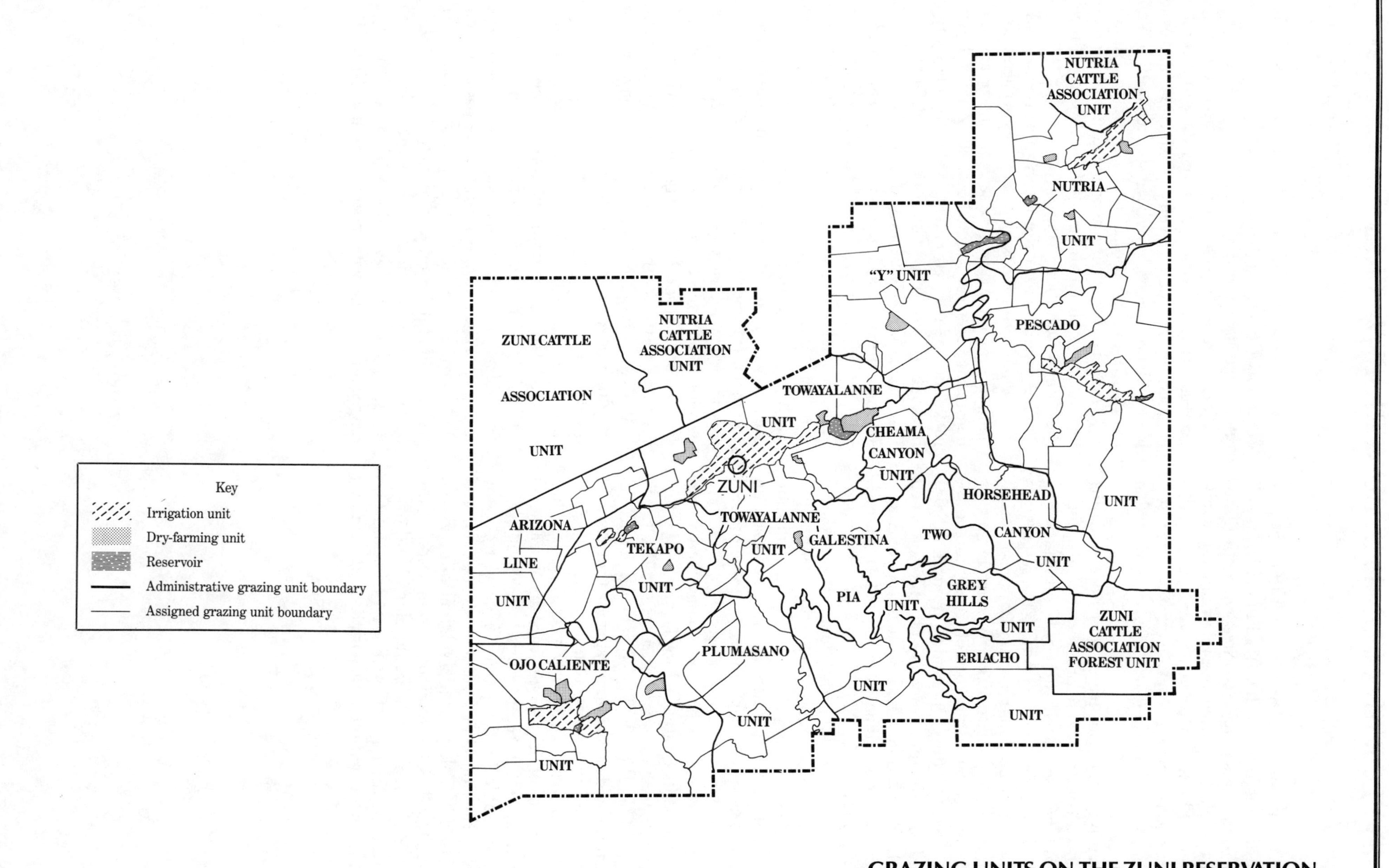

GRAZING UNITS ON THE ZUNI RESERVATION

37. GRAZING UNITS ON THE ZUNI RESERVATION

TRADITIONALLY, the Zunis grazed their sheep and cattle over large open ranges, taking advantage of the best pasture and allowing depleted grasslands time to recover. After the reservation was fenced in 1934, this system of grazing was no longer possible, and Zuni livestock was crowded into a relatively small area. This situation led to overgrazing and deterioration of the reservation rangeland. In order to better manage Zuni rangeland, the Bureau of Indian Affairs (BIA) established eighteen administrative grazing units, largely following natural physiographic units. The carrying capacity of each grazing unit was determined in terms of animal units that could be supported by the amount of forage each area produced, and the Zunis were forced to reduce their stock to the point that they did not exceed the number of animal units they were allowed. For each animal unit allowed, the stockmen were permitted to graze five sheep or one cow. It took three animal units to graze a horse.

In 1976 the Zunis adopted a Tribal Range Code that regulates grazing on the reservation. Currently, the reservation is divided into ninety-five sheep ranches or grazing units assigned to individual stockmen or "bands," and four cattle pastures operated by two cattle associations. The Zuni Range Code requires that the boundaries of each sheep ranch or cattle range be exactly delineated, and that livestock be adjusted to the carrying capacity of each separate unit. Approximately 95 percent of the reservation is currently used for grazing, supporting approximately 14,200 sheep, 50 goats and 550 beef cattle. The only areas not incorporated into grazing units are Zuni Pueblo, the four irrigated farming units, and fifteen additional fenced dry-farming units scattered across the reservation.

A typical Zuni sheep ranch consists of a main sheep camp used in the winter, several summer sheep camps, and a range with various improvements. The main sheep camp is located as close as possible to all-weather roads and water, and generally includes a small, one- or two-room house, a bread oven, sheds, woolracks, a trash dump, an outhouse, and several corrals and lambing pens. Summer camps are located to take advantage of the more remote parts of the sheep ranch during the best weather, when access around the range is easiest. Summer camps are less permanent, and often consist of rudimentary shacks, small trailers, or pick-up truck campers, sometimes with an associated tent or ramada used for shade or cooking. In addition to the camps, a sheep ranch will have about nine to eleven brush corrals scattered around the range. These brush corrals are used to pen the sheep at night so they don't have to be returned to the sheep camp. This arrangement makes grazing more flexible. The development of permanent facilities associated with grazing, such as sheep camps and similar stations associated with the cattle units, has occurred only since the reservation was fenced and individual grazing units were assigned. Before that, only temporary camps were established on the open range.

Range management practices on the Zuni Reservation have changed the landscape in many ways. Denudation of the rangeland and erosion occurred when the reservation was first fenced and the area was severely overgrazed. At this time sagebrush, rabbitbrush, and pinyon-juniper woodland invaded the reservation grasslands. Subsequently, the Zunis have participated in many governmental programs to improve the range, including plowing and reseeding projects to restore grasslands and "chaining" projects in which two large tractors drag a large chain or cable to uproot juniper trees and brush that have encroached on rangeland. These projects have had varying success rates. The development of roads, well and drinker facilities, and stockponds have reorganized grazing patterns. Since the adoption of the Tribal Range Code, many individual grazing units are being fenced for the first time. The formerly open rangeland of the reservation has gradually been developed into numerous small, intensively used grazing units.

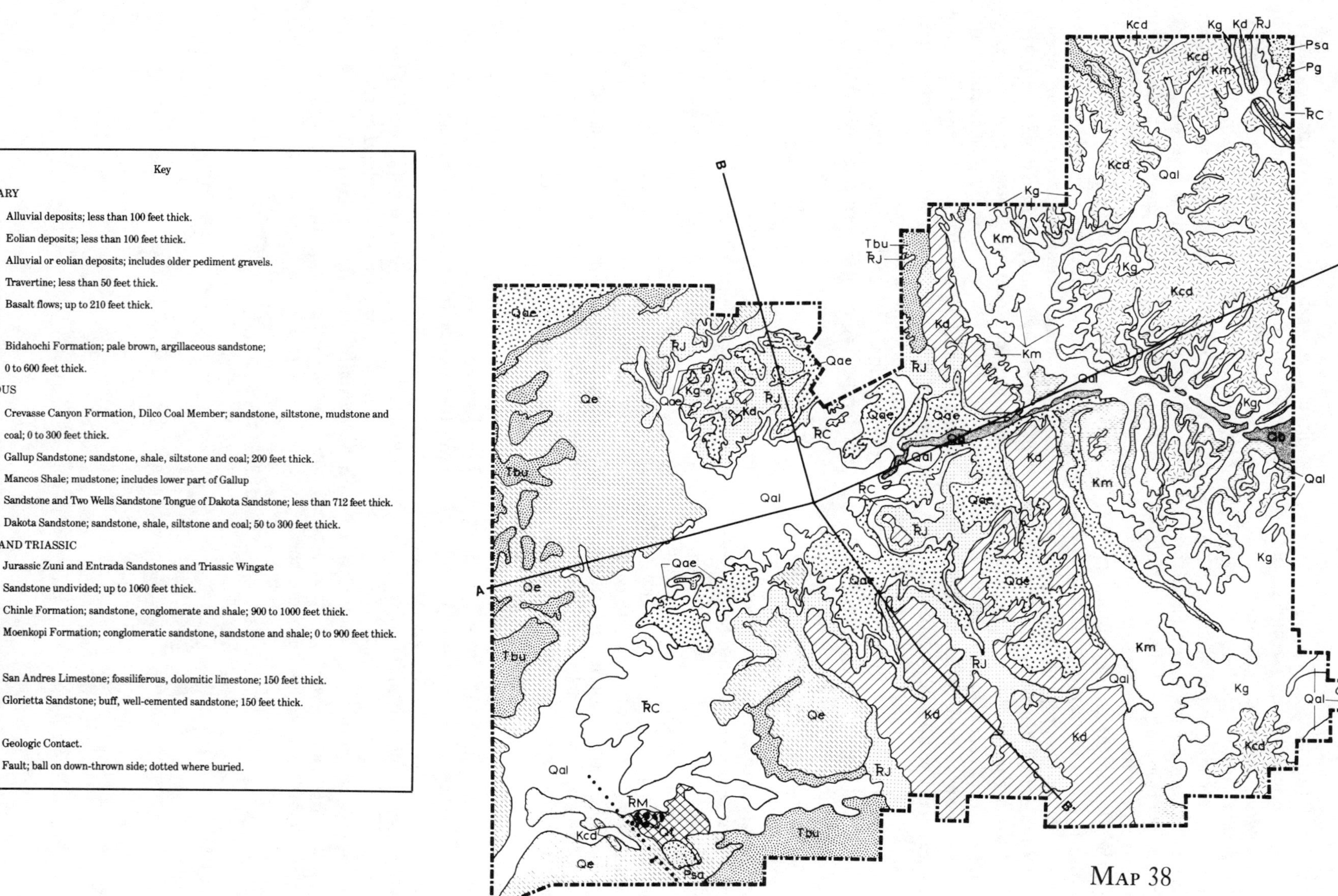

Map 38

GEOLOGY OF THE ZUNI RESERVATION

0 1 2 3 4 5 mi.

Key

QUATERNARY

- Qal — Alluvial deposits; less than 100 feet thick.
- Qe — Eolian deposits; less than 100 feet thick.
- Qae — Alluvial or eolian deposits; includes older pediment gravels.
- Qt — Travertine; less than 50 feet thick.
- Qb — Basalt flows; up to 210 feet thick.

TERTIARY

- Tbu — Bidahochi Formation; pale brown, argillaceous sandstone; 0 to 600 feet thick.

CRETACEOUS

- Kcd — Crevasse Canyon Formation, Dilco Coal Member; sandstone, siltstone, mudstone and coal; 0 to 300 feet thick.
- Kg — Gallup Sandstone; sandstone, shale, siltstone and coal; 200 feet thick.
- Km — Mancos Shale; mudstone; includes lower part of Gallup Sandstone and Two Wells Sandstone Tongue of Dakota Sandstone; less than 712 feet thick.
- Kd — Dakota Sandstone; sandstone, shale, siltstone and coal; 50 to 300 feet thick.

JURASSIC AND TRIASSIC

- R̄J — Jurassic Zuni and Entrada Sandstones and Triassic Wingate Sandstone undivided; up to 1060 feet thick.
- R̄C — Chinle Formation; sandstone, conglomerate and shale; 900 to 1000 feet thick.
- R̄M — Moenkopi Formation; conglomeratic sandstone, sandstone and shale; 0 to 900 feet thick.

PERMIAN

- Psa — San Andres Limestone; fossiliferous, dolomitic limestone; 150 feet thick.
- Pg — Glorietta Sandstone; buff, well-cemented sandstone; 150 feet thick.

Geologic Contact.

Fault; ball on down-thrown side; dotted where buried.

38. GEOLOGY OF THE ZUNI RESERVATION

The geology of the Zuni Reservation determines many aspects of the physical environment that condition human land use, including the distribution of water, soils, and exploitable minerals. The Zuni Reservation is underlain by twenty-five hundred to four thousand feet of sedimentary rocks, beneath which is a basement of Precambrian granitic rock. Sedimentary rocks include beds of limestone, sandstone, siltstone, coal, and shale formed by marine and continental deposition. Folding, faulting, uplifting, and erosion have created a geological structure in which the sedimentary deposits from different geological periods are exposed at the surface in various parts of the reservation.

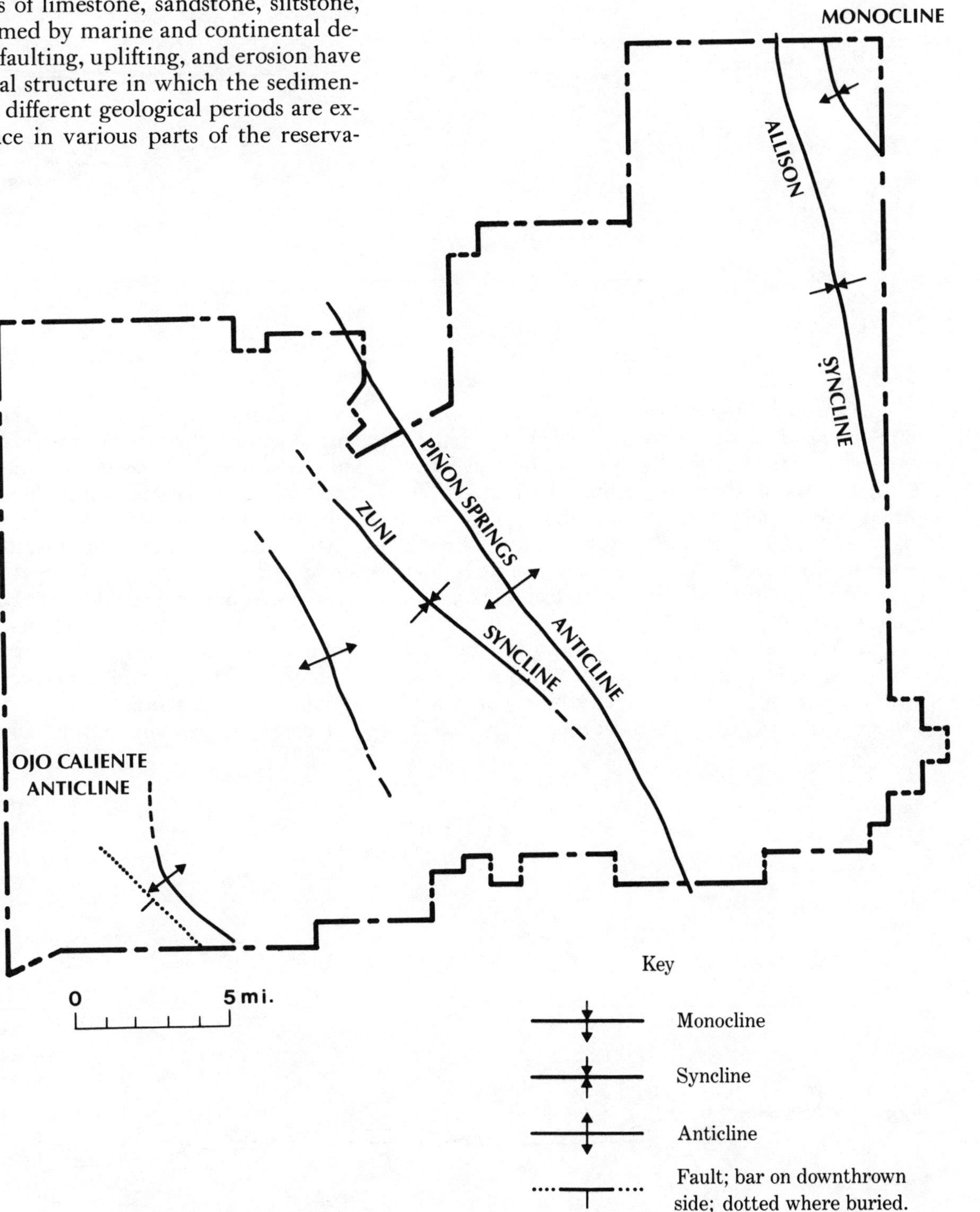

FIGURE 3. *Structural features of Zuni Reservation.*

FIGURE 4. *Schematic Profile of Cross-section A-A'. The concave fold of the Allison Syncline can be seen in this stratigraphic profile, illustrating how Cretaceous rocks are exposed at the surface in the eastern half of the reservation. The western half of this cross-section runs through the Zuni River valley, where Quaternary alluvium and basalt flows overlay earlier Triassic deposits.*

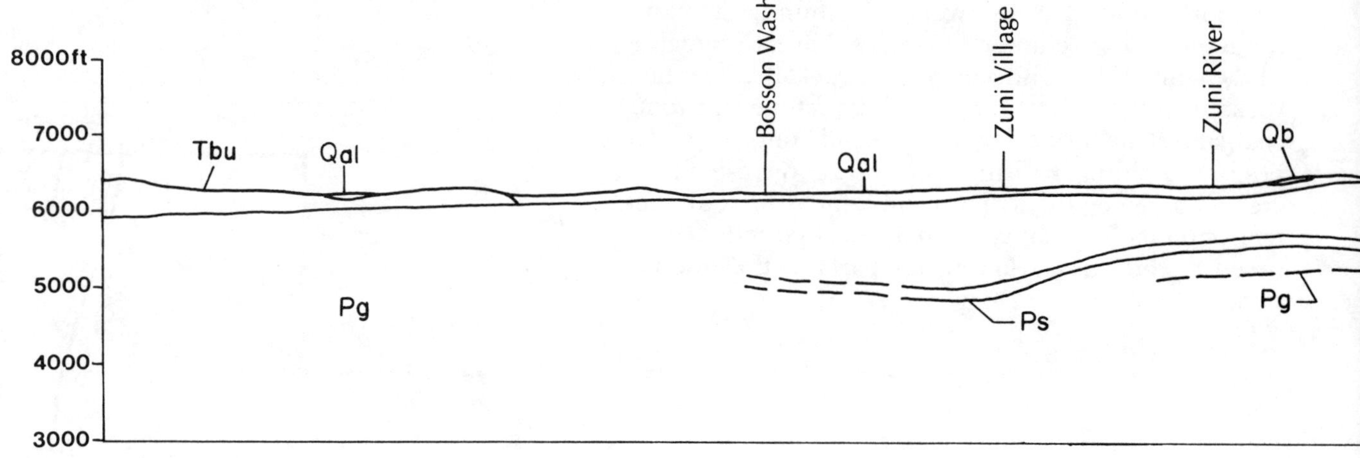

Two types of Permian rocks are exposed in the northeast corner of the reservation east of the Nutria Hogback, a dramatically tilted monocline that forms the edge of the uplift of the Zuni Mountains. The Glorieta Sandstone, about 150 feet thick, is white to buff in color and forms the floor of Nutria Canyon. Above the Glorieta is the fossiliferous gray to yellow San Andres Limestone, also about 150 feet thick, forming cliffs and steep slopes.

Rocks from the Triassic and Jurassic periods are exposed along the pronounced convex structural fold of the Pinyon Springs Anticline, whose northwest-southeast axis runs through the center of the reservation (figure 3), as well as in other low, broad fields in the western half of the reservation, and along the Nutria Hogback. Triassic rocks include the Moenkopi and Chinle formations, with as much as thirteen hundred feet of red, brown, and purple shale interbedded with sandstone and conglomerates. Wingate Sandstone, a bed of approximately 150 feet of reddish-brown siltstone and fine-grained sandstone is exposed with Entrada and Zuni Sandstones, Jurassic rocks with red and white crossbanded deposits of fine to coarse-grained sandstone forming steep escarpments, such as those at Dowa Yalanne.

Except for erosional outliers like the Zuni Buttes,

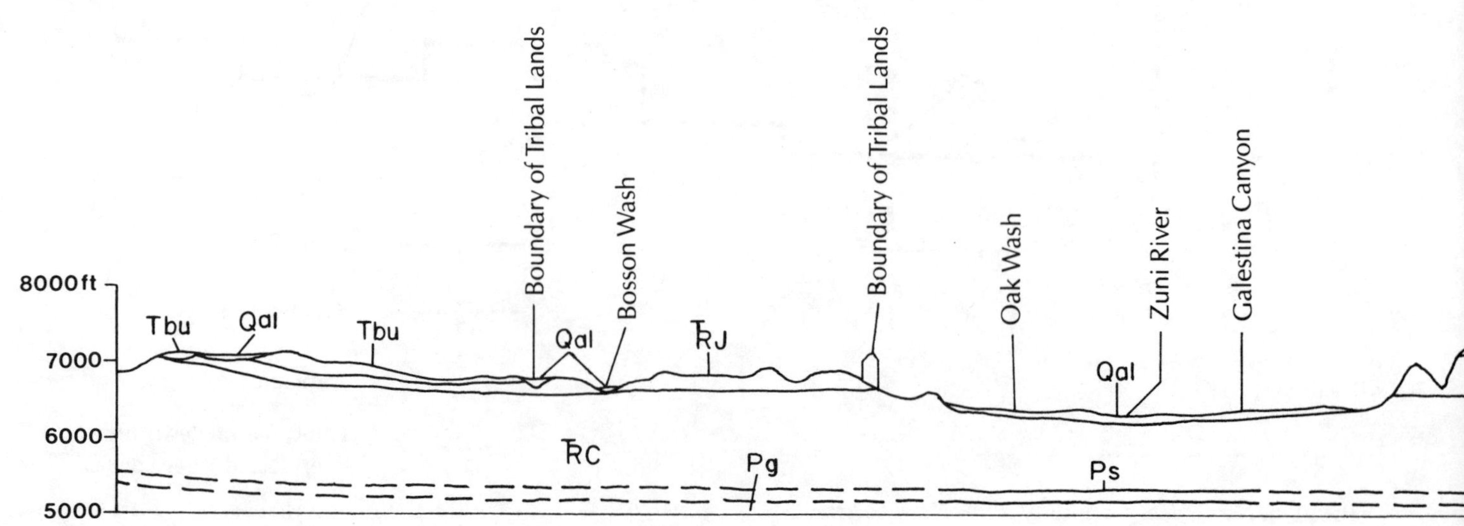

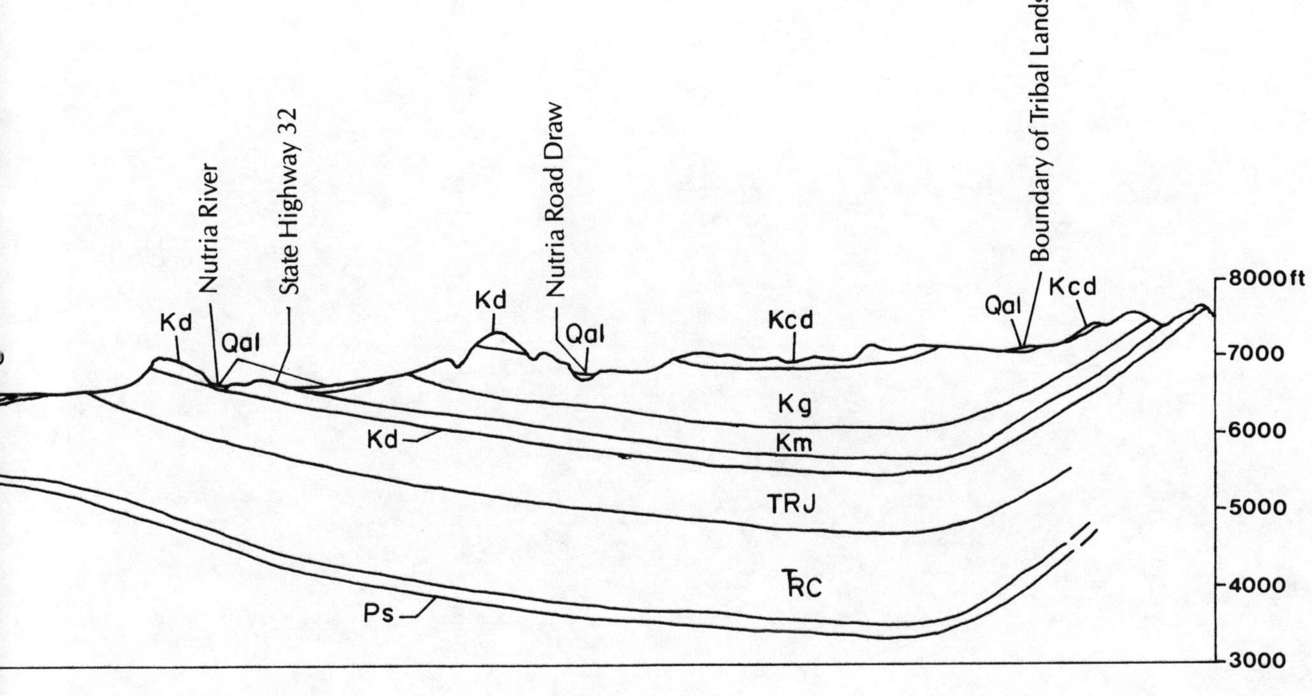

Cretaceous rocks are exposed only in the eastern half of the reservation along the convex fold of the Allison Syncline (figure 4), a trough depression that is a southern projection of the San Juan Basin. The Allison Syncline is defined by the Nutria Monocline on the east and the Pinyon Springs Anticline on the west. The earliest Cretaceous rock is the Dakota Sandstone, composed of up to three hundred feet of yellow-brown, fine- to coarse-grained sandstone with thin seams of coal, forming cliffs and slopes. Mancos Shale, consisting of three hundred to four hundred feet of bluish-gray marine deposits that form gentle slopes, intertongues with the underlying Dakota Sandstone and the overlying Gallup Sandstone. Gallup Sandstone contains a lower unit up to two hundred feet thick of interbedded brown sandstone, shale, and thin coal seams, and an upper unit of pink sandstone with interbedded carbonaceous shale and thin coal seams. The uppermost Cretaceous rock is the Crevasse Canyon Formation, with as much as three hundred feet of ledge-forming brown shale interbedded with yellow sandstone and coal seams.

Tertiary deposits on the reservation are represented by the Bidahochi Formation, a loosely consolidated fluvial apron of white to brown sands and gravels up to six hundred feet thick. The Bidahochi Formation

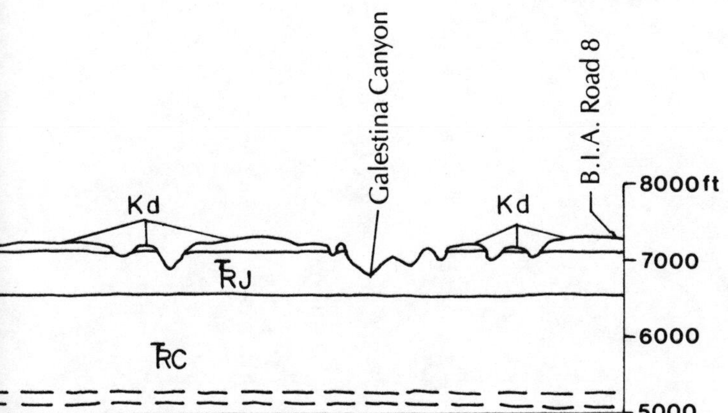

FIGURE 5. *Schematic Profile of Cross-section B-B′. The broad alluvial deposits in the Zuni River valley and adjacent drainages can be seen in the center of this profile, which also illustrates the geological stratification of Permian, Triassic, Jurassic, Cretaceous, Tertiary, and Quaternary deposits under the Zuni Reservation.*

"Waffle gardens" near the Zuni River in 1919. Photograph courtesy the Museum of the American Indian, Heye Foundation (Neg. No. 5598).

covers several large areas in the western part of the reservation, and weathers into ledges alternating with steep white slopes.

Several different types of Quaternary deposits are present on the reservation. These include eolian deposits of windblown silt, sand, and loess on mesas, benches, and broad valleys, and alluvial deposits up to seventy feet thick of silt, sand, and gravel in stream valleys and flood plains (figure 5). Volcanic flows of basalt or basaltic andesite extend from the east down the Pescado and Zuni river valleys as far as Blackrock, covered in places by alluvium. Travertine, a type of high purity limestone, occurs as a result of spring deposition in the Ojo Caliente area in the southwest corner of the reservation. The springs at Ojo Caliente are located on fractures associated with a large fault whose stratigraphic displacement of up to four thousand feet is largely obscured by alluvial and eolian deposits.

Zuni Pueblo, 1978. Photograph by Helga Teiwes, courtesy the Arizona State Museum (Neg. No. 46904).

A view of Dowa Yalanne from the Mission balcony, 1978. Photograph by Helga Teiwes, courtesy the Arizona State Museum (Neg. No. 46903).

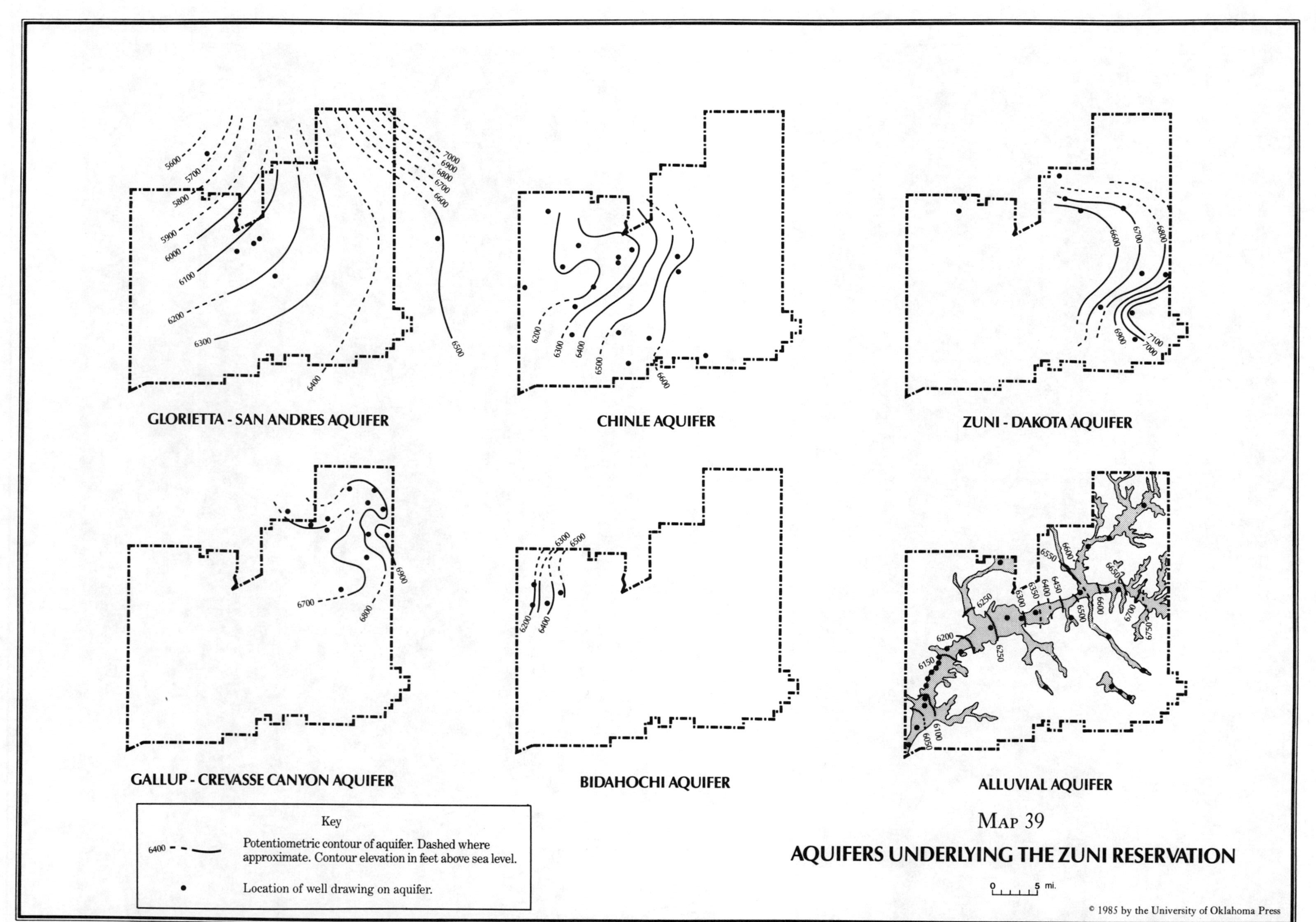

MAP 39

AQUIFERS UNDERLYING THE ZUNI RESERVATION

39. AQUIFERS UNDERLYING THE ZUNI RESERVATION

When the accumulation of thousands of years of water has saturated a geological formation to the extent that springs or wells may yield water from the formation, it it said to be an *aquifer*. In the semi-arid Southwest in general, and at Zuni in particular, where all of human history—indeed, all record of life—has been dependent upon the availability of water, underground aquifers, or *groundwater*, constitute the crucial source of water for survival. At Zuni, aquifers are dependent on large watersheds and require thousands of years to be *recharged*.

Aquifers are mapped by measuring the elevation to which water will rise within tightly cased wells—the contours of the *potentiometric* surfaces. On the Zuni Reservation, of the six geological formations, from Permian to Quaternary age, which supply groundwater for livestock, irrigation, and domestic use, the aquifers in the Permian and Triassic geological formations provide most of the water supply.

The Glorieta Sandstone and San Andres Limestone deposited in the Permian age form a hydraulically interconnected aquifer in which water is transmitted along solution channels in the limestone. This aquifer has a natural discharge at Rainbow Spring and Sacred Spring at Ojo Caliente in the southeast corner of the reservation. These springs are related to fractures associated with the Ojo Caliente anticline and fault line which permit the upward movement of water from the aquifer to the surface at a rate of discharge of about 450 gallons a minute. The four wells on the reservation that are drilled at depths of a thousand to twelve hundred feet into the Glorieta-San Andres aquifer yield as much as 150 gallons per minute. Measurements at pumping centers near Blackrock, which draw from the Glorieta-San Andreas aquifer to supply domestic water to Zuni Pueblo and the Blackrock settlement, have shown drops in the water level of as much twenty-nine feet in only ten years.

Water in the Triassic sandstones of the Chinle Formation is confined by interbedded shales and transmitted along a system of fractures. Local discharge occurs at small springs and seeps where the Chinle Formation reaches the surface, with some additional lateral discharge into alluvium-filled channels such as the Zuni River valley. Of the seventeen wells on the reservation drawing water from the Chinle Formation aquifer, yields range from 5 to 125 gallons a minute, and water-level declines of as much as twenty-seven feet in twenty years have been measured in deep domestic wells from two hundred to four hundred feet deep near Zuni Pueblo.

The Zunia and Dakota sandstones make up a single aquifer underlying the northern and eastern end of the reservation. Although eleven wells powered by windmills draw water from the Zuni-Dakota aquifer for livestock use, the potential to produce water for domestic use or irrigation from this aquifer is limited.

The water-bearing sandstones of the Gallup Sandstone and Crevasse Canyon Formation make up an aquifer that discharges water as seepage along the talus slopes and alluvium of the Rio Nutria and Rio Pescado drainages. The Gallup-Crevasse Canyon aquifer also yields water in the eastern third of the reservation to eleven stock wells. Yield from this aquifer range from four to five gallons a minute.

The sands and gravel of the Bidahochi Formation in the northwest corner of the reservation provide an aquifer that is currently used to supply water for livestock use. Well yields for the four wells drawing water from this aquifer range from three to fifteen gallons a minute. The buried channels that exist in the eroded rock underlying the Bidahochi Formation may contain thick sections of saturated sands and gravels that could be further developed for livestock and domestic use.

Alluvial deposits of sand and gravel compose an aquifer primarily limited to the main drainages, including the Rio Nutria, Rio Pescado and Zuni River. Natural discharge takes place along the channel bottoms of these drainages, supplying the perennial reaches of the watercourses. At Pescado two springs discharge about five hundred gallons of water a minute from the saturated alluvium under a basalt flow, providing water for irrigation and domestic use. A collection gallery constructed at a seep in the Zuni River near Blackrock produces between two and three hundred gallons a minute, and this water is mixed with more heavily mineralized water from the Glorieta–San Andres aquifer to provide domestic water for the Blackrock settlement. More than thirty-three wells have been dug in the alluvial aquifer, usually to depths between five and forty feet, but occasionally as deep as two hundred feet. Yields from these wells, used largely for livestock, are generally less than ten gallons a minute. The susceptibility of alluvial water to surface pollution and the small extent of the alluvial aquifers limits use of this source of groundwater.

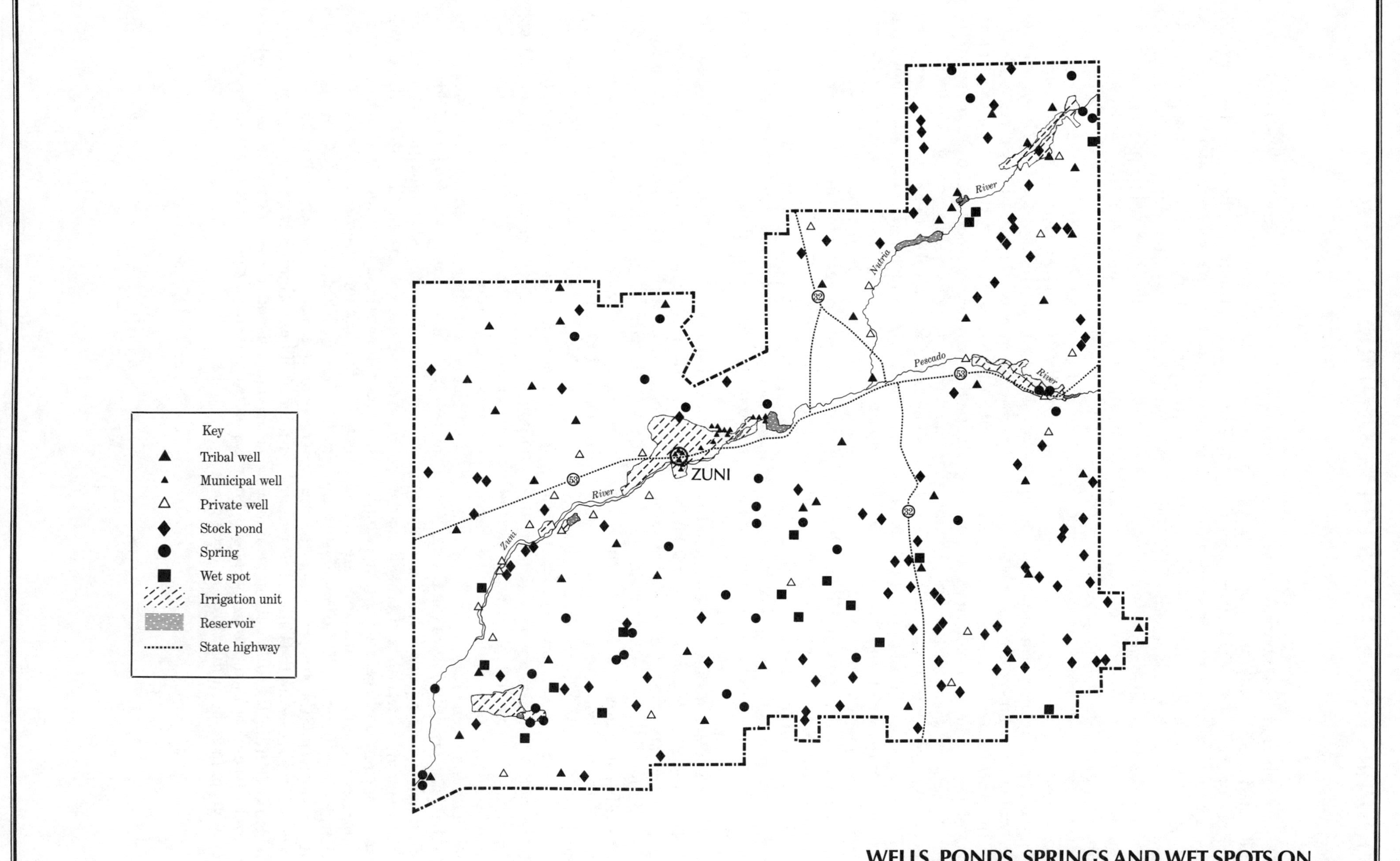

WELLS, PONDS, SPRINGS AND WET SPOTS ON THE ZUNI RESERVATION

40. WELLS, PONDS, SPRINGS, AND WET SPOTS ON THE ZUNI RESERVATION

THERE are three types of wells on the reservation. The deep municipal wells draw water from the Glorieta-San Andres and Chinle Formation aquifers to supply domestic water for Zuni Pueblo and Blackrock. A large number of wells distributed throughout the reservation rangeland draw water for livestock from all six of the aquifers underlying the reservation. These stock wells are divided into private wells developed by individual tribal members at their own expense, and tribal wells developed with government subsidy.

Dozens of small springs dot the reservation, and major springs are located at Ojo Caliente, Nutria, and Pescado. These major springs have been developed for crop irrigation and for religious and domestic use since prehistoric times, and today provide water for the irrigation units. Rainbow Spring, at Ojo Caliente, has been developed with a rock-lined pit thirty feet in diameter, from which water is piped for irrigation and domestic use. Sacred Spring, the other spring at Ojo Caliente, has been modified with earthen dikes that supply a pipe irrigation system. The seepage area between the two springs has been ditched to drain into the reservoir at Ojo Caliente, which is also fed by irrigation and waste water. The two springs in the Pescado Irrigation Unit produce about five hundred gallons of water a minute. Here, the upper spring has been developed with a small rectangular reservoir of stonemasonry, head gates, and a ditched irrigation system; and the lower spring has been improved with an earthen dike, rock retaining wall, and headgate. Recently both of these springs were incorporated into a pipeline irrigation system that discharges into the Rio Pescado from a concrete diversion structure.

Wet spots are ephemeral seeps or springs. These water sources occasionally dry up, but when they are wet provide important water resources for livestock and wild game. The importance of wet spots has somewhat diminished since the advent of deep drilled wells on the range, but wet spots are still used to water livestock whenever convenient.

The Zunis and their ancestors have been constructing small domestic water reservoirs since the thirteenth century, and Zuni stockmen began to construct small stock ponds to impound water in the early twentieth century. Most water impoundment, however, has been the result of federally funded programs to construct large dams, reservoirs, and stock ponds. These government programs began with the construction of Blackrock Dam and Reservoir in the years 1904–1909, and continued with the construction of additional reservoirs and stock ponds between 1930 and the present. In total, these stock ponds and reservoirs cover more than 1,500 acres with water, but the storage of large amounts of water is accompanied by a correspondingly large loss from evaporation, close to 7,000 acre-feet of water a year. The reservoirs also increase seepage into aquifers, and decrease the flow of the Zuni River. Approximately 30,000 acre-feet of the original storage capacity of Blackrock Dam, the additional reservoirs, and the stock ponds have been lost because of sedimentation or flood damage. In recent years the reservoirs with permanent bodies of water have been stocked with fish and developed for recreational purposes.

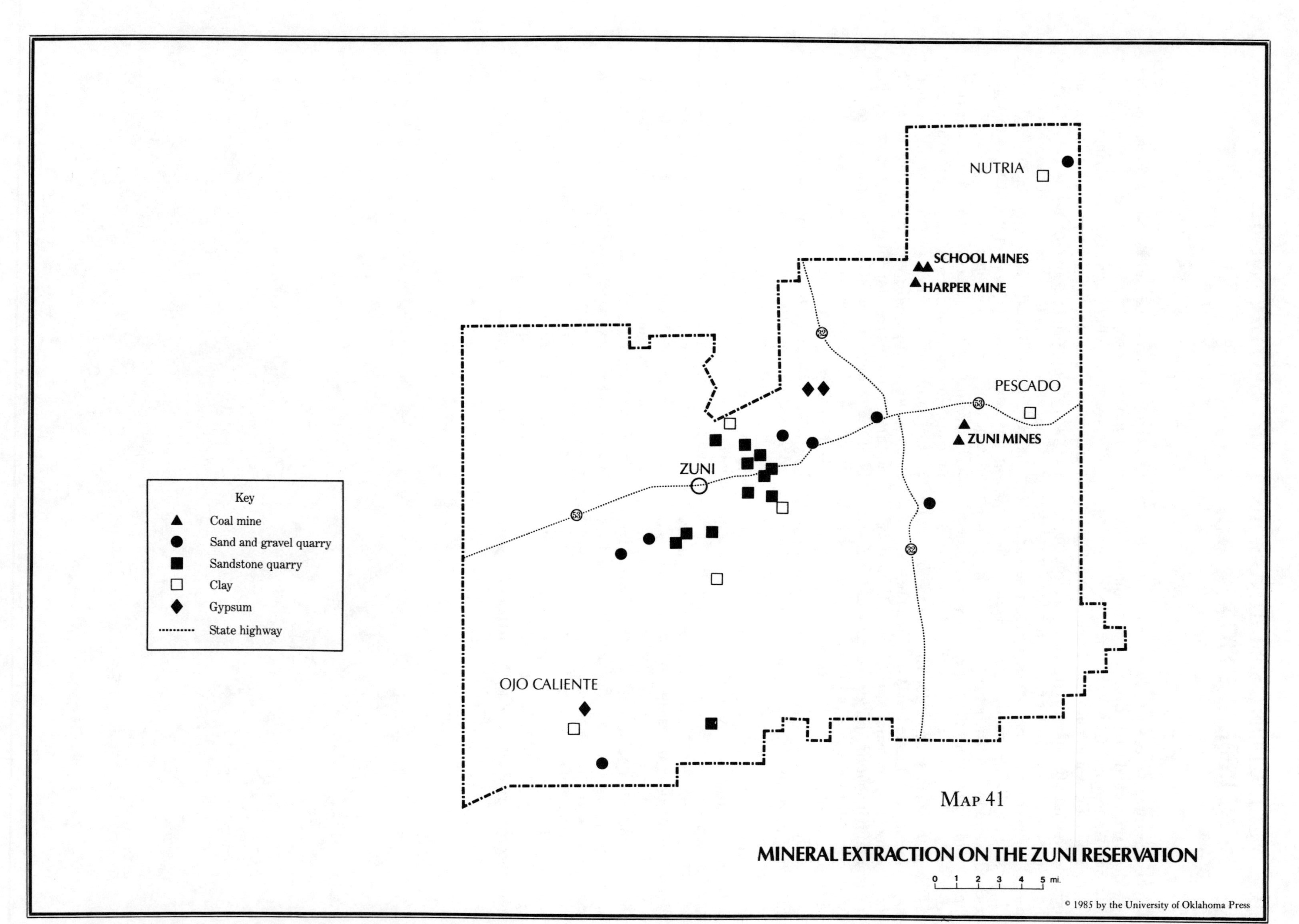

Map 41

MINERAL EXTRACTION ON THE ZUNI RESERVATION

41. MINERAL EXTRACTION ON THE ZUNI RESERVATION

OVER the centuries the Zuni Indians have used the mineral resources of their land for a variety of purposes. In the traditional Zuni economy, the most common minerals extracted for use included sandstone, basalt, clay, gypsum, and pigments. Sandstone and basalt were widely quarried to provide the building materials needed in the stonemasonry that has long been a hallmark of Zuni architecture. In addition, sandstone and basalt were used in the manufacture of *manos* and *metates*—the grinding slabs used to prepare cornmeal and other food products. A special type of fine-grained white Zuni sandstone was obtained at Dowa Yalanne to use in the ovens for making *hewe*, or paperbread. Clay sources all over the reservation were mined to provide the raw material needed to produce a wide variety of ceramics ranging from rough-surface cooking wares to highly polished and beautifully painted water jars and serving bowls. Different kinds of clay also had medicinal value. Gypsum was obtained for whitewash. Pigments were collected and used ritually as well as ground into paints. All of the mineral extraction conducted to sustain the traditional economy was on a relatively small scale, creating little adverse ecological impact. Many of these same minerals continue to be collected for the same uses today.

With the development of a modern reservation economy the scale of mineral extraction has increased on the Zuni Reservation, and a number of mineral commodities have been extracted, including coal, sand and gravel, and crushed limestone aggregate. Coal has been mined by the Bureau of Indian Affairs at four locations in the northeastern portion of the reservation, including the School Mine and Harper Mine near Nutria, and the Zuni Mine and Zuni No. 2 Mine near Pescado. These mines are abandoned at present, but they formerly supplied coal for fuel at the sub-agency, the Zuni Indian School, and for use at other localities. The Zuni Mine operated from 1928 to 1943, and produced about thirty-two thousand tons of coal. The Zuni No. 2 Mine, in operation from 1939 to 1951, produced about fourteen thousand tons of coal. Both mines produced coal from the Gallup Sandstone geological formation. Data on production of the Nutria mines is not currently available.

Road construction and paving projects on and near the Zuni Reservation have created a need for sand, gravel, and limestone aggregate. In recent years, major sand and gravel pits have been established in the Bidahochi formation west of Zuni Pueblo, as well as the basalt flow east of Blackrock. Sand from alluvial deposits has been mined in several parts of the reservation. The San Andres Limestone deposit north of Nutria has provided a quarry for crushed limestone aggregate for the past two decades; another limestone quarry was recently established near Ojo Caliente. The sale of sand, gravel and crushed limestone aggregate has generated a small source of income for the Zuni tribal government.

To date, the extraction of mineral resources on the Zuni Reservation has largely been for local use, although sand, gravel, and limestone aggregate have begun to be exported from the reservation in small quantities. The scale of mineral extraction has increased slightly, but no large underground, open pit, or strip mines have been established. Minable coal reserves are present in the Nutria area, and the possibilities of mining coal there are being considered by the Zuni Tribal Council.

Zunis being filmed during a salt-gathering ceremony at the Zuni Salt Lake, ca. 1921–23. Photograph by D. A. Cadzow, courtesy the Museum of the American Indian, Heye Foundation (Neg. No. 13117).

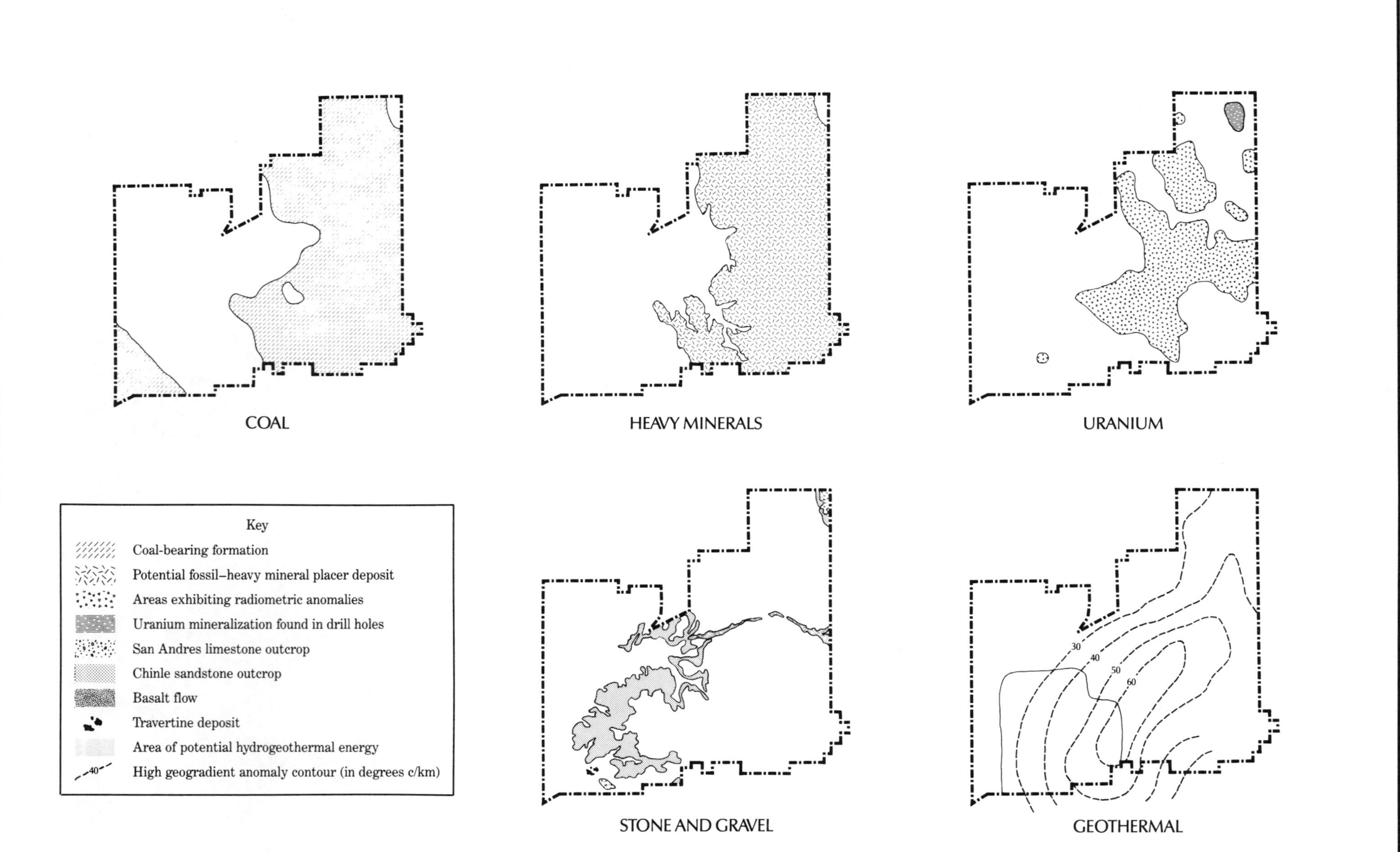

MAP 42

MINERAL AND ENERGY RESOURCES OF THE ZUNI RESERVATION

42. MINERAL AND ENERGY RESOURCES OF THE ZUNI RESERVATION

Possible sources for future economic development on the Zuni Reservation lie in mineral and energy resources; coal, heavy minerals, uranium, nonmetallic minerals, and potential geothermal power all exist or potentially exist on the reservation. While only a few of these resources have been exploited so far, and these mostly for local use, at least some of the mineral and energy resources exist in commercially valuable deposits which could be mined or developed. Which of these resources to exploit and how to exploit them constitute important developmental issues for the Zuni Tribe.

Deposits of good quality, subbituminous coal exist in the eastern half and southwestern corner of the reservation, in the Dakota Sandstone, Gallup Sandstone, and Crevasse Canyon Formation. The coal found in the Dakota Sandstone occurs as thin stringers less than a foot thick, and is not commercially minable. In the Gallup Sandstone, coals range from one to five feet in thickness, lying in two to four beds, some of which are commercially minable. The richest coal beds on the reservation, up to ten feet in thickness in seven distinct beds, occur in the Crevasse Canyon Formation. The coal deposits in several areas near Pescado and Nutria in the eastern half of the reservation have been determined suitable for strip mining. Other coal deposits could only be exploited through underground mining. The presence of coal reserves on the reservation suggests that other fossil fuels, such as petroleum and gas, might also be present, but exploration of these resources has not yet advanced to the point that they can be mapped.

Two types of metallic mineral deposits potentially exist on the reservation: red bed copper and heavy mineral placers. Red bed copper deposits are known to exist in the Zuni Mountains, and are widespread in Permian and Triassic formations throughout the Southwest. Since three-quarters of the reservation is underlain by Permian and Triassic rocks, it is possible that red bed copper deposits exist there as well. Heavy mineral placer deposits have been found in Cretaceous sedimentary rocks in many places on the Colorado Plateau. Similar geological formations are found in the eastern half of the reservation, raising the possibility that heavy mineral placers are also present in that area. Heavy mineral placers include magnetite, ilmenite, leucoxene, rutile, spinel, monazite, zircon, garnet, epidote, and tourmaline with quartz and feldspar, cemented by hematite and carbonates. These placers were concentrated by waves and currents along ancient beaches, and were later consolidated into the sandstone formation. Neither copper nor heavy mineral prospecting has been conducted on the reservation.

Uranium prospecting was conducted on the Zuni Reservation in the 1950s and 1960s, largely because many significant uranium deposits are located within sixty miles of Zuni in the Triassic and Cretaceous formations that also underlie the Zuni Reservation. Radiometric surveys of the reservation revealed 272 radiometric anomalies, but a sampling of these indicated only the presence of low-grade uranium not warranting further exploration. Similarly, test holes drilled for uranium exploration near Nutria revealed the presence of uranium, but a grade too low for commercial exploitation. Additional prospecting might locate commercially valuable deposits.

Nonmetallic minerals of economic importance on the reservation include sand and gravel aggregates, limestone, clays, gypsum, and stone. Crushed aggregate material is quarried from the San Andres Limestone near Nutria, and the travertine near Ojo Caliente provides another source of calcium carbonate. Building stone has been quarried from many different geological formations, including the Chinle Formation and basalt flows. These nonmetalic minerals are high bulk, low unit-value materials that commonly occur over a wide region. For this reason their potential for export is limited, but they remain valuable for local construction and community development.

Two geothermal anomalies exist on the Zuni Reservation. An area with a geothermal gradient twice the normal temperature exists in the central and eastern part of the reservation, and a hot spring that attains an average surface temperature of twenty-two degrees Celsius occurs at Ojo Caliente. The geothermal energy studies that have been conducted on the reservation have concluded a significant hydrogeothermal resource probably does not exist, but that the reservation does represent a good prospect for "hot dry rock" geothermal development. The Precambrian granitic rocks at a depth of 2,500 to 4,000 feet constitute the "hot dry rock," which could be developed by artificially fracturing the rock to provide a heat transfer pathway for introduced water. The water and its heat could then be pumped out and used to produce electricity and space heating.

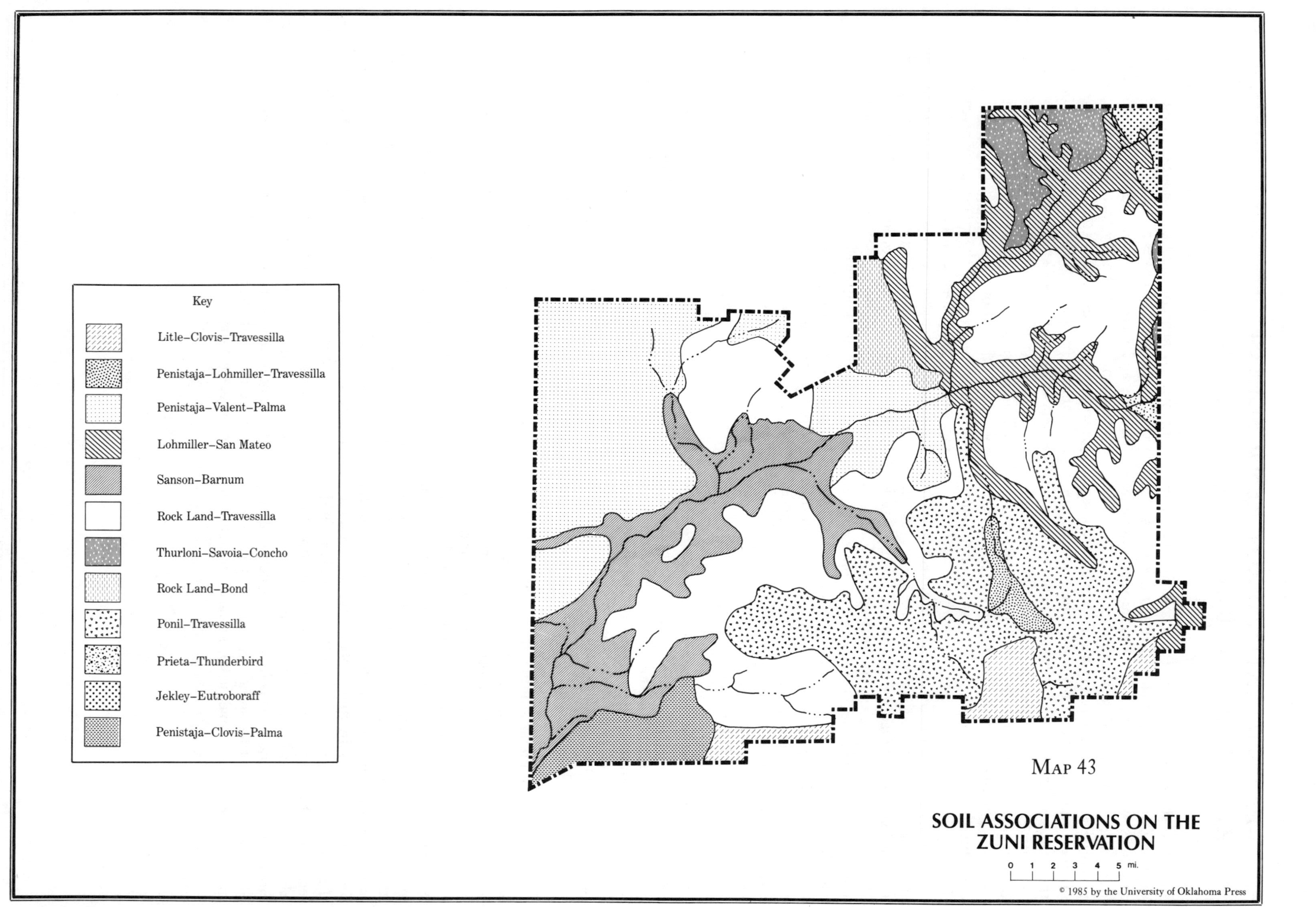

Map 43

SOIL ASSOCIATIONS ON THE ZUNI RESERVATION

43. SOIL ASSOCIATIONS ON THE ZUNI RESERVATION

Soils are often perceived as simply "dirt," but are really complex geological structures of great importance, which vary widely across the landscape. These uppermost layers of the earth's surface are capable of supporting rooted plants and are important because the type of soil will help determine the natural vegetation in an area and thus the capability of the area to sustain human land uses. For instance, agricultural areas require soils with adequate moisture retention, drainage, and nutrients, while land to be used for construction should have soils firm enough to support building foundations.

Variation in soils results from the different types of geological materials and processes that combine to form surface deposits. Decomposition of the underlying geological parent material or bedrock, and deposition of windblown (eolian) and water transported (alluvial) sediments, as well as the addition of organic material from the vegetative cover, all play a role in the formation of soils. Soils take eons to form, and are a resource that needs careful conservation. Erosion of soils, especially by gullying and arroyo cutting, can take place in a few years, and redeposition may never restore it to its former state, even over centuries.

Individual soils often occur in small deposits, and while areas are mapped for two or more of their major soils, they often contain additional soils as well. Gullied land and alluvial land, both containing highly variable sediments in the flood plains of arroyos and drainage channels, cross cut many other soils. The major emphasis of the soil studies on the Zuni Reservation has been to identify potentially irrigable land.

The highest-rated irrigable land on the Zuni Reservation (and in McKinley and Cibola counties), consists of the Sanson-Barnum soil association, which occurs on the gently sloping floodplains of the Zuni River and tributary drainages, as well as in small areas of gently sloping alluvial plains and fans that extend from adjoining uplands towards the Zuni River. At Ojo Caliente, the site of one of the Zuni farming villages, the Zuni Indians have long irrigated Sanson-Barnum soils with water available from springs. In areas where water is not presently available, the soils of the Sanson-Barnum association support a good vegetative cover of grasses and forbs used to graze livestock and wildlife.

To the north and west of the Sanson-Barnum soil association lies the Penistaja-Valent-Palma soil association, an area of deep, well-drained soils occurring mainly on gently sloping and undulating landscapes formed from alluvial and aeolian sediments, also including a few small areas of steep breaks and rolling uplands. The Penistaja-Valent-Palma soil association is also rated highly in terms of irrigation potential, but since there is less water available here, the area is mostly used for grazing livestock and supports a vegetative cover of grasslands and pinyon-juniper woodland.

The loamy, Penistaja-Clovis-Palma association occurs south of the Sanson-Barnum association near the Arizona state line in an area of sloping and undulating landscapes. This potentially irrigable soil association supports a vegetative cover of mixed grasses and trees, including scattered stands of pinyon-juniper.

A fourth potentially irrigable soil is the Lohmiller–San Mateo association which occurs on the valley bottoms, floodplains, and terraces of the Rios Pescado and Nutria in the eastern half of the Zuni Reservation, where the Zunis have developed productive farming villages. Deep, vertical-walled arroyos have been cut through the valley bottoms of this area. Areas of the Lohmiller–San Mateo soil association not used for irrigated agriculture support a vegetative cover of grasses and shrubs, and are currently used to graze livestock.

Bordering the valleys of the Zuni River and its tributaries on most of the reservation are large areas of the Rockland-Travessilla soil association, areas characterized by a rough, broken topography where narrow valley floors and upland summits are separated by steep canyon walls and escarpments, but also includes gently to steeply sloping alluvial fans between the valley floors and canyon sides, and undulating uplands. In general, the major soils in this association are shallow and rocky or sandy, with no potential for modern irrigated agriculture. In several of the canyon bottoms, however, there are areas appropriate for less intensive agriculture, many of which show evidence they were used for farming by the ancestors of the Zuni Indians. In addition to pinyon-juniper woodland, this soil association also supports coniferous forest and extensive livestock grazing, and it is important as wildlife habitat for deer and other animals.

Another soil association with a low rating for potential irrigation but that nonetheless contains small areas suitable for agriculture is the Penistaja-Lohmiller-Travessilla association, occurring in a small area near the southeastern corner of the reservation. In this association, the best agricultural soils occur in small patches intermixed in areas of poor soils. The Penistaja-Lohmiller-Travessilla association occurs in a landscape consisting of a broad, nearly level valley bottom, supports a good vegetative cover, including pinyon-juniper woodland, and is used primarily for grazing livestock.

The Ponil-Travessilla soil association occurs on the broad, gently sloping and undulating mesa tops to the southeast of Zuni Pueblo. The soils of this association range from shallow to moderately deep, formed largely from parent material eroded from the underlying sand-

A Zuni woman making pottery, ca. 1921–23. Photograph by D. A. Cadzow, courtesy the Museum of the American Indian, Heye Foundation (Neg. No. 13102).

stone, occasionally mixed with aeolian and alluvial sediments. Although in general it has very little potential for irrigated agriculture, the association supports a fair to good vegetative cover, including extensive areas of pinyon-juniper woodlands, and is used to graze livestock.

Five other soil associations occur in small areas on the Zuni Reservation. The Rockland-Bond soil association occurs in an area of gently sloping mesa tops in the north-central portion of the reservation, the residual soils of which support a good vegetative cover of pinyon-juniper woodland. The Jekley-Eutroboraff association present in the northeast corner of the reservation, where the slopes are often steep, has moderate to deep soils supporting a vegetative cover dominated by trees, especially Ponderosa pine. The Thurloni-Savoia-Concho association, which occurs in a small, narrow strip along the eastern border of the reservation, consists of moderately deep residual soils, along with some shale and rock outcrops, and supports a good vegetative cover, including some coniferous forest as well as pinyon-juniper woodland. The Prieta-Thunderbird association, which also occurs in a small area at the eastern edge of the reservation where soils are forming from volcanic materials on old lava flows in the low-lying areas, supports a thin vegetative cover of pinyon-juniper and grasses. The Litle-Clovis-Travessilla association, present in several areas in the uplands along the southern border of the reservation, supports a moderate to good vegetative cover including pinyon-juniper woodland and grasses. None of these five soil associations are well suited to irrigated agriculture.

44. ZUNI PUEBLO, 1972, AS MAPPED by Perry E. Borchers

As THE Zuni people developed their reservation in the twentieth century, they also substantially reconstructed Zuni Pueblo to keep up with the changing times. In 1972, Perry E. Borchers mapped the old pueblo at Zuni for the National Park Service and the Historic American Buildings Survey, using photogrammetrical mapping techniques. Using aerial photographs taken by the New Mexico State Highway Department in September, 1972, Borchers produced his highly accurate plan view of Zuni Pueblo, showing both architectural continuity and change.

In the old pueblo there has been a marked tendency for the architecture to change rapidly in detail, while keeping the same general outline; many changes in the form and amount of open space within the pueblo are clearly evident, but there is still continuity to the past outlines of the house blocks. The three linear house blocks to the east are no longer contiguous, but they are still discernable, and the clustering of the western house blocks is still oriented around the dance plazas northwest of the Mission, which was restored in 1966.

While the general outline of the old pueblo at Zuni has been preserved, this part of the village has otherwise undergone a complete architectural transformation. Less than fifty structures dating before 1937 still stand, and the pueblo today consists primarily of recently constructed single-storied houses sitting on top of the mounded remains of the earlier multi-storied village. The impact of the automobile has been immense, and virtually all exterior space, except for the small dance plaza used for religious ceremonies, has been modified so that it can be used as a roadway. New masonry styles, gabled roofs, and building materials such as cinderbrick have become popular, and the new construction has tended to obscure the old

FIGURE 6. *Zuni Pueblo and suburbs, 1972. From U.S.G.S. 7.5 minute quad, Zuni Quadrangle, courtesy United States Geological Survey.*

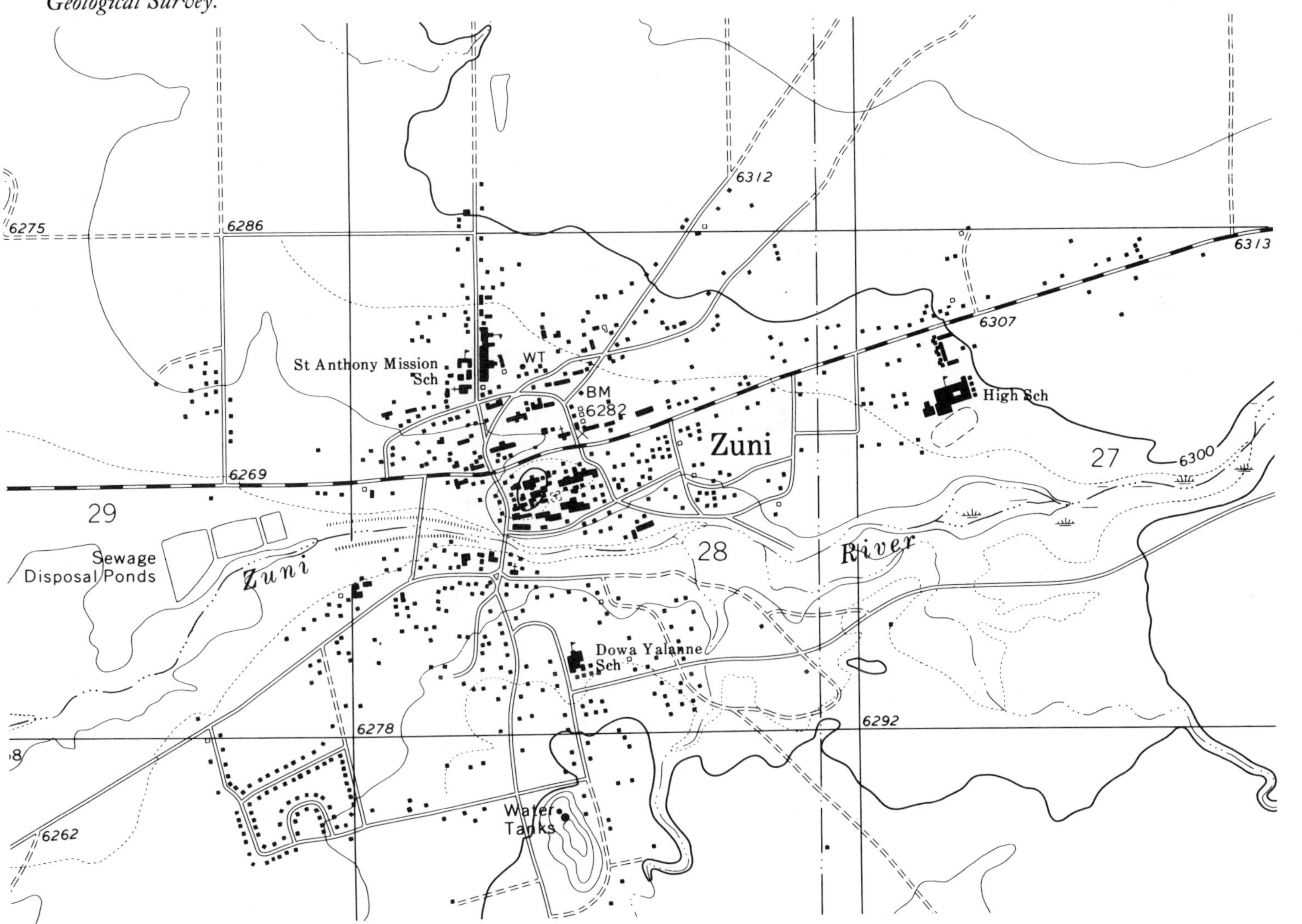

10
20
30
40
50
60
70
80
90
100
150
SCALE IN METERS
PLAN OF ZUNI

AERIAL PHOTOGRAPHY BY NEW MEXICO STATE HIGHWAY DEPARTMENT
SEPTEMBER 1972
PLOTTED ON THE WILD A7 AUTOGRAPH, THE OHIO STATE UNIVERSITY, OCTOBER–NOVEMBER 1972, BY PERRY E. BORCHERS, RESEARCH SUPERVISOR
SCALE IN FEET
HISTORIC AMERICAN BUILDINGS SURVEY
SHEET OF SHEETS
SURVEY NO.
NAME AND LOCATION OF STRUCTURE
THE CENTRAL AND ORIGINAL PORTION OF THE PUEBLO OF ZUNI
ZUNI RESERVATION, McKINLEY COUNTY, NEW MEXICO U.S.A.
DRAWN BY: JAMES LAMSAM, RESEARCH ASSISTANT
PREPARED AT THE SCHOOL OF ARCHITECTURE, THE OHIO STATE UNIVERSITY, COLUMBUS OHIO

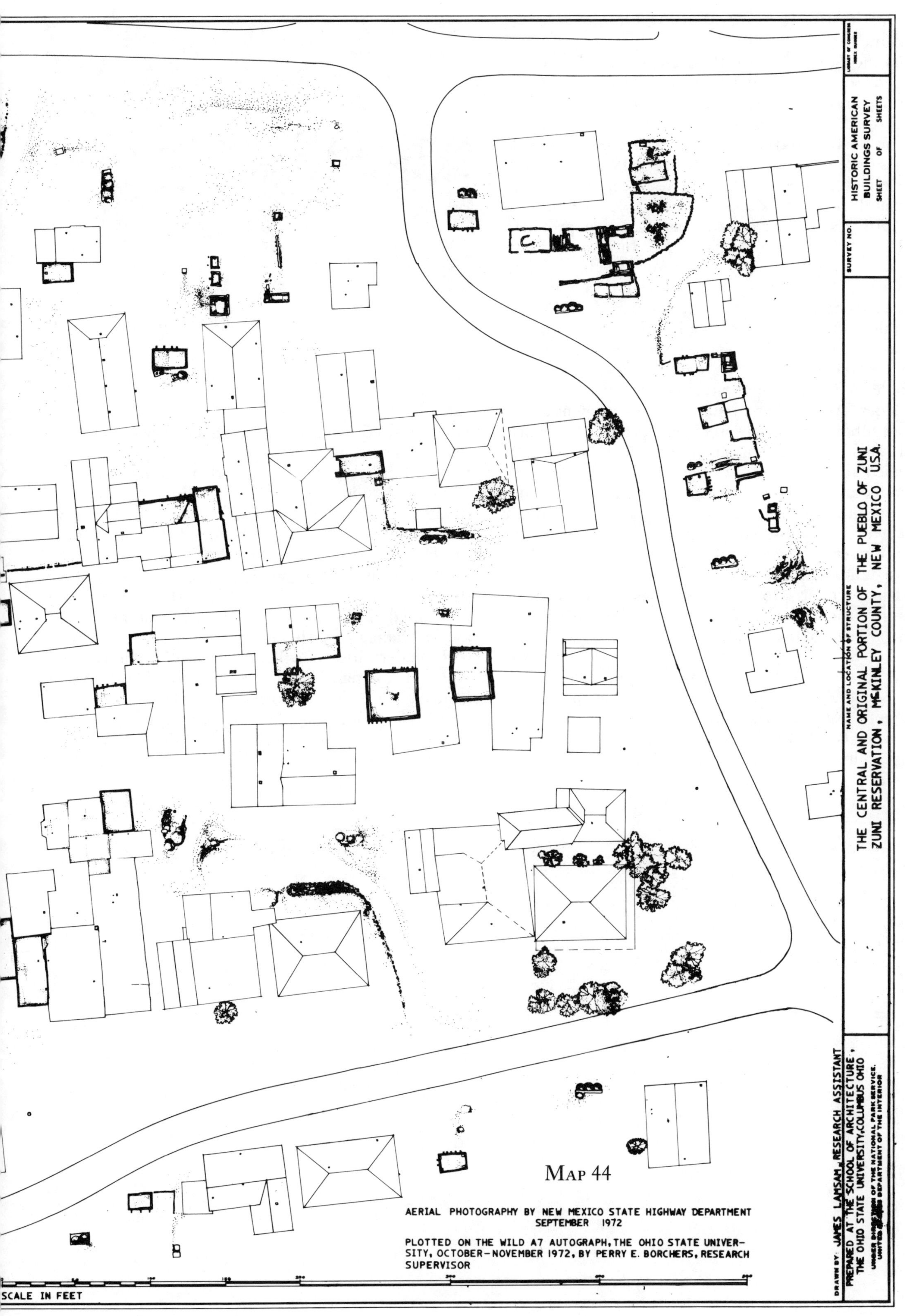

Map 44

terraces that were formerly such a prominent aspect of Zuni architecture.

As the Zunis changed the architecture of their village to serve their changing needs, they also introduced a number of modern conveniences to improve their standard of living. In 1950 electricity was installed in the pueblo, and in 1954 the first piped municipal water system was constructed. In the 1950s and 1960s the major streets were paved to accommodate the cars and trucks the Zunis obtained in great numbers. In 1961 a sewer system was installed that provided indoor plumbing for the first time. In the late 1970s the water and sewer systems were upgraded, providing service to all remaining households that wanted it.

The trend toward suburban living at Zuni Pueblo has also continued, accompanied by a rapid growth in the population of the Zuni tribe, which expanded from 1,600 people in the 1880s to more than 7,000 people in 1980. The old pueblo is now surrounded on all sides by outlying houses and government-subsidized subdivisions. New architectural forms and materials, such as woodframe and cinderblock houses with pitched and gabled roofs, have greatly diversified the architectural character of the village. Zuni Pueblo has grown into a small town more than a square mile in size, with the layout of the larger settlement following patterns set by paved roads and utilities (figure 6). A large building housing the tribal government complex and five schools provide institutional nodes in community orientation, but the old pueblo remains the central focus of the village.

Architectural change at Zuni in the twentieth century has been swift and seemingly complete. Many visitors to Zuni today have difficulty distinguishing the core historic pueblo from the rest of the village, because its appearance is so changed. Nonetheless, many culturally important aspects of Zuni architecture have endured. Kiva locations, dance plazas, and religious pathways have maintained an integrity of position to a much greater extent than habitation structures, and it is around these traditionally oriented points that the pueblo has been reconstructed. Although religious areas have been enlarged, they have rarely been encroached on. The roofs around the plazas are still used as galleries from which to observe the many social and religious dances that are regularly performed. Thus, while the old pueblo has been drastically changed by the Zunis in order to keep pace with modern life, the village core still functions much like it always has. During Shalako, the Winter Night Dances, and other important religious events, great numbers of Zuni people still congregate in the old pueblo to participate in and observe the ancient ceremonies that are the heartbeat of the Zuni tribe.

Zuni homes, 1979. Photograph by Rick Dingus, courtesy of T. J. Ferguson.

Appendix 1. ZUNI LAND USE SITES

1. *Shiba:bulima*
LOCATION: Stone Lions Shrine, Bandelier National Monument, New Mexico.
PLANT COLLECTION: Big Fire Society collects herbs.
RELIGIOUS USE: The origin place of medicine societies and prey animals; the shrine is still in use today.

2. *Chi:biya Yalanne*
LOCATION: Sandia Mountains, New Mexico.
PLANT COLLECTION: The Big Fire Society collects herbs here, and also a medicine for swelling is collected here.
MINERAL COLLECTION: Galena, used for paint for masks, and also malachite and azurite are collected here.
RELIGIOUS USE: It is the origin place for the Big Fire Society and a shrine for the Shuma:que Society, which is still in use. The whole mountain is considered sacred.

3. *Łemmulle or Łemmul'a*
LOCATION: Ice Caves, Valencia County, New Mexico.
PLANT COLLECTION: The Big Fire Society collects herbs here.
MINERAL COLLECTION: Obsidian is obtained here.
GRAZING: The Laweeka family grazed from Nutria Canyon and McGaffey to here.
RELIGIOUS USE: A religious area for Big Fire Society and Sword Swallowing Society, it is also used annually by Longhorn groups; area is important in religion and songs and is used by curing groups to pray for rain and snow.

4. *Nałuwala:wa*
LOCATION: East end of the Zuni Mountains, New Mexico.
HUNTING: It is a deer hunting area.
RELIGIOUS USE: It is a shrine area important for the hunting society in particular, and for all hunters in general.
OTHER: This is a Zuni place name for "where the deer people dwell."

5. *Dowa Yalanne*
LOCATION: Zuni Indian Reservation, New Mexico.
PLANT COLLECTION: Bark from peach trees on east side is used for red dye.
MINERAL COLLECTION: Mineral for black paint is obtained here.
RELIGIOUS USE: It is a shrine area, but the whole mountain is sacred.

6. *Kwili Yala: A:chi*
LOCATION: Zuni Indian Reservation, New Mexico.
HUNTING: It is a Zuni hunting area.
RELIGIOUS USE: A War God Shrine is located here.

7. *Lhak/alhonatah-na*
LOCATION: North of the Zuni Indian Reservation, New Mexico.
FARMING: The area here and to the north was farmed by Zunis.
RELIGIOUS USE: It is a War God Shrine and an area associated with the Mudhead group.

8. *Lhaulhetah-na*
LOCATION: North of Zuni Indian Reservation, New Mexico.
PLANT COLLECTION: Herbs are collected in this area.
FARMING: This area has been farmed by Zunis.

9. *Dwankwin Onan Baniyna'a*
LOCATION: Zuni Indian Reservation, New Mexico.
RELIGIOUS USE: This War God Shrine is in an area associated with the Sword Swallowing Society.

10. *Hanłibinkya*
LOCATION: Southwest of Witchwells, Arizona.
PLANT COLLECTION: The Sword Swallower Society collects herbs and medicine here. A medicine called "Owaylu" is collected here.
HUNTING: Eagles were captured here in 1923.
GRAZING: It is a traditional Zuni grazing area.
RELIGIOUS USE: This is the origin place of the War Gods and of Zuni clans. It is also an ancestral site in the Zuni migration narrative.

11. *Kołuwala:wa*
LOCATION: Confluence of the Zuni and Little Colorado rivers, Arizona.
PLANT COLLECTION: Willow and herbs are collected in this area.
MINERAL COLLECTION: Pink clay, yellow clay, and red paint are collected in this area.
GRAZING: This is a traditional Zuni grazing area.
RELIGIOUS USE: Every four years a pilgrimage is made to this area by religious leaders who are asking for rain and portentous signs concerning the future. It is especially important to the Mudheads and is an ancestral site in the Zuni migration narrative. All Zunis go to Kołuwala:wa after death.

12. *Beya K'okshi'a*
LOCATION: North of St. Johns, Arizona.
RELIGIOUS USE: This is a ritual camping site on the pilgrimage to no. 11, Koluwala:wa.

13. *K'ya'na'a or K'yapkwayina'a (Ojo Caliente)*
LOCATION: Zuni Indian Reservation.
MINERAL COLLECTION: Sandstone for construction is found there.
FARMING: This is one of the important and ancient Zuni farming villages.
GRAZING: It is a traditional Zuni grazing area.

14. *Do:k'yana'a or Do:k'yan'a or Do:k'yana*
LOCATION: Zuni Indian Reservation, New Mexico.
RELIGIOUS USE: A sacred spring used by kiva groups is located here.

NOTE: Consult the index listing for the individual site to find the map where it is shown.

15. *Ma'k'yaya'a or Ma'k'yay'a or Ma'k'yaya*
Location: Zuni Salt Lake, New Mexico.
Mineral Collection: The Zunis have obtained salt here for centuries.
Hunting: Eagle nestlings are collected and other hunting is carried out in this area.
Grazing: It is a traditional Zuni grazing area.
Religious Use: Ritualized collection of salt and other ceremonial and religious activities take place at this sacred lake.

16. *Ahayu:t an Yalanne*
Location: A cindercone within the Zuni Salt Lake.
Plant Collection: Herbs belonging to the War Gods are collected here and used as medicine to strengthen children.
Mineral Collection: Salt and mud are collected here.
Religious Use: The area is associated with the War Gods.

17. *Chimik'yana'kya dey'a*
Location: Colorado River, Grand Canyon, Arizona.
Plant Collection: Willows and herbs are collected here.
Mineral Collection: Sands and clay are collected here.
Religious Use: This is the original point of origin in the Zuni origin and migration narrations. It is visited regularly by the Galaxy Fraternity.

18. *Denatsali Im'a or Imme*

Location: Woodruff Butte, Arizona.
Plant Collection: Herbs, flowers, and medicine plants are collected at this site.
Religious Use: This is a very sacred place mentioned in the migration narration and is a place name in the Kyaklo prayer.

19. *Da:biliyanku*
Location: East of no. 18, Denatsali Im'a, Arizona.
Plant Collection: Plants are obtained here.
Mineral Collection: Soils are obtained here.
Religious Use: This is a site mentioned in the Zuni migration narrative.

20. *Heshoda Bitsulliya or Ki:wihtsi Bitsulliya*
Location: Chaco Canyon, New Mexico.
Religious Use: This is an ancestral site in the Zuni migration narratives. It is associated with the Sword Swallowing Society and is a place where prayer offerings are deposited.

21. *Canyon de Chelly*
Location: Canyon De Chelly, Arizona.
Religious Use: An ancestral site in Zuni migration narrative, it is associated with the Sword Swallowing Society and is a site where prayers are made and offerings deposited.

22. *Mesa Verde*
Location: Mesa Verde, Colorado.
Religious Use: An ancestral site in the Zuni migration narrative, it is a place where prayers are made and offerings deposited.

23. *Sunha: K'yaba:chu Yalanne*
Location: San Francisco Peaks, Arizona.
Plant Collection: Willows, aspen and medicine herbs are collected here. The Big Fire Society collects herbs in this locale.
Mineral Collection: Soils are collected here.
Religious Use: An ancestral site in the Zuni migration narrative, it is a major medicinal herb collection place and is associated with the Big Fire Society.

24. *Dewankwin K'yaba:chu Yalanne*
Location: Mt. Taylor, New Mexico.
Plant Collection: Willows, aspen, mahogany, and herbs are collected here.
Mineral Collection: Obsidian is obtained in this area.
Hunting: Feathers and birds are hunted and snared here, including blue jays, woodpeckers, red-shafted flickers, sparrows, hawks, orioles, turkeys, and robins.
Religious Use: The whole mountain is considered a religious area. It is associated with the */uhuuque* Medicine Society and the Big Fire Society. It is a major medicinal herb collection area.

25. *K'yak'yali an Yalanne*
Location: Eagle Peak, New Mexico.
Plant Collection: Willows, aspen, mahogany, and medicinal herbs are collected here, the latter by the Big Fire Society.
Hunting: It is an important hunting area where birds and feathers are collected.
Religious Use: It is a shrine area.

26. *Sa'do:w Yalanne*
Location: Hardcastle Peak, New Mexico
Plant Collection: Willow, aspen, mahogany, and herbs are collected here.
Hunting: Birds and feathers are collected in this area.
Grazing: This is a traditional Zuni grazing area.
Religious Use: It is a shrine area.

27. *Piliayalla:we*
Location: Willow Mountain, New Mexico.
Plant Collection: Zunis collect willow, aspen, mahogany, and herbs in this area.
Hunting: This is a hunting area where birds and feathers are also collected.
Religious Use: It is a shrine area.

28. *Dona Yala:we*
Location: South of the Datil Mountains, New Mexico.
Plant Collection: Willow, aspen, mahogany, and herbs are collected here.
Hunting: In this hunting area turkeys and other birds are also snared and caught in order to obtain feathers.
Religious Use: It is a shrine and sacred area.

29. *U'laɫɫimna: Yala:we*
Location: White Mountain, Arizona.
Plant Collection: Willow, aspen, mahogany, and herbs are obtained in this area.
Hunting: It is a hunting area where birds and feathers are also collected.
Religious Use: It is a shrine and sacred area.

30. *Deshukt Ina:wa*
Location: Southwest of El Morro, New Mexico.
Plant Collection: Herbs are collected here.
Hunting: It is a hunting area where birds are among the game.
Grazing: People from Pescado grazed this area and farther to the south.

31. *He:mushina Yala:we*
LOCATION: Jemez Mountains, New Mexico.
PLANT COLLECTION: Medicinal herbs are collected here.
MINERAL COLLECTION: This site is the exclusive source for white powder medicine.
HUNTING: It is a general hunting area.
RELIGIOUS USE: The site is the source for materials for kiva initiations and is a place name in medicine prayers.

32. *Du:shi an K'yan'a*
LOCATION: Horse Lake, Dulce, New Mexico.
HUNTING: It is a hunting area.

33. *Wilats'ukwena:wa*
LOCATION: General northern mountain area, New Mexico.
OTHER: It is the place name for the mountains near the Jicarilla Apache.

34. *Ku'k'ohanna or Ku'k'ohan'a*
LOCATION: South of Sanders, Arizona.
HUNTING: It is an antelope hunting area.
OTHER: It is a campsite on the trail to the Hopi villages.

35. *Bayye [Paiya Mesa]*
LOCATION: Zuni Indian Reservation, New Mexico.
PLANT COLLECTION: Pinyon nuts are collected here.
HUNTING: It is a hunting area for wild pigs.

35a. *Nobonni Dahna'a*
LOCATION: Zuni Indian Reservation.
RELIGIOUS USE: It is a religious use area.

35b. *K'ya:dechi'a or K'ya:dech'a or K'ya:dechi' K'yan'a*
LOCATION: Zuni Indian Reservation.
OTHER: It is a Zuni place name.

36. *Udeya: Yalanne*
LOCATION: Bandera Crater, New Mexico.
PLANT LOCATION: Various flowers, aspen and other wood are collected here.
RELIGIOUS USE: It is a shrine area for the Longhorns and the Council of the Gods and also is used by the Sword Swallowing Society.

37. *Wimanbowa Yalanne*
LOCATION: North of El Morro, New Mexico.
RELIGIOUS USE: This is a Zuni religious area.

38. *Akwałina: Yala:we*
LOCATION: Zuni Mountains.
PLANT COLLECTION: Herbs.
MINERAL COLLECTION: Two kinds of blue paint (malachite and azurite) and turquoise are collected here.
OTHER: Land snails are collected here for religious use.

39. *Heshoda Yałt'a*
LOCATION: Ruins on top of El Morro, New Mexico.
RELIGIOUS USE: Religious offerings are made here.
OTHER: It is a place name for an ancestral Zuni village.

40. *A'ts'in'a*
LOCATION: Inscription Rock, El Morro National Monument.
HUNTING: This is an eagle gathering place.
RELIGIOUS USE: It is a shrine and religious area at which the Council of the Gods makes offerings at the water pool.

41. *Ts'u'yala'a*
LOCATION: Cerillos Hills, New Mexico.
MINERAL COLLECTION: Turquoise is found in this locale.
RELIGIOUS USE: It is a shrine area for the Shumaque Society and is the Home of Turquoise Man.

42. *Łi'akwa k'yakwe'a*
LOCATION: It is in the White Mountains, Arizona.
MINERAL COLLECTION: Turquoise.
RELIGIOUS USE: It is a sacred spring.

43. *Bi'k'yay'a*
LOCATION: San Rafael, New Mexico.
RELIGIOUS USE: This sacred spring used by medicine societies and Rain Priests is also associated with the Suskikwe (Coyote/Hunting Society).

44. *K'ya:dul Ullapna'a*
LOCATION: OCEANS.
RELIGIOUS USE: This is the referent for the "surrounding waters" for the Rain Priests. Water is sometimes collected for religious use.

45. *Shohk'onan Im'a*
LOCATION: Escudilla Peak, Arizona.
PLANT COLLECTION: The Big Fire Society collects herbs and medicines here, including medicine belonging to bear and snake.
MINERAL COLLECTION: Banded stone for fetishes or */esho/ mayak/awe* is collected here.
HUNTING: It is a hunting area.
RELIGIOUS USE: It is a shrine area.

46. *K'ya:ts'i' K'yan'a*
LOCATION: North of Lyman Lake, Arizona.
HUNTING: Turtles are collected in this area.
RELIGIOUS USE: It is considered a sacred area.

47. *Tamaya*
LOCATION: Rio Grande River, New Mexico.
HUNTING: It is a turtle collection area.

48. *K'ya:k'yałna' K'ya:kwayinna*
LOCATION: Jemez Mountains, New Mexico.
MINERAL COLLECTION: Mud and silt are collected here.
RELIGIOUS USE: It is a curing area.

49. *Tsi'iyama (Laguna word)*
LOCATION: Seama, New Mexico.
MINERAL COLLECTION: Clay used for white paint is found here.

50. *Bolan Akkwen Kwayin'a*
LOCATION: Cottonwood Canyon, Arizona.
OTHER: Trading area and boundary between Hopi and Zuni.

51. *Ha:milili*
LOCATION: Petrified Forest, Arizona.
MINERAL COLLECTION: Ha:milili, or petrified wood is collected here.

52. *Kumanch an A'l Akkwe'a*
LOCATION: Canyon Diablo, Arizona.
RELIGIOUS USE: It is a religious area which is an ancestral site on migration to Zuni.

53. *Lu:k'yan'a*
LOCATION: Zuni Indian Reservation, New Mexico.
RELIGIOUS USE: It is a sacred spring to the Galaxy Society.

54. *Uhana'a or Uhan'a*
LOCATION: Zuni Indian Reservation, New Mexico.
RELIGIOUS USE: It is a sacred spring to the Galaxy Society.

55. *A'łabattsi'a*
LOCATION: Zuni Indian Reservation, New Mexico.
RELIGIOUS USE: It is a sacred spring to the Galaxy Society.

56. *Wikk'yal'a*
LOCATION: Zuni Indian Reservation, New Mexico.
RELIGIOUS USE: The Galaxy Society makes offerings here.

57. *Yala Łana*
LOCATION: Zuni Indian Reservation, New Mexico.
RELIGIOUS USE: The Galaxy Society makes offerings here.

58. *Kyaki:ma*
LOCATION: Zuni Indian Reservation, New Mexico.
RELIGIOUS USE: An ancestral site in the Zuni migration narration, it is a place where the Galaxy Society makes offerings.

59. *Shohk'ona: Yalanne*
This is the same place as no. 45, Shohk'onan Im'a.

60. *Sha'lak'ona:wa*
LOCATION: Zuni Indian Reservation, New Mexico.
RELIGIOUS USE: It is a sacred spring associated with Kyaklo.

61. *K'yabe' Kwayin'a or K'yapkwayin'a*
LOCATION: Along the Zuni River, Arizona.
RELIGIOUS USE: It is a sacred spring along the pilgrimage trail to no. 11, Koluwala:wa, and associated with Kyaklo.

62. *Ts'oklik Ikna:wa or Ts'oklik'ona:wa*
Same place as no. 12, Beya K'okshi'a.

63. *K'ya:dul Łana*
LOCATION: North of Saint Johns, Arizona.
RELIGIOUS USE: It is an ancestral site in the migration narration (commonly spelled "Kiatuthlanna") on the trail to no. 11 and associated with Kyaklo.

64. *He/epat/chi:wa*
LOCATION: North of Saint Johns, Arizona.
RELIGIOUS USE: An ancestral site in the Zuni migration, it is a sacred site associated with Kyaklo.

65. *K'yawa:n Ahonna*
LOCATION: Saint Johns, Arizona.
GRAZING: It is a traditional Zuni grazing area.

66. *Idwa K'yan'a*
LOCATION: Zuni Indian Reservation, New Mexico.
RELIGIOUS USE: It is a ritual campsite used on the return from the pilgrimage to no. 11 and associated with Kyaklo.

67. *Kolo:wisi An K'yakw'a (or K'yakwe'a)*
LOCATION: Along the Zuni River in Arizona.
RELIGIOUS USE: It is a sacred spring used during the pilgrimage to no. 11 and associated with Kyaklo.

68. *K'ya:ts'i' K'yan'a*
LOCATION: Zuni Indian Reservation, New Mexico.
RELIGIOUS USE: A sacred spring used on the pilgrimage to no. 11 and associated with Kyaklo.

69. *Bo'sho'wa or Bo'sho'w'a*
LOCATION: Zuni Indian Reservation, New Mexico.
RELIGIOUS USE: It is a religious area used on pilgrimage to no. 11.

70. *Shoya K'oskwi'a*
LOCATION: Zuni Indian Reservation, New Mexico.
PLANT COLLECTION: Pinyon nuts, yucca, yucca fruits, and other subsistence plants are collected here.

71. *Ishan'an Dek'yapbow'a or Ishan An Dek'yapbow'a*
LOCATION: Zuni Indian Reservation, New Mexico.
RELIGIOUS USE: It is an area used by the Small Fire Society.

72. *Mats'a:kya*
LOCATION: Zuni Indian Reservation, New Mexico.
RELIGIOUS USE: It is an ancestral ruin associated with Kyaklo, the House of Sun, for Head Cacique offerings and has special significance to the Small Fire Society.

73. *Idiwa Dahn'a*
LOCATION: Zuni Indian Reservation, New Mexico.
RELIGIOUS USE: It is on the trail of Salt Mother from Blackrock to the Zuni Salt Lake and has special significance to the Small Fire Society.

74. *Akkwe Łana*
LOCATION: Zuni Indian Reservation, New Mexico.
PLANT COLLECTION: Curing plants and medicines for the Small Fire Society are collected here.

75. *A'mossi'a*
LOCATION: Zuni Indian Reservation, New Mexico.
FARMING: It is a Zuni farming area.
OTHER: It is a camping area along the trail to the Hopi villages.

76. *Ma/ettude*
LOCATION: Puerco River at Manuelito Canyon, Arizona.
OTHER: It is a place along the trail to Hopi.

77. *Donashi An K'yan'a*
LOCATION: Zuni Indian Reservation, New Mexico.
OTHER: It is a camping area near a spring along the trail to Hopi.

78. */Oh/emm/a*
LOCATION: North of the Puerco River, Arizona.
OTHER: It is a campsite for the third day along the trail to the Hopi villages.

79. *Mo:chikwana:wa*
LOCATION: Awatovi, Arizona.
OTHER: It is the Zuni place name for the first Hopi village or place on the trail to the Hopi villages.

80. *Bolan Akken Kwayin'a*
LOCATION: Northwest of Ganado, Arizona.
OTHER: It is the boundary between Zuni and Hopi on the trail to the Hopi villages. It has the same name as, but is in a different location from, no. 50.

81. *Bibałłi Yal'a*
Location: North of Zuni Salt Lake, Arizona.
Other: It is a campsite on the trail to the Zuni Salt Lake.

82. *Shodo: K'yawa:n Ahon'a*
Location: Concho, Arizona
Farming: It was a planting area used in the "old days" (ca. 1850).

83. *Idiwananne*
Location: Zuni Indian Reservation, New Mexico.
Religious Use: It is the Zunis' "center place" and the end of the Zuni migration.

84. *Yalan K'ohanna*
Location: South of Show Low, Arizona.
Other: It is a place name for an area where the Apaches lived in old times as well as recently.

85. *Shohk'onan Im'a*
This is the same place as no. 45.

86. *Chishe:na:/A'l'akkwe'a*
Location: Apache Creek, New Mexico.
Plant Collection: Medicine, herbs, and wood are collected here, as well as materials collected by the Big Fire Society.
Hunting: It is a deer hunting area.
Grazing: Zunis grazed from no. 26 (Sa'do:w Yalanne) to here.
Religious Use: It is a shrine area.
Other: It is an area in which Apaches used to assemble before raiding Zuni. A large battle once occurred here when Zunis surprised Apaches in a camp near caves and killed many of them.

87. *Adela K'ohan'a*
Location: Atarque, New Mexico.
Plant Collection: Medicinal herbs for spider medicine are collected here.
Hunting: It is an eagle collection area.
Grazing: It is remembered as a Zuni grazing area at least as early as the 1920s.

88. */amequelleyawa*
Location: Near Manuelito, Arizona.
Religious Use: It is an ancestral site in the Zuni migration narrations.

89. *Shoya K'yaba'a*
Location: Southwest of Ganado, Arizona.
Religious Use: It is an ancestral site in the Zuni migration narrations.

90. *Ahayu:t A:chiya' Delashhin'a (War God Shrine)*
Location: South of Gallup, New Mexico.
Religious Use: It is a War God Shrine.

91. *K'ya: Łi'anna' K'ya:kwayinna*
Location: Blue Lake, Zuni Mountains, New Mexico.
Mineral Collection: Blue stones used to paint prayer sticks are collected here.

92. *Kiwaikuluk/a*
Location: Jemez Mountains, New Mexico.
Religious Use: Medicine Society Prayers are made here.

93. *Dahna K'ohanna*
Location: Near San Isidro, New Mexico.
Plant Collection: Apache plume and mahogany are collected here.
Mineral Collection: Sands and clays are collected here.
Religious Use: It is associated with the Nadir Kiva, and the Longhorn visits here annually.

94. *Ts'iya'a:wa*
Location: Jemez Mountains.
Religious Use: It is a ritual area for prayer offerings.

95. *K'yawihkya*
Location: Laguna Pueblo, New Mexico.
Religious Use: It is a place name in prayers.

96. *Shak'yaya'a*
Location: Peak on Mt. Taylor, New Mexico.
Plant Collection: Herbs and other materials for spiritual support are gathered here.

97. *Kashi:kuk/a:tu*
Another name for no. 4, Nałhuwala:wa.

98. *A'su'wa*
Location: Zuni Indian Reservation, New Mexico.
Religious Use: It is a place name in songs, a rock pierced by Salt Mother during her flight to the Zuni Salt Lake.

99. *U'k'yahayan El'a*
Location: Zuni Indian Reservation.
Religious Use: A place name in songs, "Feather Rock" was dropped by Salt Mother during her flight to the Zuni Salt Lake.

100. *Da'wi Dabak'i:wa*
Location: Zuni Indian Reservation, New Mexico.
Plant Collection: Brushes and two kinds of medicines are collected here.
Mineral Collection: Clay and sand are collected here.

101. */iyanik/a:waisha*
Location: Rio Grande, New Mexico.
Religious Use: It is known in songs and visited by elders.

102. *Yash:tik/u:tu*
Location: Rio Grande, New Mexico
Religious Use: It is known in songs and visited by elders.

103. *Mi/ashu:k/awa/ka*
Location: Rio Grande, New Mexico.
Religious Use: It is a religious area visited by elders.

104. *Heshe/aleto:wa*
Location: Malpais south of Grants, New Mexico.
Other: This is the Zuni place name for the lava flow at the east end of the Zuni Mountains.

105. *Dewankwin Onan Baniyn'a*
This is the same place as no. 9.

106. *K'ya:ts'i' K'yan'a*
Location: Zuni Indian Reservation, New Mexico.
Religious Use: It is a sacred spring where water is collected for religious ceremonials.

107. *Amidola: Debow Ul'a*
LOCATION: Zuni Indian Reservation, New Mexico.
FARMING: It is a peach orchard.
RELIGIOUS USE: It is associated with scalp ceremonies of the War Chiefs.

108. *Debo'kwin Im'a*
LOCATION: Zuni Reservation, New Mexico.
RELIGIOUS USE: It is a religious area.

109. *Sho' Dek'yapbow'a*
LOCATION: Zuni Indian Reservation, New Mexico.
RELIGIOUS USE: It is an area associated with the War Chiefs.

110. *Hebadin'a*
LOCATION: Zuni Indian Reservation.
RELIGIOUS USE: It is a shrine used by a kiva group; no. 156 is a different area from no. 110 but has the same name.

111. *Danin K'yay'a*
LOCATION: Grand Canyon, Arizona.
RELIGIOUS USE: It is known in prayers and songs of the origin and migration and is important to the Galaxy Society.

112. *Yamun K'yay'a*
LOCATION: Grand Canyon, Arizona.
RELIGIOUS USE: Known in prayers and songs of origin and migration, it is an important area for the Galaxy Society.

113. *Ts'ik'on K'yay'a*
LOCATION: Grand Canyon, Arizona.
RELIGIOUS USE: It is known in prayers and songs of the Zuni origin and migration and is important to the Galaxy Society.

114. *Awisho K'yay'a*
LOCATION: Grand Canyon, Arizona.
RELIGIOUS USE: It is known in prayers and songs of origin and migration and is important to the Galaxy Society.

115. *Kumanch An A'l'akkwe'a*
This is the same place as no. 52.

116. *Bittsemi Deyatchi:wa*
LOCATION: Second Mesa, Arizona.
RELIGIOUS USE: It is associated with the Zuni Migration and the group that went to the north.
OTHER: It is a Zuni place name for the Hopi village on Second Mesa and is associated with the Cotton Twins, who used to be in Zuni, but who moved to Hopi for some reason.

117. *Mokkwi: Deyatchi:wa*
LOCATION: Third Mesa, Arizona.
RELIGIOUS USE: It is associated with the Zuni migration narration and the group that went to the north.
OTHER: It is a Zuni place name for the Hopi Village of Hotevilla, meaning "Onion Field."

118. *Kyane:lu Yala:we*
LOCATION: Near Shiprock, New Mexico.
RELIGIOUS USE: It is a shrine area where offerings are made to request growth and security of sheep herds.

119. *Deshukt Dina:wa*
LOCATION: West of the Malpais, New Mexico.
PLANT COLLECTION: Pinyons, oak seeds, juniper seeds, yucca, and cactus for subsistence are gathered here.
RELIGIOUS USE: It is associated with the Hunting Society.

120. *Deshukt Łan Im'a*
LOCATION: West of the Malpais, New Mexico.
RELIGIOUS USE: It is associated with the Hunting Society.

121. *K'yana:wa*
LOCATION: Zuni Indian Reservation, New Mexico.
RELIGIOUS USE: It is the original home of Salt Mother, before it was defiled (Blackrock Lake).

122. *Hak'win A'deyałt'a*
LOCATION: Zuni Indian Reservation, New Mexico.
MINERAL COLLECTION: Black paint is obtained in this area.
RELIGIOUS USE: It is along the trail of Salt Mother to the Zuni Salt Lake.

123. *Dona A:de'ana:wa*
LOCATION: Zuni Indian Reservation, New Mexico.
RELIGIOUS USE: It is along the trail of Salt Mother to the Zuni Salt Lake.

124. *Deshamik'ya Im'a*
LOCATION: Zuni Indian Reservation, New Mexico.
RELIGIOUS USE: It is a place along the trail of Salt Mother to the Zuni Salt Lake where offerings are made and omens discerned.

125. *Ma'baniykya Dey'a*
This is the same place as no. 81.

126. *Demossi Dahna'a*
LOCATION: South of the Zuni Indian Reservation, New Mexico.
HUNTING: This is a traditional hunting area used to surround and corral deer and to hunt by magic.

127. *Kyama:kya*
LOCATION: Near Atarque, New Mexico.
RELIGIOUS USE: This is the home of the Kanakwe, a special kind of katchina.

128. *Habana: A'l'akkwe'a*
LOCATION: Northeast of Ramah, New Mexico.
RELIGIOUS USE: This an ancestral site in the Zuni migration narration.

129. *Nadatdekwi:wa*
LOCATION: Zuni Indian Reservation, New Mexico.
HUNTING: It is a deer hunting area.
RELIGIOUS USE: It is a ritual hunting area.

130. *Dełak Akwe'a*
LOCATION: Zuni Indian Reservation, New Mexico.
HUNTING: It is a deer hunting area.
RELIGIOUS USE: It is an area in which ritual traps for deer hunting are set.

131. *Bilan Akkwe'a (or Akkwe'a)*
LOCATION: Zuni Indian Reservation, New Mexico.
HUNTING: Zunis impounded deer from here to Ojo Caliente in the past.

132. *Dek'yapbowa:wa* [*Tekapo*]
LOCATION: Zuni Indian Reservation, New Mexico.
HUNTING: It is a place to catch minnows.

133. *K'yawa:na Łana'a (Dekwankwin K'yawa:na Łana)*
LOCATION: Rio Grande, New Mexico.
PLANT COLLECTION: Herbs and medicines are collected here by the Sword Swallowing Society.
RELIGIOUS USE: It is a place mentioned in the Zuni migration narration.

134. *Tsilhinn/yalh/a*
LOCATION: Rio Grande, New Mexico.
RELIGIOUS USE: It is a place mentioned in the Zuni migration narration.

135. *Dopbolliya:K'yan'a*
LOCATION: Taos Blue Lake, New Mexico.
RELIGIOUS USE: It is associated with the migration of the Sword Swallowing Society.

136. *Anshe K'yan'a*
LOCATION: Ft. Wingate, New Mexico.
MINERAL COLLECTION: "Soaprock" for fetishes is obtained here.
OTHER: It is the Zuni place name for Bear Springs.

137. *Komkwayikya dey'a*
LOCATION: Zuni Indian Reservation.
RELIGIOUS USE: It is a sacred area associated with Kyaklo.

138. *Da:melank'yay'a*
LOCATION: East-central Arizona.
RELIGIOUS USE: It is a place name for a site between no. 17 (Chimik'yana'kya dey'a) and no. 11 (Koluwala:wa) in songs and prayers of Kyaklo.

139. *Banelunan K'yay'a*
LOCATION: East-central Arizona.
RELIGIOUS USE: It is the place name for a site between no. 17 and no. 11 in songs and prayers of Kyaklo.

140. *Ladaw K'yay'a or Lada:w K'yay'a*
LOCATION: East-central Arizona.
RELIGIOUS USE: It is a place name for a site between no. 17 and no. 11 in songs and prayers of Kyaklo.

141. *Ubulemi*
LOCATION: East-central Arizona.
RELIGIOUS USE: It is a place name for a site between no. 17 and no. 11 in songs and prayers of Kyaklo.

142. *Batsikchina:wa*
LOCATION: East-central Arizona.
RELIGIOUS USE: It is a place for a site between no. 17 and no. 11 in songs and prayers of Kyaklo.

143. *To:papik/a-ya*
LOCATION: East-central Arizona.
RELIGIOUS USE: It is a place name for a site between no. 17 and no. 11 in songs and prayers of Kyaklo.

144. *K'yashhida K'yay'a*
LOCATION: East-central Arizona.
RELIGIOUS USE: It is a place name for a site between no. 17 and no. 11 in songs and prayers of Kyaklo.

145. *Molan K'yay'a*
LOCATION: East-central Arizona.
RELIGIOUS USE: It is a place name for a site between no. 17 and no. 11 in songs and prayers of Kyaklo.

146. *Hadin K'yay'a*
This is another name for no. 11 (Kołuwala:wa).

147. *A'ts'ina:wa*
LOCATION: Zuni Indian Reservation, New Mexico.
RELIGIOUS USE: It is a place name for a Sacred Spring in Kyaklo prayer.

148. *A'łabatts'i'a*
LOCATION: Zuni Indian Reservation, New Mexico.
RELIGIOUS USE: It is place name for a site in Kyaklo prayer.

149. *Bi:shu'k'yay'a*
LOCATION: Zuni Indian Reservation, New Mexico.
RELIGIOUS USE: It is a place name for a sacred spring in Kyaklo prayer.

150. *K'yan Ul'a*
LOCATION: Zuni Indian Reservation, New Mexico.
RELIGIOUS USE: It is the place name for a sacred spring in Kyaklo prayer.

151. *K'ya:dechi'a*
LOCATION: Zuni Indian Reservation, New Mexico.
RELIGIOUS USE: It is the place name for a sacred spring in Kyaklo prayer.

152. *A:yaya'kya*
LOCATION: Zuni Indian Reservation, New Mexico.
RELIGIOUS USE: It is a place name for a sacred spring in Kyaklo prayer.

153. *Idełakukya dey'a or Idełakunapkya dey'a or Idełakupk'yan'*
LOCATION: Zuni Indian Reservation, New Mexico.
RELIGIOUS USE: It is a place name in Kyaklo prayer.

154. *Sumk'yana'a or Sumk'yan'a*
LOCATION: Zuni Indian Reservation, New Mexico.
RELIGIOUS USE: It is a place name in Kyaklo prayer.

155. *Wilatsu'u:kw An K'yan'a*
LOCATION: Zuni Indian Reservation, New Mexico.
RELIGIOUS USE: It is a place name in Kyaklo prayer before no. 58 (Kyaki:ma) and no. 72 (Mats'a:kya).

156. *Hebadin'a*
LOCATION: Zuni Indian Reservation, New Mexico.
RELIGIOUS USE: It is a place name in Kyaklo prayer. See no. 110.

157. *Sak'yaya Yalanne*
LOCATION: North of the Zuni Indian Reservation, New Mexico.
GRAZING: The Quam family grazed cattle and sheep in this area.

158. *Abak'in Shilow Im'a*
LOCATION: North of the Zuni Indian Reservation, New Mexico.
GRAZING: The Quam family grazed sheep and cattle here.

159. *Yaladeyałdo:wa*
LOCATION: McGaffey, New Mexico.
HUNTING: It is a hunting area where birds and feathers were among the things obtained.
GRAZING: Zuni herders grazed their flocks in this area at least as late as the 1920s.
OTHER: The Quam family had a log cabin here as a part of their livestock operation.

160. *Lhep/tequ/aqu/a*
LOCATION: North of the Zuni Indian Reservation, New Mexico.
GRAZING: The Quam family grazed sheep and cattle in this area.

161. *Billena:wa*
LOCATION: Zuni Indian Reservation, New Mexico.
PLANT COLLECTION: Timber for roof beams was obtained here.

162. *Adel Ahonna*
This is the same place as no. 87 (Adela K'ohan'a).

163. *Suski:kw A:wan K'yan'a*
LOCATION: Paxton Springs, New Mexico.
RELIGIOUS USE: It is a Hunting Society shrine.

164. *Wałbi'a*
LOCATION: First Mesa, Arizona.
OTHER: It is the Zuni place name for First Mesa.

165. *A'l El'a*
LOCATION: Second Mesa, Arizona.
OTHER: It is the Zuni place name for Second Mesa.

166. *Pat/chi:wa*
LOCATION: Oraibi, Arizona.
OTHER: It is the Zuni place name for Oraibi.

167. *Biha An Yal'a*
LOCATION: Beaver Mountain, Arizona.
HUNTING: It is a Zuni hunting area.

168. *Hek'o' Yal'a*
LOCATION: Southeast of Fencelake, New Mexico.
OTHER: It is a camping area along the pilgrimage route to the Zuni Salt Lake.

169. *Talapa/k/a-na*
LOCATION: Zuni Indian Reservation, New Mexico.
OTHER: It is the Zuni place name for Grasshopper Spring, on the old trail to Ft. Wingate.

170. *K'ya:dechi' K'yan'a*
LOCATION: North of the Zuni Indian Reservation, New Mexico.
OTHER: It is on the old trail to Ft. Wingate.

171. *Achiya: Dek'yapbow'a (chuwap A:chuya)*
LOCATION: Zuni Indian Reservation, New Mexico.
PLANT COLLECTION: Pinyon nuts are collected in this area.

172. *Heshodan Imk'oshkwi'a*
LOCATION: East of the Zuni Indian Reservation, New Mexico.
GRAZING: It is a Zuni grazing area.
OTHER: This is the Zuni place name for Box "S" Canyon and the old ruins in the area.

173. *Sokkwi'a*
LOCATION: Near Atarque, New Mexico.
GRAZING: The Gaspar family grazed in this area at least as late as the 1920s.
OTHER: It is the campsite for the first night on the trail to the Zuni Salt Lake.

174. *Kechiba:wa*
LOCATION: Zuni Indian Reservation, New Mexico.
MINERAL COLLECTION: Red and yellow paint pigment and gypsum for whitewash are collected here.

175. *Hawikku*
LOCATION: Zuni Indian Reservation, New Mexico.
RELIGIOUS USE: It is an ancestral site in the Zuni migration.

176. *Halona:wa*
LOCATION: Zuni Indian Reservation, New Mexico.
RELIGIOUS USE: It is an ancestral site and portion of the current Zuni Village that has been occupied for centuries.

177. *Awisho Yala:we*
LOCATION: All mountain tops with fog and rain.
RELIGIOUS USE: All mountain tops around Zuni are revered as a source of rain.

178. *Doloknana'a*
LOCATION: Zuni Indian Reservation, New Mexico.
RELIGIOUS USE: This is a sacred spring.

179. *Onan Dełakwi'a*
LOCATION: Zuni Indian Reservation, New Mexico.
RELIGIOUS USE: This is a sacred spring.

180. *Opbon Biya'a*
LOCATION: Zuni Indian Reservation, New Mexico.
RELIGIOUS USE: This is a sacred spring.

181. *Banidan Im'a*
LOCATION: Zuni Indian Reservation, New Mexico.
RELIGIOUS USE: It is a sacred spring.

182. *Aneła:wa Im'a*
LOCATION: Zuni Indian Reservation, New Mexico.
RELIGIOUS USE: It is a sacred spring.

183. *Sum A'shokda'a*
LOCATION: Zuni Indian Reservation, New Mexico.
RELIGIOUS USE: It is a sacred spring.

184. *A:k'ohanna' Dina:wa*
LOCATION: Zuni Indian Reservation, New Mexico.
Religious Use: It is a sacred spring.

185. *K'eyadi:wa or K'eyadina:wa*
LOCATION: Grand Canyon, Arizona.
RELIGIOUS USE: It is a sacred spring, known in prayers.

186. *Yala Łi'anna*
LOCATION: Blue Mountain, Utah.
HUNTING: It is a Zuni hunting area.

187. */ashokta:piyan/a*
LOCATION: Tinaja, New Mexico.
GRAZING: It is a former Zuni grazing area.
OTHER: It is a Zuni place name for a site on the trail to the east.

188. *Sanana:wohan'a*
LOCATION: Zuni Mountains, New Mexico.
OTHER: It is a Zuni place name for a site on the trail to the east.

189. *Tsi:k/auk/osk/a*
LOCATION: Zuni Mountains, New Mexico.
OTHER: It is a Zuni place name for a site on the trail to the east.

190. *Sha:k/aya*
LOCATION: Datil Mountains, New Mexico.
HUNTING: It is a Zuni hunting area.
RELIGIOUS USE: The area is used by the Hunting Society.

191. *K'emaya: k'yan'a*
LOCATION: North of the Puerco River, Arizona.
OTHER: It is a Zuni place name.

192. *Awatu*
LOCATION: Southwest of Keams Canyon, Arizona.
OTHER: It is a Hopi village on the Zuni/Hopi Trail.

193. *Ko:chali:wa*
LOCATION: North of the Zuni Indian Reservation, New Mexico.
HUNTING: Ravens nest and are hunted here.
GRAZING: The Nastacio family grazed in this area.

194. *Wilats'ukwe A:wan Yal'a (Yala:wa)*
LOCATION: White Mountains, Arizona.
OTHER: It is the Zuni place name for the White Mountains.

195. *Doya'a or Doya (Nutria)*
LOCATION: Zuni Indian Reservation, New Mexico.
MINERAL COLLECTION: Hematite, jet, and petrified wood (or ha:milili) are gathered in this vicinity.
FARMING: Irrigated farming takes place at Nutria, and Zunis also farmed to the northeast towards the mountains.

196. *Salt River Canyon*
LOCATION: Northeast of Globe, Arizona.
MINERAL COLLECTION: Serpentine is obtained here.

197. *(unnamed)*
LOCATION: Near Reserve, New Mexico.
MINERAL COLLECTION: Soft stone for fetishes is obtained here.

198. *K/na/tsi/yall/a*
LOCATION: Lyman Lake, New Mexico.
HUNTING: Turtles are obtained at this site.
RELIGIOUS USE: It is a religious area.

199. *K'yawa:n Ahonna*
LOCATION: Near Holbrook, Arizona.
HUNTING: It is an antelope hunting area.

200. *Luna*
LOCATION: Luna, New Mexico.
HUNTING: It is a deer hunting area.

201. *Sandy Flats*
LOCATION: Plains of San Augustin.
HUNTING: It is an antelope hunting area.

202. *Nigger Ridge*
LOCATION: Negrito Creek, New Mexico.
HUNTING: It is a hunting area south of Eagle Peak.

203. *Du:sh an K'yan'a*
LOCATION: Horsesprings, Plains of San Augustin, New Mexico.
HUNTING: It is a Zuni hunting area. The Zunis also hunted at Dog Springs, and from there to mountains on the southern edge of the Plains.

204. *Kyalap Onanne*
LOCATION: The road to Gallup between Zuni and Gallup, New Mexico.
PLANT COLLECTION: Beeweed and pinyon nuts are gathered here.

205. *Ganado Area*
LOCATION: Ganado, Arizona.
PLANT COLLECTION: Pinyon nuts are gathered here.

206. *K'yabachu'a/Sunha:kwin or K'yaba:ch Wohnanne*
LOCATION: The Flagstaff, Arizona, area.
PLANT COLLECTION: Pinyon nuts are collected here.

207. *Quemado*
LOCATION: Quemado, New Mexico.
PLANT COLLECTION: Pinyon nuts are collected here.

208. *Piney Park*
LOCATION: Piney Park, New Mexico.
HUNTING: A hunting area is near Eagle Peak.
OTHER: It is a camping area for hunting.

209. *Fence Lake*
LOCATION: Fence Lake, New Mexico.
GRAZING: Zuni grazing area.

210. *Mu:man'a*
LOCATION: Ramah, New Mexico.
GRAZING: It is a Zuni grazing area.

211. *Page*
LOCATION: Zuni Mountains, New Mexico.
GRAZING: It is a Zuni grazing area.

212. *Wimaya: Akkwe'a*
LOCATION: The Vanderwagen–Oak Wash area north of the Zuni Reservation.
GRAZING: The Tekala family grazed this area.

213. *Shuminkya*
LOCATION: South of the Zuni Indian Reservation, New Mexico.
GRAZING: It is a Zuni grazing area. Zuni livestock operators built Red Dam in this area.

214. *Witch Wells*
LOCATION: Witch Wells, Arizona.
GRAZING: Zunis grazed from Zuni west to Witch Wells and beyond.

215. *Sanders*
LOCATION: Sanders, Arizona.
GRAZING: It is a Zuni grazing area. Cedarwood shelters for sheepcamps were built here by Zunis as recently as two generations ago.

216. *Yucca Gathering Place*
LOCATION: Northwest of Lyman Lake, Arizona.
PLANT COLLECTION: Yucca was gathered here as recently as the late 1970s.

217. */awak/on:yellan/a*
LOCATION: Between Luna and Reserve, New Mexico.
PLANT COLLECTION: Herbs are gathered in this area.
HUNTING: It is a Zuni hunting area.
RELIGIOUS USE: A sacred spring is located in this area.

218. *Granite Mountain*
LOCATION: North of Magdalena, New Mexico.
HUNTING: It is a Zuni hunting area.

219. *Granite Peak*
LOCATION: Mogollon Mountains, New Mexico.
HUNTING: It is a traditional Zuni hunting area used at least as recently as 1900.

220. *Gila Cliff Dwellings*
LOCATION: Mogollon Mountains, New Mexico.
HUNTING: The Zunis hunted turkeys in this area.

221. *Jewett Gap*
LOCATION: Gallo Mountains, New Mexico.
HUNTING: It is a Zuni deer hunting area.

222. *Eagle Nesting Area*
LOCATION: South of Zuni Salt Lake, New Mexico.
MINERAL COLLECTION: Clay is collected here.
HUNTING: It is an eagle gathering area used traditionally and recently.

223. *Hepetsulia:wa*
LOCATION: North of St. Johns, Arizona.
HUNTING: It is an eagle gathering place.

224. *Piliayalla:we*
LOCATION: Willow Mountain, Arizona.
HUNTING: It is a Zuni hunting area.

225. *Łi'akwa Yal'a*
LOCATION: North of Clifton, Arizona.
MINERAL COLLECTION: "When ancestors would trade into Mexico they would pick up some stones in this area" (turquoise and chalcedony).

226. *Shu'ts'ina Yal'a*
LOCATION: Near Eagle Peak, New Mexico.
HUNTING: It is a Zuni hunting area.

227. *McNary Area*
LOCATION: McNary, Arizona.
PLANT COLLECTION: Aspens, wood for prayer plumes, and other plants are collected in this area.

228. *Upper Little Colorado River Valley*
LOCATION: Between St. Johns and Springerville, Arizona.
GRAZING: It is a traditional Zuni grazing area. In the nineteenth century the Zunis paid for grazing rights here.

229. *Mo'yachun Biyahkya Dey'a*
LOCATION: Meteor Crater, Arizona.
OTHER: This is the Zuni place name.

230. *Satabiyana*
LOCATION: Houck, Arizona.

231. *Amaquewilawa*
LOCATION: Lupton, Arizona.
HUNTING: It is a Zuni hunting area.
RELIGIOUS USE: It is the site of a Zuni Hunting Society shrine.

232. *Plant Collection Area*
LOCATION: Mogollon Rim, Chevelon Creek, Arizona.
PLANT COLLECTION: It is a traditional Zuni area for collection of subsistence plants like wild spinach and pinyon nuts. Plants were collected on a need basis all along the Mogollon Rim from Show Low to here.

233. *Shundek'yay'a*
LOCATION: Zuni Indian Reservation, New Mexico.
RELIGIOUS USE: It is used by the Small Fire Society.
OTHER USE: It is also a small village site that was occupied in the 1700s and 1800s.

234. *Bibał'a or Bibałłi'a*
This is another name for no. 81 and no. 125.

SOURCES: The body of information contained in Appendix 1 came mostly from Zuni religious leaders, who provided depositions to the United States Court of Claims in support of Docket 161-79L. Depositions were taken from Tom Awelagte, Oscar Nastacio, Fred Bowannie, Chester Mahooty, Frank Vacit, Alonzo Hustito, Ralph Quam, Theodore Edaakie, Mecalito Wytsalucy, Sefferino Eriacho, Chester H. Gaspar, and Alvin L. Nastacio. Edmund J. Ladd acted as interpreter. T. J. Ferguson indexed and compiled the appendix and accompanied the religious leaders as they pointed out land use areas. The following Zunis participated in the field trips: Alonzo Hustito, Allen Kallestewa, Edmund J. Ladd, Pesancio Lasiloo, Chester Mahooty, Victor Niihi, Jack Peynetsa, and Albert Peywa. T. J. Ferguson's field notes were also used in the compilation of the appendix and in locating the sites on the maps in the atlas.

Appendix 2. SUMMARY OF LAND USE BY SITE

	Name	Plant Collection	Mineral Collection	Hunting	Farming	Grazing	Religious	Other
1.	Shiba:bulima	x					x	
2.	Chi:biya Yalanne	x	x				x	
3.	Łemmulle	x	x			x	x	
4.	Nałuwala:wa			x			x	
5.	Dowa Yalanne	x	x				x	
6.	Kwili Yala: A:chi			x			x	
7.	Lhak/alhonatah-na				x		x	
8.	Lhualhetah-na	x			x		x	
9.	Dwankwin Onan Baniyna'a						x	
10.	Hanłibinkya	x		x		x	x	
11.	Kołuwala:wa	x	x			x	x	
12.	Beya K'okshi'a						x	
13.	K'ya'na'a		x		x	x		
14.	Do:k'yana'a						x	
15.	Ma'k'yaya'a		x	x		x	x	
16.	Ahayu:t an Yalanne	x	x				x	
17.	Chimik'yana'kya dey'a	x	x				x	
18.	Denatsali Im'a	x					x	
19.	Da:biliyanku	x	x				x	
20.	Heshoda Bitsulliya						x	
21.	Canyon de Chelly						x	
22.	Mesa Verde						x	
23.	Sunha: K'yaba:chu Yalanne	x	x				x	
24.	Dewankwin K'yaba:chu Yalanne	x	x	x			x	
25.	K'yak'yali an Yalanne	x		x			x	
26.	Sa'do:w Yalanne	x		x		x	x	
27.	Piliayalla:we	x		x			x	
28.	Dona Yala:we	x		x			x	
29.	U'lałłimna: Yala:we	x		x			x	
30.	Deshukt Ina:wa	x		x		x		
31.	He:mushina Yala:we	x	x	x			x	
32.	Du:shi an K'yan'a			x				
33.	Wilats'ukwena:wa							x
34.	Ku'k'ohanna			x				x
35.	Bayye [Paiya Mesa]	x		x				
35a.	Nobonni Dahna'a						x	
35b.	K'ya:dechi'a							x
36.	Udeya: Yalanne	x					x	
37.	Wimanbowa Yalanne						x	
38.	Akwałina: Yala:we	x	x					x
39.	Heshoda Yałt'a						x	x
40.	A'ts'in'a			x			x	
41.	Ts'u'yala'a		x				x	
42.	Łi'akwa k'yakwe'a		x				x	
43.	Bi'k'yay'a						x	
44.	K'ya:dul Ullapna'a						x	
45.	Shohk'onan Im'a	x	x	x			x	
46.	K'ya:ts'i' K'yan'a			x			x	
47.	Tamaya			x				
48.	K'ya:k'yałna' K'ya:kwayinna		x				x	
49.	Tsi'iyama (Laguna word)		x					
50.	Bolan Akkwen Kwayin'a						x	

	Name	Plant Collection	Mineral Collection	Hunting	Farming	Grazing	Religious	Other
51.	Ha:milili		x					
52.	Kumanch an A'l Akkwe'a						x	
53.	Lu:k'yan'a						x	
54.	Uhana'a or Uhan'a						x	
55.	A'łabattsi'a						x	
56.	Wikk'yal'a						x	
57.	Yala Łana						x	
58.	Kyaki:ma						x	
59.	Shohk'ona: Yalanne (see #45)							
60.	Sha'lak'ona:wa						x	
61.	K'yabe' Kwayin'a						x	
62.	Ts'oklik Ikna:wa (see #12)							
63.	K'ya:dul Łana						x	
64.	He/epat/chi:wa						x	
65.	K'yawa:n Ahonna					x		
66.	Idwa K'yan'a						x	
67.	Kolo:wisi An K'yakw'a						x	
68.	K'ya:ts'i' K'yan'a						x	
69.	Bo'sho'wa or Bo'sho'w'a						x	
70.	Shoya K'oskwi'a						x	
71.	Ishan'an Dek'yapbow'a						x	
72.	Mats'a:kya						x	
73.	Idiwa Dahn'a						x	
74.	Akkwe Łana	x						
75.	A'mossi'a				x			x
76.	Ma/ettude							x
77.	Donashi An K'yan'a							x
78.	/Oh/emm/a							x
79.	Mo:chikwana:wa							x
80.	Bolan Akkwen Kwayin'a							x
81.	Bibałłi Yal'a							x
82.	Shodo: K'yawa:n Ahon'a				x			
83.	Idiwananne						x	
84.	Yalan K'ohanna							x
85.	Shohk'onan Im'a (see #45)							
86.	Chishe:na:/A'l'akkwe'a	x		x		x	x	x
87.	Adela K'ohan'a	x		x		x		x
88.	/amequelleyawa						x	
89.	Shoya K'yaba'a						x	
90.	Ahayu:t A:chiya' Delashhin'a						x	
91.	K'ya: Łi'anna' K'ya:kwayinna		x					
92.	Kiwaikuluk/a						x	
93.	Dahna K'ohanna	x	x				x	
94.	Ts'iya'a:wa						x	
95.	K'yawihkya						x	
96.	Shak'yaya'a	x					x	
97.	Kashi:kuk/a:tu (see #4)							
98.	A'su'wa						x	
99.	U'k'yahayan El'a						x	
100.	Da'wi Dabak'i:wa	x	x					
101.	/iyanik/a:waisha						x	
102.	Yash:tik/u:tu						x	
103.	Mi/ashu:k/awa/ka						x	
104.	Heshe/aleto:wa						x	
105.	Dewankwin Onan Baniyn'a (see #9)							
106.	K'ya:ts'i' K'yan'a						x	

	Name	Plant Collection	Mineral Collection	Hunting	Farming	Grazing	Religious	Other
107.	Amidola: Debow Ul'a				x		x	
108.	Debo'kwin Im'a						x	
109.	Sho' Dek'yapbow'a						x	
110.	Hebadin'a						x	
111.	Danin K'yay'a						x	
112.	Yamun K'yay'a						x	
113.	Ts'ik'on K'yay'a						x	
114.	Awisho K'yay'a						x	
115.	Kumanch An A'l'akkwe'a (see #52)							
116.	Bittsemi Deyatchi:wa						x	x
117.	Mokkwi: Deyatchi:wa						x	x
118.	Kyane:lu Yala:we						x	
119.	Deshukt Dina:wa	x					x	
120.	Deshukt Łan Im'a						x	
121.	K'yana:wa						x	
122.	Hak'win A'deyałt'a		x				x	
123.	Dona A:de'ana:wa						x	
124.	Deshamik'ya Im'a						x	
125.	Ma'baniykya Dey'a (see #81)							
126.	Demossi Dahna'a			x				
127.	Kyama:kya						x	
128.	Habana: A'l'akkwe'a						x	
129.	Nadatdekwi:wa			x			x	
130.	Dełak Akwe'a			x			x	
131.	Bilan Akkwe'a (or Akkwe'a)			x				
132.	Dek'yapbowa:wa [Tekapo]			x				
133.	K'yawa:na łana'a	x					x	
134.	Tsilhinn/yalh/a						x	
135.	Dopbolliya: K'yan'a						x	
136.	Anshe K'yan'a		x					x
137.	Komkwayikya dey'a						x	
138.	Da:melank'yay'a						x	
139.	Banelunan K'yay'a						x	
140.	Ladaw K'yay'a						x	
141.	Ubulemi						x	
142.	Batsikchina:wa						x	
143.	To:papik/a-ya						x	
144.	K'yashhida K'yay'a						x	
145.	Molan K'yay'a						x	
146.	Hadin K'yay'a (see #11)							
147.	A'ts'ina:wa						x	
148.	A'łabatts'i'a						x	
149.	Bi:shu'k'yay'a						x	
150.	K'yan Uł'a						x	
151.	K'ya:dechi'a						x	
152.	A:yaya'kya						x	
153.	Idełakukya dey'a						x	
154.	Sumk'yana'a						x	
155.	Wilatsu'u:kw An K'yan'a						x	
156.	Hebadin'a						x	
157.	Sak'yaya Yalanne					x		
158.	Abak'in Shilow Im'a					x		
159.	Yaladeyałdo:wa			x		x		x
160.	Lhep/tequ/aqu/a					x		
161.	Billena:wa	x						
162.	Adel Ahonna (see #87)							

	Name	Plant Collection	Mineral Collection	Hunting	Farming	Grazing	Religious	Other
163.	Suski:kw A:wan K'yan'a						x	
164.	Wałbi'a							x
165.	A'l El'a							x
166.	Pat/chi:wa							x
167.	Biha An Yal'a			x				
168.	Hek'o' Yal'a							x
169.	Talapa/k/a-na							x
170.	K'ya:dechi' K'yan'a							x
171.	Achiya: Dek'yapbow'a	x						
172.	Heshodan Imk'oshkwi'a							x
173.	Sokkwi'a					x		x
174.	Kechiba:wa		x					
175.	Hawikku						x	
176.	Halona:wa						x	
177.	Awisho Yala:we						x	
178.	Doloknana'a						x	
179.	Onan Dełakwi'a						x	
180.	Opbon Biya'a						x	
181.	Banidan Im'a						x	
182.	Anела:wa Im'a						x	
183.	Sum A'shokda'a						x	
184.	A:k'ohanna' Dina:wa						x	
185.	K'eyadi:wa or K'eyadina:wa						x	
186.	Yala Łi'anna			x				
187.	/ashokta:piyan/a					x		x
188.	Sanana: wohan'a							x
189.	Tsi:k/auk/osk/a							x
190.	Sha:k/aya			x			x	
191.	K'emaya: k'yan'a							x
192.	Awatu							x
193.	Ko:chali:wa					x	x	
194.	Wilats'ukwe A:wan Yal'a (Yala:wa)							x
195.	Doya'a or Doya (Nutria)		x		x			
196.	Salt River Canyon		x					
197.	(unnamed)		x					
198.	K/na/tsi/yall/a			x			x	
199.	K'yawa:n Ahonna			x				
200.	Luna			x				
201.	Sandy Flats			x				
202.	Nigger Ridge			x				
203.	Du:sh an K'yan'a			x				
204.	Kyalap Onanne	x						
205.	Ganado Area	x						
206.	K'yabachu'a / Sunha:kwin	x						
207.	Quemado	x						
208.	Piney Park			x				x
209.	Fence Lake					x		
210.	Mu:man'a					x		
211.	Page					x		
212.	Wimaya: Akkwe'a					x		
213.	Shuminkya					x		
214.	Witch Wells					x		
215.	Sanders					x		
216.	Yucca Gathering Place	x						
217.	/awak/on:yellan/a	x		x			x	
218.	Granite Mountain			x				

	Name	Plant Collection	Mineral Collection	Hunting	Farming	Grazing	Religious	Other
219.	Granite Peak			x				
220.	Gila Cliff Dwellings			x				
221.	Jewett Gap			x				
222.	Eagle Nesting Area			x				
223.	Hepetsulia:wa			x				
224.	Piliayalla:we			x				
225.	Łi'akwa Yal'a		x					
226.	Shu'ts'ina Yal'a			x				
227.	McNary Area	x						
228.	Upper Little Colorado River Valley					x		
229.	Mo'yachun Biyahkya Dey'a							x
230.	Satabiyana							x
231.	Amaquewilawa			x			x	x
232.	Plant Collection Area	x						
233.	Shundek'yay'a						x	
234.	Bibaɫ'a or Bibaɫɫi'a (same place as no. 81)							

SOURCES

The depositions listed below, as well as expert testimony from various historians, archaeologists, and anthropologists, were submitted to the United States Court of Claims (now renamed the United States Claims Court), as evidence in the Zuni land-claim litigation (Zuni Indian Tribe v. United States, *Docket 161-79L), and are part of the court record in Washington, D.C.*

1. **Location of the Zuni Area**

Awelagte, T., Deposition, *Zuni Indian Tribe v. United States,* Docket 161-79L (Ct. Cl., filed April 27, 1979), pp. 10–20.

Bowannie, F., Deposition, *Zuni Indian Tribe v. United States,* Docket 161-79L (Ct. Cl., filed April 27, 1979), p. 26.

Edaakie, T., Deposition, *Zuni Indian Tribe v. United States,* Docket 161-79L (Ct. Cl., filed April 27, 1979), p. 19.

Eggan, F., "Aboriginal Land Use of the Zuni Indian Tribe," Written testimony submitted to the U.S. Court of Claims in behalf of the Zuni Indian Tribe, *Zuni Indian Tribe of New Mexico v. United States,* Docket 161-79L, 1980.

Eriacho, S., Sr., Deposition, *Zuni Indian Tribe v. United States,* Docket 161-79L (Ct. Cl., filed April 27, 1979), p. 25.

Ferguson, T. J., "Zuni Settlement and Land Use: An Archaeological Perspective," written testimony submitted to the U.S. Court of Claims in behalf of the Zuni Indian Tribe, *Zuni Indian Tribe of New Mexico v. United States,* Docket 161-79L, 1980.

Gaspar, C. H., Deposition, *Zuni Indian Tribe v. United States,* Docket 161-79L (Ct. Cl., filed April 27, 1979), p. 26.

Hart, E. R., "Boundaries of Zuni Land: With Emphasis on Details Relating to Incidents Occurring 1846–1946," Expert Witness Testimony Submitted December, 1980, to the U.S. Court of Claims on Behalf of the Zuni Tribe, 2 vols., *Zuni Tribe v. United States of America.*

Hustito, A., Deposition, *Zuni Indian Tribe v. United States,* Docket 161-79L (Ct. Cl., filed April 27, 1979), pp. 23–26, 39.

Jenkins, M. E., "The Pueblo of Zuni and United States Occupation," written testimony submitted to the U.S. Court of Claims in behalf of the Zuni Indian Tribe, *Zuni Indian Tribe of New Mexico v. United States,* Docket No. 161-79L, 1980.

Mahooty, C., Deposition, *Zuni Indian Tribe v. United States,* Docket 161-79L (Ct. Cl., filed April 27, 1979), pp. 11, 13.

Minge, W. A., "Zuni in Spanish and Mexican History," written testimony submitted to the U.S. Court of Claims in behalf of the Zuni Indian Tribe, *Zuni Indian Tribe of New Mexico v. United States,* Docket 161-79L, 1980.

Nastacio, A., Deposition, *Zuni Indian Tribe v. United States,* Docket 161-79L (Ct. Cl., filed April 27, 1979), pp. 29–39.

Nastacio, O., Deposition, *Zuni Indian Tribe v. United States,* Docket 161-79L (Ct. Cl., filed April 27, 1979), pp. 12–13.

Pandey, T. N., "Some Reflections on Aboriginal Land Use of the Zuni Indian Tribe," written testimony submitted to the U.S. Court of Claims in behalf of the Zuni Indian Tribe, *Zuni Indian Tribe of New Mexico v. United States,* Docket 161-79L, 1980.

Quam, R., Deposition, *Zuni Indian Tribe v. United States,* Docket 161-79L (Ct. Cl., filed April 27, 1979), p. 25.

Tyler, S. L., "The Zuni Indians Under the Laws of Spain, Mexico, and the United States," written testimony submitted to the U.S. Court of Claims in behalf of the Zuni Indian Tribe, *Zuni Indian Tribe of New Mexico v. United States,* Docket 161-79L, 1980.

Vacit, F., Deposition, *Zuni Indian Tribe v. United States,* Docket 161-79L (Ct. Cl., filed April 27, 1979), p. 21.

Wytsalucy, M., Deposition, *Zuni Indian Tribe v. United States,* Docket 161-79L (Ct. Cl., filed April 27, 1979), p. 8.

2. **Landforms of the Zuni Area**

Fenneman, N. M., *Physiography of the Western United States.* New York: McGraw-Hill, 1931.

Raisz, E., Landforms of the United States Map, 1957.

3. **Geology of the Zuni Area**

Darton, N. H., "The Zuni Salt Lake," *Journal of Geology* 13(3) (1905): 185–93.

Fitzsimmons, J. P., "The structure and geomorphology of west-central New Mexico," Guidebook of West-Central New Mexico, New Mexico Geological Society, Tenth Field Conference, 1959.

Foster, R. W., "Southern Zuni Mountains, Zuni-Cibola Trail," *Scenic Trips to the Geologic Past,* no. 4, New Mexico Bureau of Mines and Mineral Resources, 1971.

Heindl, L. A., "Topographic, Physiographic, and Structural Subdivisions of Arizona," *Arizona Geology Society Digest* 3 (1960): 12–18.

United States Geological Survey, Geologic Map of the United States.

4. **Drainages and Hydrology**

Orr, Brennon R., "Water Resources of the Zuni Tribal Lands, McKinley and Cibola Counties, New Mexico," Water Supply of Indian Reservations, Geological Survey Water Supply Paper (open file); Washington: GPO, 1982.

U.S. Geological Survey, State maps of Arizona and New Mexico at scale of 1:500,000.

5. **Precipitation and Climate**

Jurwitz, L. R. and P. C. Kangieser, "The climate of Arizona," *Climates of the States,* Vol. 2, Western States including Alaska and Hawaii, by Officials of the National Oceanic and Atmospheric Administration, U.S. Department of Commerce, 1974 (originally written in 1959).

Houghton, F. E., "The climate of New Mexico," *Climates of the States,* Vol. 2, Western States including Alaska and Hawaii, by Officials of the National Oceanic and Atmospheric Administration, U.S. Department of Commerce, 1974 (originally written 1972).

United States Department of Commerce, *Climatic atlas of the United States,* Washington: Environmental Science Services; Environmental Data Service, 1968.

6. **Temperature and Frost-free Season**

Tuan, Y., C. E. Everard, J. G. Widdison and I. Bennett, *The Climate of New Mexico,* (Revised edition). Santa Fe: State Planning Office, 1973.

United States Department of Commerce, *Climatic Atlas of the United States.* Washington: Environmental Science Services; Environmental Data Service, 1968.

7. **Biotic Communities**

Brown, D. E. and C. H. Lowe, Biotic Communities of the Southwest Map, General Technical Report RM-78. Rocky Mountain Forest and Range Experimental Station, U.S. Forest Service, U.S. Department of Agriculture, 1980.

Castetter, E. F., "The vegetation of New Mexico," *New Mexico Quarterly* 26 (1957): 257–88.

Lowe, C. H., *Arizona's Natural Environment.* Tucson: University of Arizona Press, 1964.

8. **Zuni Origin and Migration**

Awelagte, T., Deposition, *Zuni Indian Tribe v. United States,* Docket 161-79L (Ct. Cl., filed April 27, 1979), pp. 10–20.

Bowannie, F., Deposition, *Zuni Indian Tribe v. United States,* Docket 161-79L (Ct. Cl., filed April 27, 1979), p. 26.

Bunzel, R. L., "Zuni origin myths," *Forty-seventh Annual Report of the Bureau of American Ethnology, 1929–1930,* Washington, 1932; pp. 454–609.

Cushing, F. H., "Outlines of Zuni creation myths," *Thirteenth Annual Report of the Bureau of American Ethnology; 1891–1892,* Washington, 1896; pp. 321–447.

Edaakie, T., Deposition, *Zuni Indian Tribe v. United States,* Docket 161-79L (Ct. Cl., filed April 27, 1979), p. 19.

Eriacho, S., Sr., Deposition, *Zuni Indian Tribe v. United States,* Docket 161-79L (Ct. Cl., filed April 27, 1979), p. 25.

Gaspar, C. H., Deposition, *Zuni Indian Tribe v. United States,* Docket 161-79L (Ct. Cl., filed April 27, 1979), p. 26.

Hustito, A., Deposition, *Zuni Indian Tribe v. United States,* Docket 161-79L (Ct. Cl., filed April 27, 1979), pp. 23–26, 39.

Mahooty, C., Deposition, *Zuni Indian Tribe v. United States,* Docket 161-79L (Ct. Cl., filed April 27, 1979), pp. 11, 13.

Nastacio, A., Deposition, *Zuni Indian Tribe v. United States,* Docket 161-79L (Ct. Cl., filed April 27, 1979), pp. 29–39.

Nastacio, O., Deposition, *Zuni Indian Tribe v. United States,* Docket 161-79L (Ct. Cl., filed April 27, 1979), pp. 12–13.

Parsons, E. C., "The origin myth of Zuni," *Journal of Amercan Folklore* 36 (1923): 135–62.

Quam, R., Deposition, *Zuni Indian Tribe v. United States,* Docket 161-79L (Ct. Cl., filed April 27, 1979), p. 25.

Stevenson, M. C., "The Zuni Indians: their mythology, esoteric fraternities, and ceremonies," *Twenty-third Annual Report of the Bureau of American Ethnology, 1901–1902,* Washington, 1904, pp. 3–634.

Tedlock, D., *Finding the Center: Narrative Poetry of the Zuni Indians, from Performances in Zuni, by Andrew Peynetsa and Walter Sanchez.* New York: Dial Press, 1972.

Vacit, F., Deposition, *Zuni Indian Tribe v. United States,* Docket 161-79L (Ct. Cl., filed April 27, 1979), p. 21.

Wytsalucy, M., Deposition, *Zuni Indian Tribe v. United States,* Docket 161-79L (Ct. Cl., filed April 27, 1979), p. 8.

9. **Zuni Archaeology and Culture History**

Ferguson, T. J. and B. J. Mills, "Archaeological investigations at Zuni Pueblo, 1977–1980," *Zuni Archaeology Program Report* 183, Pueblo of Zuni, 1982.

Roberts, F. H. H., "The ruins at Kiatuthlanna, Eastern Arizona," *Bureau of American Ethnology Bulletin* 100, Washington, 1931.

———, "The Village of the Great Kivas on the Zuni Indian Reservation, New Mexico," *Bureau of American Ethnology Bulletin* 111, Washington, 1932.

Smith, W., R. B. Woodbury and N. S. Woodbury, "The excavation of Hawikuh by Frederick Webb Hodge: Report of the Hendricks-Hodge Expedition, 1917–1923," *Contributions from the Museum of the American Indian, Heye Foundation* 20, New York, 1966.

Spier, L., "An outline for a chronology of Zuni ruins," *Anthropological Papers of the American Museum of Natural History* 18, no. 3 (New York, 1916): 363–87.

Woodbury, R. B., "Zuni prehistory and history to 1850," *Handbook of the North American Indians,* vol. 9, edited by A. Ortiz. Washington: Smithsonian Institution, 1979, pp. 473–76.

10. **Sixteenth Century Zuni Villages and Spanish Entradas**

Bandelier, A. F., "An Outline of the Documentary History of the Zuni Tribe," *A Journal of American Ethnology and Archaeology,* vol. 3, Boston and New York: Houghton, Mifflin and Company, 1892.

———, *The Gilded Man.* Chicago: Rio Grande Press, 1962 (originally published 1873), 302 pp.

Bolton, H. E., *Coronado: Knight of Pueblos and Plains.* Albuquerque: University of New Mexico Press and Whittlesey House, 1949.

Hammond, G. P. and A. Rey, eds., *Narratives of the Coronado Expedition, 1540–1542.* Albuquerque: University of New Mexico Press, 1940 (reprinted AMS, 1977).

———, *Oñate, Colonizer of New Mexico, 1598–1628.* 2 vols. Albuquerque: University of New Mexico Press, 1953.

———, *The Rediscovery of New Mexico, 1580–1594.* Albuquerque: University of New Mexico Press (Coronado Historical Fund), 1966.

Hodge, F. W., *History of Hawikuh, New Mexico: One of the So-called Cities of Cibola.* Los Angeles: Hodge Publication Fund, 1937.

Kintigh, K., "Settlement, Subsistence and Society in Late Zuni Prehistory," *Anthropological Papers of the University of Arizona, no. 44,* Tucson: University of Arizona Press, 1985.

Turrell, M. R., trans. and ed., *Adolph F. Bandelier's The Discovery of New Mexico.* Tucson: University of Arizona Press, 1981.

11. **The Maps of Don Bernardo Miera y Pacheco, 1775–79**

Adams, E. B., "Fray Silvestre and the Obstinate Hopi," *New Mexico Historical Review* 38 (1963): 97–138.

Adams, E. B., and Angelico Chavez, eds. and trans., *The Missions of New Mexico, 1776: A Description by Fray Francisco Atanasio Dominguez, with other Contemporary Documents.* Albuquerque: University of New Mexico Press, 1956.

Chavez, A., trans., *The Dominguez-Escalante Journal: Their Expedition through Colorado, Utah, Arizona, and New Mexico in 1776,* ed. by T. J. Warner. Provo, Utah: Brigham Young University Press, 1976.

Fireman, J. R., *The Spanish Royal Corps of Engineers in the Western Borderlands: Instrument of Bourbon Reform, 1764 to 1815.* Glendale, California: Arthur H. Clark Company, 1977.

Jones, O. L., Jr., *Los Paisanos: Spanish Settlers on the Northern Frontier of New Spain.* Norman: University of Oklahoma Press, 1979.

Kessell, J. L., *Kiva, Cross, and Crown: The Pecos Indians and New Mexico, 1540–1840.* Washington, D.C.: National Park Service, 1979.

Minge, W. A., "Zuni in Spanish and Mexican History," written testimony submitted to the U.S. Court of Claims in behalf of the Zuni Indian Tribe, *Zuni Indian Tribe of New Mexico v. United States,* Docket 161-79L, 1980.

Thomas, A. B., trans. and ed., *Forgotten Frontiers: A Study of the Spanish Indian Policy of Don Juan Bautista de Anza, Governor of New Mexico, 1777–1787.* Norman: University of Oklahoma Press, 1932 (reprinted 1969).

Twitchell, R. E., "Colonel Juan Bautista de Anza . . . ," *Historical Society of New Mexico,* no. 21 (1918).

12. Core Area of Zuni Settlement in the Historic Period

Bandelier, A. F., "An Outline of the Documentary History of the Zuni Tribe," *A Journal of American Ethnology and Archaeology,* vol. 3, Boston and New York: Houghton, Mifflin and Company, 1892 (Republished by AMS 1977).

Cushing, F. H., "Outlines of Zuni creation myths," *Thirteenth Annual Report of the Bureau of American Ethnology; 1891–1892,* Washington, 1896, pp. 321–447.

Kroeber, A. L., "Zuni potsherds," *Papers of the American Museum of Natural History,* vol. 18, pt. 1, pp. 1–37.

Mindeleff, V., "A Study of Pueblo Architecture: Tusayan and Cibola," *Eighth Annual Report of the Bureau of Ethnology,* Washington, 1891.

Spier, L., "An Outline for a chronology of Zuni ruins," Anthropological Papers of the American Museum of Natural History, vol. 18, pt. 3, pp. 363–87.

13. Zuni Agriculture

Awelagte, T., Deposition, *Zuni Indian Tribe v. United States,* Docket 161-79L (Ct. Cl., filed April 27, 1979), pp. 10–20.

Bohrer, V. L., "Zuni agriculture," *El Palacio* 67, no. 6 (1960): 181–82.

———, "Chinchweed (Pectis Papposa), a Zuni Herb," *El Palacio* 64, nos. 11–13 (Nov., Dec., 1957): 365.

Bowannie, F., Deposition, *Zuni Indian Tribe v. United States,* Docket 161-79L (Ct. Cl., filed April 27, 1979), p. 26.

Bunzel, R., *Zuni Texts;* Publications of the American Ethnological Society, vol. 15. New York: G. E. Stechert & Co., 1933.

Cushing, F. H., "Zuni breadstuff," *Indian Notes and Monographs* 8. New York: Museum of the American Indian, Heye Foundation (1974 reprint of 1920 edition).

———, "Life at Zuni," Lecture before the Buffalo Society, n.d. [1893?], H-C MS E214, Southwest Museum, Los Angeles.

Douglas, F. H., "Main Types of Pueblo Cotton Textiles," *Denver Art Museum Indian Leaflet Series* vols. 92–93, 1940, pp. 166–73.

———, "Weaving at Zuni Pueblo," *Denver Art Museum Indian Leaflet Series* vols. 96–97, 1940, pp. 182–87.

———, "Main Types of Pueblo Woven Textiles," *Denver Art Museum Indian Leaflet Series* vols. 94–95, 1940, pp. 174–80.

Ferguson, T. J., "The Emergence of Modern Zuni Culture and Society; A Summary of Zuni Culture History, A.D. 1450 to 1700." In "The Protohistoric Period in the North American Southwest, AD 1450–1700," edited by David R. Wilcox and W. Bruce Masse. *Arizona State University Anthropological Research Papers, no. 24.*

Goodman, I., "The Zuni Indians of New Mexico," in *Cooperation and Competition among Primitive Peoples.* Boston: Beacon Press, 1939 (reprinted Cloncester, Mass.: Peter Smith, 1976).

Hart, E. R., "Rebuttal Report," submitted in behalf of the Zuni Indian Tribe, Docket No. 161-79L, United States Court of Claims, March, 1981.

———, "Zuni Agriculture: An Historical Application of Ethnological Research," a paper presented at the Laurier Conference on Ethnohistory and Ethnology, Wilfred Laurier University, Canada, October 20, 1980.

———, "Boundaries of Zuni Land: With Emphasis on Details Relating to Incidents Occurring 1846–1946," Expert Witness Testimony Submitted December, 1980, to the U.S. Court of Claims on behalf of the Zuni Tribe, 2 vols., *Zuni Tribe v. United States of America.*

Holmes, B. E. and A. P. Fowler, *The Alternate Dams Survey: An Archaeological Sample Survey and Evaluation of the Burned Timber and Coalmine Dams,* Zuni Archaeology Program, Zuni, N.Mex., 1980.

Leighton, D. C., and J. Adair, *People of the Middle Place.* New Haven, Conn.: Human Relations Area Files, Inc., 1971, p. 28.

Nastacio, O., Deposition, *Zuni Indian Tribe v. United States,* Docket 161-79L (Ct. Cl., filed April 27, 1979), pp. 12–13.

Spier, L., "Zuni Weaving Technique," *American Anthropologist* 26 (1924): 64–85.

Stewart, G. R., "Conservation in Pueblo agriculture," *Scientific Monthly* 51 (1940): 201–20, 329–40.

Woodbury, R. B., and E. B. W. Zubrow, "Agricultural Beginnings, 2000 B.C.–A.D. 500," *Handbook of North American Indians: Southwest,* vol. 9, ed. by A. Ortiz. Washington: Smithsonian Institution, 1979, pp. 43–60.

14. Zuni Grazing Lands

Bowannie, F., Deposition, *Zuni Indian Tribe v. United States,* Docket 161-79L (Ct. Cl., filed April 27, 1979), p. 26.

Cushing, F. H., "Outlines of Zuni Creation Myths," *Thirteenth Annual Report of the Bureau of American Ethnology, 1891–1892,* Washington, 1896.

———, "Zuni breadstuff," *Indian Notes and Monographs* 8. New York: Museum of the American Indian, Heye Foundation, 1974 (Reprint of 1920 edition).

Eriacho, S., Sr., Deposition, *Zuni Indian Tribe v. United States,* Docket 161-79L (Ct. Cl., filed April 27, 1979), p. 25.

Gaspar, C. H., Deposition, *Zuni Indian Tribe v. United*

States, Docket 161-79L (Ct. Cl., filed April 27, 1979), p. 26.

Green, J., ed., *Zuni: Selected Writings of Frank Hamilton Cushing.* Lincoln, Neb.: University of Nebraska Press, 1979, pp. 182–83.

Hart, E. R., "Boundaries of Zuni Land: With Emphasis on Details Relating to Incidents Occurring 1846–1946," Expert Witness Testimony Submitted December, 1980, to the U.S. Court of Claims on behalf of the Zuni Tribe, 2 vols., *Zuni Tribe v. United States of America* (Docket 161-79L).

Ladd, E. J., "Zuni Economy," *Handbook of North American Indians, Southwest, vol. 9,* ed. by A. Ortiz. Washington: Smithsonian Institution, 1979, pp. 492–98.

Leighton, D. C., and J. Adair, *People of the Middle Place.* New Haven, Conn.: Human Relations Area Files, Inc., 1971, p. 28.

Mahooty, C., Deposition, *Zuni Indian Tribe v. United States,* Docket 161-79L (Ct. Cl., filed April 27, 1979), pp. 11, 13.

Quam, R., Deposition, *Zuni Indian Tribe v. United States,* Docket 161-79L (Ct. Cl., filed April 27, 1979), p. 25.

Stevenson, M. C., "The Zuni Indians: their mythology, esoteric fraternities, and ceremonies," *Twenty-third Annual Report of the Bureau of American Ethnology, 1901–1902,* Washington, 1904, pp. 3–634.

Trotter, G. A., *From Feather, Blanket and Tepee.* New York: Vantage Press, Inc., 1955, p. 125.

Vacit, F., Deposition, *Zuni Indian Tribe v. United States,* Docket 161-79L (Ct. Cl., filed April 27, 1979), p. 21.

Wytsalucy, M., Deposition, *Zuni Indian Tribe v. United States,* Docket 161-79L (Ct. Cl., filed April 27, 1979), p. 8.

15. **Zuni Hunting**

Bandelier, A. F., *The Gilded Man.* Chicago: Rio Grande Press, 1962 (originally published 1873).

———, *The Southwestern Journals of Adolph F. Bandelier, 1883–1884,* ed. and annot. by C. H. Lange and C. L. Riley. Albuquerque: University of New Mexico Press, 1970, pp. 81–82.

Benavides, Fr. Alonso de, *Benavides Memorial of 1630,* trans. by P. P. Forrestal. Washington: Academy of American Franciscan History, 1954, pp. 40–41.

Bourke, J. G., "Sacred Hunts of the American Indians," *International Congress of Americanists,* vol. 8 (1890), pp. 357–68.

Bowannie, F., Deposition, *Zuni Indian Tribe v. United States,* Docket 161-79L (Ct. Cl., filed April 27, 1979), p. 26.

Bunzel, R. L., "Introduction to Zuni Ceremonialism," *Forty-seventh Annual Report of the Bureau of American Ethnology, 1929–1930,* Washington, 1932, pp. 467–544.

———, "Zuni Origin Myths," *Forty-seventh Annual Report of the Bureau of American Ethnology, 1929–1930,* Washington, 1932, pp. 545–609.

———, "Zuni Ritual Poetry," *Forty-seventh Annual Report of the Bureau of American Ethnology, 1929–1930,* Washington, 1932, pp. 611–835.

Culin, S., "Report of a Museum Expedition in 1907—Zuni Notes," typescript in the collection of the Brooklyn Museum.

Cushing, F. H., "Life at Zuni," Lecture before the Buffalo Society, n.d. [1893?], H-C MS E214, SWM.

———, "Zuni breadstuff," *Indian Notes and Monographs* 8, New York: Museum of the American Indian, Heye Foundation, 1974 (Reprint of 1920 edition).

———, "Pueblos and Ruins of the United States," MS, H-C #222, SWM.

———, *Zuni folk tales.* New York: AMS Press, 1976 (originally published 1901).

———, *Zuni fetishes,* with an introduction by Tom Bahti, facsimile edition. Flagstaff: K. C. Publications, 1970 (original printed in the *Second Annual Report of the Bureau of Ethnology, 1880–1881,* Washington, 1883).

Edaakie, T., Deposition, *Zuni Indian Tribe v. United States,* Docket 161-79L (Ct. Cl., filed April 27, 1979), p. 19.

Eggan, F., "Pueblos: Introduction," *Handbook of North American Indians, Southwest,* vol. 9, ed. by A. Ortiz. Washington: Smithsonian Institution, 1979, pp. 224–35.

Eggan, F., and T. N. Pandey, "Zuni History, 1850–1970," *Handbook of North American Indians: Southwest, vol. 9* (ed. by A. Ortiz), Washington: Smithsonian Institution, 1979, pp. 474–81.

Eriacho, S., Sr., Deposition, *Zuni Indian Tribe v. United States,* Docket 161-79L (Ct. Cl., filed April 27, 1979), p. 25.

Gaspar, C. H., Deposition, *Zuni Indian Tribe v. United States,* Docket 161-79L (Ct. Cl., filed April 27, 1979), p. 26.

Hustito, A., Deposition, *Zuni Indian Tribe v. United States,* Docket 161-79L (Ct. Cl., filed April 27, 1979), pp. 23–26, 39.

Kirk, R. F., "Buffalo Hunting Fetish Jar," *El Palacio* 57 (May, 1950), pp. 131–41.

Ladd, E. J., "Zuni Ethno-Ornithology," M.S. Thesis in Anthropology, University of New Mexico, 1963.

Mahooty, C., Deposition, *Zuni Indian Tribe v. United States,* Docket 161-79L (Ct. Cl., filed April 27, 1979), pp. 11, 13.

Nastacio, A., Deposition, *Zuni Indian Tribe v. United States,* Docket 161-79L (Ct. Cl., filed April 27, 1979), pp. 29–39.

Nastacio, O., Deposition, *Zuni Indian Tribe v. United States,* Docket 161-79L (Ct. Cl., filed April 27, 1979), pp. 12–13.

Owens, J. G., "Some Games of the Zunis," *Popular Science Monthly* 38 (1891): 47.

Reports of Explorations and Surveys to Ascertain the Most Practicable and Economical Route for a Railroad from the Mississippi River to the Pacific Ocean, 1853–1854, 33d Cong., 2d Sess., Exec. Doc. #91, vol. 3, p. 63.

Stevenson, M. C., "The Zuni Indians: their mythology, esoteric fraternities, and ceremonies," *Twenty-third Annual Report of the Bureau of American Ethnology, 1901–1902,* Washington, 1904, pp. 3–634.

Ten Broek, P. G. S., "Manners and Customs of the Moqui and Navajo," in vol. 1, pt. 4 of *Historical and Statistical Information Respecting the History, Condition and Prospects of the Indian Tribes of the United States by Henry R. Schoolcraft.* Philadelphia: Lippincott, Granbo & Co., 1854, pp. 80–81.

Vacit, F., Deposition, *Zuni Indian Tribe v. United States,* Docket 161-79L (Ct. Cl., filed April 27, 1979), p. 21.

16. **Zuni Plant Collection**

Awelagte, T., Deposition, *Zuni Indian Tribe v. United States,* Docket 161-79L (Ct. Cl., filed April 27, 1979), pp. 10–20.

Bowannie, F., Deposition, *Zuni Indian Tribe v. United States,* Docket 161-79L (Ct. Cl., filed April 27, 1979), p. 26.

Cushing, F. H., "Zuni breadstuff," *Indian Notes and Monographs* 8, New York: Museum of the American Indian,

Heye Foundation, 1974 (Reprint of 1920 edition).
Edaakie, T., Deposition, *Zuni Indian Tribe v. United States*, Docket 161-79L (Ct. Cl., filed April 27, 1979), p. 19.
Eriacho, S., Sr., Deposition, *Zuni Indian Tribe v. United States*, Docket 161-79L (Ct. Cl., filed April 27, 1979), p. 25.
Gaspar, C. H., Deposition, *Zuni Indian Tribe v. United States*, Docket 161-79L (Ct. Cl., filed April 27, 1979), p. 26.
Hart, E. R., "Boundaries of Zuni Land: With Emphasis on Details Relating to Incidents Occurring 1846–1946," Expert Witness Testimony Submitted December, 1980, to the U. S. Court of Claims on Behalf of the Zuni Tribe, 2 vols., *Zuni Tribe v. United States of America.*
Hustito, A., Deposition, *Zuni Indian Tribe v. United States*, Docket 161-79L (Ct. Cl., filed April 27, 1979), pp. 23–26, 39.
Mahooty, C., Deposition, *Zuni Indian Tribe v. United States*, Docket 161-79L (Ct. Cl., filed April 27, 1979), pp. 11, 13.
Nastacio, A., Deposition, *Zuni Indian Tribe v. United States*, Docket 161-79L (Ct. Cl., filed April 27, 1979), pp. 29–39.
Nastacio, O., Deposition, *Zuni Indian Tribe v. United States*, Docket 161-79L (Ct. Cl., filed April 27, 1979), pp. 12–13.
Quam, R., Deposition, *Zuni Indian Tribe v. United States*, Docket 161-79L (Ct. Cl., filed April 27, 1979), p. 25.
Smith, W., R. B. Woodbury and N. S. Woodbury, "The excavation of Hawikuh by Frederick Webb Hodge: Report of the Hendricks-Hodge Expedition, 1917–1923," *Contributions from the Museum of the American Indian, Heye Foundation* 20, New York, 1966.
Stevenson, M. C., "Ethnobotony of the Zuni Indians," *Thirtieth Annual Report of the Bureau of American Ethnology*, Washington, 1915; pp. 31–102.
Vacit, F., Deposition, *Zuni Indian Tribe v. United States*, Docket 161-79L (Ct. Cl., filed April 27, 1979), p. 21.
Wytsalucy, M., Deposition, *Zuni Indian Tribe v. United States*, Docket 161-79L (Ct. Cl., filed April 27, 1979), p. 8.

17. **Zuni Mineral Collection**

Adair, J., *The Navajo and Pueblo Silversmiths.* Norman: University of Oklahoma Press, 1944, pp. 121–36.
Awelagte, T., Deposition, *Zuni Indian Tribe v. United States*, Docket 161-79L (Ct. Cl., filed April 27, 1979), pp. 10–20.
Bandelier, A. F., *The Southwestern Journals of Adolph F. Bandelier, 1883–1884*, ed. and annot. by C. H. Lange and C. L. Riley. Albuquerque: University of New Mexico Press, 1970, pp. 81–82.
Bowannie, F., Deposition, *Zuni Indian Tribe v. United States*, Docket 161-79L (Ct. Cl., filed April 27, 1979), p. 26.
Bunzel, R. L., *The Pueblo Potter, a Study of Creative Imagination in Primitive Art.* New York: Dover Publications, 1972 (originally published 1929), pp. 5–6.
Curtis, E. S., "Zuni," *The North American Indian*, vol. 27, ed. by F. W. Hodge. New York: Johnson Reprint Corp., 1970 (first published 1926), p. 102.
Cushing, F. H., "A Study of Pueblo Pottery as Illustrative of Zuni Culture-Growth," *Fourth Annual Report of the Bureau of Ethnology, 1882–1883*, Washington, 1886, p. 4.
———, "Primitive Copper Working: An Experimental Study," *The American Anthropologist* 7 (1894): 93–97.
———, *My Adventures at Zuni*, with an introduction by O. L. Jones, Jr. (reprint). Palmer Lake, Colo.: Filter Press, 1967, p. 28.
———, "Search for the Tchalchuitl Mines," unpublished MS, Southwest Museum, Los Angeles.
———, "Zuni Fetishes," *Second Annual Report of the Bureau of Ethnology*, Washington, 1883 (Republished Flagstaff, Ariz.: D. C. Publications, 1970), 3–45.
———, "Zuni breadstuff," *Indian Notes and Monographs* 8, New York: Museum of the American Indian, Heye Foundation (Reprint of 1920 edition).
Edaakie, T., Deposition, *Zuni Indian Tribe v. United States*, Docket 161-79L (Ct. Cl., filed April 27, 1979), p. 19.
Eriacho, S., Sr., Deposition, *Zuni Indian Tribe v. United States*, Docket 161-79L (Ct. Cl., filed April 27, 1979), p. 25.
Gaspar, C. H., Deposition, *Zuni Indian Tribe v. United States*, Docket 161-79L (Ct. Cl., filed April 27, 1979), p. 26.
Hart, E. R., "Boundaries of Zuni Land: With Emphasis on Details Relating to Incidents Occurring 1846–1946," Expert Witness Testimony Submitted December, 1980, to the U.S. Court of Claims on Behalf of the Zuni Tribe, 2 vols., *Zuni Tribe vs. United States of America.*
Hodge, F. W., "Early Metalworking by Pueblo Indians," *The Masterkey* 8 (1934): 157.
———, "How Old is Southwestern Indian Silverwork?" *El Palacio* 25 (1928): 224–33.
Hustito, A., Deposition, *Zuni Indian Tribe v. United States*, Docket 161-79L (Ct. Cl., filed April 27, 1979), pp. 23–26, 39.
Mahooty, C., Deposition, *Zuni Indian Tribe v. United States*, Docket 161-79L (Ct. Cl., filed April 27, 1979), pp. 11, 13.
Nastacio, A., Deposition, *Zuni Indian Tribe v. United States*, Docket 161-79L (Ct. Cl., filed April 27, 1979), pp. 29–39.
Nastacio, O., Deposition, *Zuni Indian Tribe v. United States*, Docket 161-79L (Ct. Cl., filed April 27, 1979), pp. 12–13.
Simpson, Lt. J. H., *Navajo Expedition: Journal of a Military Reconnaissance from Santa Fe, New Mexico to the Navajo Country Made in 1849 by Lieutenant James H. Simpson*, ed. and annot. by F. McNitt. Norman: University of Oklahoma Press, 1964, p. 126n.
Sitgreaves, Capt. L., *Report of an Expedition down the Zuni and Colorado Rivers in 1851* (U.S. Senate Executive Document 59, 32d Cong., 2d Sess., 1853), Chicago: Rio Grande Press, Inc., 1962.
Smith, W., R. B. Woodbury and N. S. Woodbury, "The excavation of Hawikuh by Frederick Webb Hodge: Report of the Hendricks-Hodge Expedition, 1917–1923," *Contributions from the Museum of the American Indian, Heye Foundation* 20, New York, 1966.
Telling, I., "History of Ramah," 1939, p. 2. Unpublished MS, American West Center files.
U.S. Congress, *Wagon Road—Fort Smith to Colorado River*, 36th Cong., 1st Sess., House Exec. Doc. No. 42, March 9, 1860, pp. 38–39.
Vacit, F., Deposition, *Zuni Indian Tribe v. United States*, Docket 161-79L (Ct. Cl., filed April 27, 1979), p. 21.
Wytsalucy, M., Deposition, *Zuni Indian Tribe v. United States*, Docket 161-79L (Ct. Cl., filed April 27, 1979), p. 8.

18. **Zuni Traditional Religious Use Area**

Awelagte, T., Deposition, *Zuni Indian Tribe v. United States*, Docket 161-79L (Ct. Cl., filed April 27, 1979), pp. 10–20.
Bowannie, F., Deposition, *Zuni Indian Tribe v. United States*, Docket 161-79L (Ct. Cl., filed April 27, 1979), p. 26.
Cushing, F. H., "Outlines of Zuni Creation Myths," *Thir-*

teenth Annual Report of the Bureau of American Ethnology, 1891–1892,* Washington, 1896.

———, "The Discovery of Zuni or the Ancient Province of Cibola [and] the Seven Cities," unpublished MS Hodge-Cushing Collection, Southwest Museum, Los Angeles, 1885, p. 65.

———, *The Nation of the Willows.* Flagstaff: Northland Press, 1965 (originally published in *Atlantic Monthly,* 1882).

———, *Zuni folk tales.* New York: AMS Press, 1976 (originally published 1901).

Domenech, Abbe Em., *Seven Years Residence in the Great Deserts of North America,* vol. 1. London: Longman, Green, Longman and Roberts, 1860, p. 201.

Edaakie, T., Deposition, *Zuni Indian Tribe v. United States,* Docket 161-79L (Ct. Cl., filed April 27, 1979), p. 19.

Eggan, F., "Aboriginal Land Use of the Zuni Indian Tribe," Written testimony submitted to the U.S. Court of Claims in behalf of the Zuni Indian Tribe, *Zuni Indian Tribe of New Mexico v. United States,* Docket 161-79L, 1980.

Eggan, F., and T. N. Pandey, "Zuni History, 1850-1970," *Handbook of North American Indians: Southwest, vol. 9* ed. by A. Ortiz. Washington: Smithsonian Institution, 1979; pp. 474–81.

Eriacho, S., Sr., Deposition, *Zuni Indian Tribe v. United States,* Docket 161-79L (Ct. Cl., filed April 27, 1979), p. 25.

Ferguson, T. J., "Zuni Settlement and Land Use: An Archaeological Perspective," written testimony submitted to the U.S. Court of Claims in behalf of the Zuni Indian Tribe, *Zuni Indian Tribe of New Mexico v. United States,* Docket 161-79L, 1980.

Gaspar, C. H., Deposition, *Zuni Indian Tribe v. United States,* Docket 161-79L (Ct. Cl., filed April 27, 1979), p. 26.

Hart, E. R., and J. R. Barton, "Primary Area of Original Zuni Land Use," drawn by J. R. Barton, data compiled by E. R. Hart, produced by the Pueblo of Zuni, 1974.

Hustito, A., Deposition, *Zuni Indian Tribe v. United States,* Docket 161-79L (Ct. Cl., filed April 27, 1979), pp. 23–26, 39.

Mahooty, C., Deposition, *Zuni Indian Tribe v. United States,* Docket 161-79L (Ct. Cl., filed April 27, 1979), pp. 11, 13.

Nastacio, A., Deposition, *Zuni Indian Tribe v. United States,* Docket 161-79L (Ct. Cl., filed April 27, 1979), pp. 29–39.

Nastacio, O., Deposition, *Zuni Indian Tribe v. United States,* Docket 161-79L (Ct. Cl., filed April 27, 1979), pp. 12–13.

Pandey, T. N., "Some Reflections on Aboriginal Land Use of the Zuni Indian Tribe," written testimony submitted to the U.S. Court of Claims in behalf of the Zuni Indian Tribe, *Zuni Indian Tribe of New Mexico v. United States,* Docket 161-79L, 1980.

Parsons, E. C., "Hopi and Zuni Ceremonialism," *Memoirs of the American Anthropological Association* no. 39 (1933). New York: Kraus Reprint, Millwood, 1976, p. 92.

Quam, R., Deposition, *Zuni Indian Tribe v. United States,* Docket 161-79L (Ct. Cl., filed April 27, 1979), p. 25.

Roberts, F. H. H., Jr., "The Ruins of Kiatuthlanna Eastern Arizona," *Bureau of American Ethnology Bulletin* 100, Washington, 1931, p. 6.

Saunders, C. F., *The Indians of the Terraced Houses: An Account of the Pueblo Indians of New Mexico and Arizona, 1902–1920.* Glorieta, N. Mex.: Rio Grande Press, Inc., 1973 (originally published 1912 by Putnam), pp. 151–52.

Stevenson, M. C., "The Zuni Indians," extract from the *Twenty-third Annual Report of the Bureau of American Ethnology,* Washington. 1904, pp. 78–79.

Tedlock, D., "Zuni Religion and World View," in *Handbook of North American Indians: Southwest, vol. 9* ed. by A. Ortiz. Washington: Smithsonian Institution, 1979.

19. **Zuni Trade Relationships**

Awelagte, T., Deposition, *Zuni Indian Tribe v. United States,* Docket 161-79L (Ct. Cl., filed April 27, 1979), pp. 10–20.

Bandelier, A. F., "An Outline of the Documentary History of the Zuni Tribe," *A Journal of American Ethnology and Archaeology,* vol. 3. Boston and New York: Houghton, Mifflin and Company, 1892.

———, "Final Report of the Investigations Among the Indians of the Southwestern United States, Carried on Mainly in the Years from 1880 to 1885, Part 1." *Papers of the Archaeological Institute of America.* Cambridge: John Wilson and Son, 1890, p. 106.

Baxter, S., "The Father of the Pueblos," *Harper's New Monthly Magazine,* 65, no. 385 (June, 1882): 79.

Bell, W. A., *New Tracks in North America: A Journal of Travel and Adventure Whilst Engaged in the Survey for a Southern Railroad to the Pacific Ocean in 1867–1868.* London: Chapman and Hall, 1870, pp. 169–70.

Bowannie, F., Deposition, *Zuni Indian Tribe v. United States,* Docket 161-79L (Ct. Cl., filed April 27, 1979), p. 26.

Cushing, F. H., "Outlines of Zuni Creation Myths," *Thirteenth Annual Report of the Bureau of American Ethnology, 1891–1892,* Washington, 1896.

———, "Zuni Fetishes," *Second Annual Report of the Bureau of Ethnology,* Washington, 1883, pp. 3–45 (Republished Flagstaff, by D. C. Publications, 1970).

———, *The Nation of the Willows.* Flagstaff: Northland Press, 1965 (originally published in *Atlantic Monthly,* 1882).

Edaakie, T., Deposition, *Zuni Indian Tribe v. United States,* Docket 161-79L (Ct. Cl., filed April 27, 1979), p. 19.

Eriacho, S., Sr., Deposition, *Zuni Indian Tribe v. United States,* Docket 161-79L (Ct. Cl., filed April 27, 1979), p. 25.

Ferguson, T. J., "Zuni Settlement and Land Use: An Archaeological Perspective," written testimony submitted to the U.S. Court of Claims in behalf of the Zuni Indian Tribe; *Zuni Indian Tribe of New Mexico v. United States;* Docket 161-79L, 1980.

Frazer, R. W., ed., *Mansfield on the Condition of the Western Forts, 1853–54.* Norman: University of Oklahoma Press, 1963, p. 47.

Gaspar, C. H., Deposition, *Zuni Indian Tribe v. United States,* Docket 161-79L (Ct. Cl., filed April 27, 1979), p. 26.

Hack, J. T., "The Changing Physical Environment of the Hopi Indians of Arizona," *Papers of the Peabody Museum of American Archaeology and Ethnology,* vol. 35 (1941) (reprinted Millwood, N.Y., by Kraus-Reprint Co., 1974).

Hammond, G. P. and A. Rey, *The Rediscovery of New Mexico, 1580–1594.* Albuquerque: University of New Mexico Press (Coronado Historical Fund), 1966.

Hart, E. R., "Zuni Trade," Submitted in behalf of the Zuni Indian Tribe, Docket No. 161-79L, United States Court of Claims, March, 1981.

Hodge, F. W., *History of Hawikuh, New Mexico: One of the So-called Cities of Cibola,* Hodge Publication Fund, Los Angeles, 1937.

Kirk, B., "Flood-Water Farming," *The Geographical Review*

19 (1929): 444–555.
Kirk, R. F., "Buffalo Hunting Fetish Jar," *El Palacio* 57 (May, 1950): 131–41.
Luomala, K., ed., "Tipai-Ipai," in *Handbook of North American Indians: California, vol. 8* ed. by R. F. Heizer. Washington: Smithsonian Institution, 1978.
Mahooty, C., Deposition, *Zuni Indian Tribe v. United States,* Docket 161-79L (Ct. Cl., filed April 27, 1979), pp. 11, 13.
McCall, Col. G. A., *New Mexico in 1850: A Military View,* ed. and with an intro. by R. W. Frazer. Norman: University of Oklahoma Press, 1968, pp. 160–61.
Nastacio, A., Deposition, *Zuni Indian Tribe v. United States,* Docket 161-79L (Ct. Cl., filed April 27, 1979), pp. 29-39.
Nastacio, O., Deposition, *Zuni Indian Tribe v. United States,* Docket 161-79L (Ct. Cl., filed April 27, 1979), pp. 12–13.
Riley, C. L., "The Road to Hawikuh: Trade and Trade Routes to Cibola-Zuni during Late Prehistoric and Early Historic Times," *The Kiva* 41 (1975): 137–39.
Schoolcraft, H. R., *Historical and Statistical Information Respecting the History, Condition, and Prospects of the Indian Tribes of the United States.* Philadelphia: Lippincott, Brambo, & Co., 1854, vol. 1, pt. 4, p. 33.
Simpson, Lt. J. H., *Navajo Expedition: Journal of a Military Reconnaissance from Santa Fe, New Mexico to the Navajo Country Made in 1849 by Lieutenant James H. Simpson,* ed. and annot. by F. McNitt. Norman: University of Oklahoma Press, 1964, p. 126n.
Sitgreaves, Capt. L., *Report of an Expedition down the Zuni and Colorado Rivers in 1851* (U.S. Senate Executive Document 59, 32d Cong., 2d Sess., 1853), Chicago: Rio Grande Press, Inc., 1962.
Stevenson, M. C., "The Zuni Indians: their mythology, esoteric fraternities, and ceremonies," *Twenty-third Annual Report of the Bureau of American Ethnology, 1901–1902,* Washington, 1904, pp. 3–634.
Winship, G. P., "The Coronado Expedition, 1539–1542," *Fourteenth Annual Report of the Bureau of Ethnology,* Washington, 1896, pp. 357–58.

20. **Zuni Trails**

Cushing, F. H., *The Nation of the Willows.* Flagstaff: Northland Press, 1965 (originally published in *Atlantic Monthly,* 1882).
Hart, E. R., "Zuni Trade," Submitted in behalf of the Zuni Indian Tribe, Docket No. 161-79L, United States Court of Claims, March, 1981.

21. **Area of Zuni Sovereignty in 1846**

See entries for maps 8–20.

22. **Significant Incidents of Violence in Zuni Area**

Abel, A. H., "The Journal of John Greiner," *Old Santa Fe: A Magazine of History, Archaeology, Genealogy and Biography* 3, no. 11 (July, 1916).
Adams, E. B., and Fr. A. Chavez, trans. and annot., *The Missions of New Mexico, 1776: A Description by Fray Francisco Atanasio Dominguez with Other Contemporary Documents.* Albuquerque: University of New Mexico Press, 1956, p. 197.
———, "Historical Introduction to Studies among the Sedentary Indians of New Mexico," *Papers of the Archaeological Institute of America.* Boston: Cupples, Upham & Co., 1883.
Bandelier, A. F., "An Outline of the Documentary History of the Zuni Tribe," *A Journal of American Ethnology and Archaeology,* vol. 3. Boston and New York: Houghton Mifflin and Company.
Bolton, H. E., *Coronado: Knight of Pueblos and Plains.* Albuquerque: University of New Mexico Press and Whittlesey House, 1949.
Burial Records, Nuestra Senora de Guadalupe de Alona, May 22, 1700 to 1719, Book 45, Archives of the Archdiocese of Santa Fe.
Chavez, A., *Archives of the Archdiocese of Santa Fe, 1678–1900,* Washington: Academy of American Franciscan History, 1957.
Connelley, W. E., *Doniphan's Expedition and the Conquest of New Mexico and California.* Kansas City, Mo.: Bryant & Douglas Book and Stationery Co., 1907, pp. 592–97.
Denver Federal Center, RG 75.
Hackett, C. W., ed., and C. C. Shelby, trans., *Revolt of the Pueblo Indians of New Mexico and Otermin's Attempted Reconquest, 1680–1682.* Albuquerque: University of New Mexico Press, 1970 (originally published 1940), vol. 1, p. 183.
Hart, E. R., "Boundaries of Zuni Land: With Emphasis on Details Relating to Incidents Occurring 1846–1946," Expert Witness Testimony Submitted December, 1980, to the U.S. Court of Claims on Behalf of the Zuni Tribe, 2 vols., *Zuni Tribe v. United States of America.*
Hammond, G. P. and A. Rey, *Onate, Colonizer of New Mexico, 1598–1628,* 2 vols. Albuquerque: University of New Mexico Press, 1953.
———, *The Rediscovery of New Mexico, 1580–1594.* Albuquerque: University of New Mexico Press (Coronado Historical Fund), 1966.
Hodge, F. W., *History of Hawikuh, New Mexico: One of the So-called Cities of Cibola,* Hodge Publication Fund, Los Angeles, 1937.
Hodge, F. W., G. P. Hammons, and A. Rey, eds., *Fray Alonso de Benavides' Revised Memorial of 1634.* Albuquerque: University of New Mexico Press, 1945, pp. 73–74, 214, 294.
Jenkins, M. E., "The Pueblo of Zuni and United States Occupation," written testimony submitted to the U.S. Court of Claims in behalf of the Zuni Indian Tribe, *Zuni Indian Tribe of New Mexico v. United States,* Docket No. 161-79L, 1980.
Jenkins, M. E., and W. A. Minge, "Navajo Activities Affecting the Acoma-Laguna Area, 1746–1910," in *Navajo Indians,* vol. 2. New York: Garland Publishing Inc., 1974, p. 38.
Jones, O. L., *Pueblo Warriors and Spanish Conquest.* Norman: University of Oklahoma Press, 1966.
Leighton, D. C., and J. Adair, *People of the Middle Place;* Human Relations Area Files, Inc., New Haven, Conn., 1966.
Lesley, L. B., ed., *Uncle Sam's Camels: The Journal of May Humphreys Stacey Supplemented by the Report of Edward Fitzgerald Beale (1857–1858).* Cambridge: Harvard University Press, 1929, pp. 188–89.
McNitt, F., *Navaho Expedition: Journal of a Military Reconnaissance from Santa Fe, New Mexico to the Navaho Country Made in 1849 by Lieutenant James H. Simpson.* Norman: University of Oklahoma Press, 1964, p. 114.
———, *Navajo Wars: Military Campaigns, Slave Raids and Reprisals.* Albuquerque: University of New Mexico Press, 1972, p. 35.
Minge, W. A., "Zuni in Spanish and Mexican History," written testimony submitted to the U.S. Court of Claims

in behalf of the Zuni Indian Tribe; *Zuni Indian Tribe of New Mexico v. United States;* Docket 161-79L, 1980.
National Archives, RG 94
National Archives, RG 393
National Archives, New Mexico Superintendency
National Archives, RG 75
Proposed Findings of Fact in Behalf of the Navaho Tribe of Indians in Area of the Overall Navajo Claim, Before the Indian Claims Commission (Docket 229), vol. 5, Findings 20, 21, & 22, n.d., selected exhibits.
State of New Mexico Archives Center, *Calendar of the Microfilm of the Spanish Archives of New Mexico, 1621–1821,* Santa Fe, 1968.
Thomas, A. B., *Forgotten Frontiers: A Study of the Spanish Indian Policy of Don Juan Bautista de Anza, Governor of New Mexico, 1777–1787.* Norman: University of Oklahoma Press, 1969 (first edition 1932).
Twitchell, R. E., *The Spanish Archives of New Mexico,* 2 vols. Cedar Rapids, Iowa: The Torch Press, 1914.
———, *The Leading Facts of New Mexican History.* Cedar Rapids, Iowa: The Torch Press, 1912.

23. American Expeditions in the Nineteenth Century

Bieber, R. P., *Marching with the Army of the West, 1846–1848 by Abraham Robinson Johnson, Marcellus Ball Edwards, Phillip Gosch Ferguson.* Philadelphia: Porcupine Press, 1974.
Bolton, H. E., *Coronado: Knight of Pueblos and Plains.* Albuquerque: University of New Mexico Press and Whittlesey House, 1949.
Chaput, D., *Francois X. Aubrey: Trader, Trailmaker and Voyageur in the Southwest, 1846–1854.* Glendale, Ca.: Arthur H. Clark Company, 1975.
Connelley, W. E., *Doniphan's Expedition and the Conquest of New Mexico and California.* Kansas City, Mo.: Bryant & Douglas Book and Stationery Co., 1907, pp. 592–97.
Foreman, G., ed. and annot., *A Pathfinder in the Southwest: The Itinerary of Lieutenant A. W. Whipple during his Explorations for a Railway Route from Fort Smith to Los Angeles in the Years 1853 & 1854.* Norman: University of Oklahoma Press, 1941.
Hague, H., *The Road to California: The Search for a Southern Overland Route, 1540–1848.* Glendale, Ca.: Arthur H. Clark Co.,1978.
Hart, E.R., "Boundaries of Zuni Land: With Emphasis on Details Relating to Incidents Occurring 1846–1946," Expert Witness Testimony Submitted December, 1980, to the U.S. Court of Claims on Behalf of the Zuni Tribe, 2 vols., *Zuni Tribe v. United States of America,*
Kern, R. H., "Map of the Territory of New Mexico," Santa Fe, 1851, Huntington Libary.
Lesley, L. B., ed., *Uncle Sam's Camels: The Journal of May Humphreys Stacey Supplemented by the Report of Edward Fitzgerald Beale (1845–1858).* Cambridge: Harvard University Press, 1929, pp. 188–89.
McNitt, F., *Navajo Expedition: Journal of a Military Reconnaissance from Santa Fe, New Mexico to the Navajo Country Made in 1849 by Lieutenant James H. Simpson.* Norman: University of Oklahoma Press, 1964, p. 114.
Sitgreaves, L., *Report of an Expdition down the Zuni and Colorado Rivers*; 32nd Congress, 2nd Session, Executive No. 59; (originally published Washington; Robert Armstrong; 1853). Chicago: Rio Grande Press, Inc., 1962.

24. Historical Descriptions of the Extent of Zuni Land

Cushing, F. H., "The Discovery of Zuni or the Ancient Province of Cibola [and] the Seven Cities," unpublished MS, 1885, Hodge-Cushing Collection, Southwest Museum, Los Angeles, pp. 62–63.
Klett, F., "The Zuni Indians of New Mexico," *Popular Science Monthly;* May–Oct., 1874, pp. 585–86.
Tenney, A. M., "Journal 1875–76," unpublished MS, Archives, LDS Church Historical Department, back cover.
Wheeler, G. M., *Report upon United States Geographical Surveys West of the One Hundredth Meridian*, vol. 1 (Geographical), Washington, 1889, p. 61.

25. "Map Hastily Sketched from Memory, to Show Localities of Caves and Ruins," by F. H. Cushing

Cushing, F. H., Letter of January 13, 1881 to Professor Baird and Major Powell. Hodge-Cushing Collection Lot No. 48, Southwest Museum, Los Angeles.
———, Catalogue of prehistoric and Zuni cave remains. Hodge-Cushing Collection, Lot No. 159, Southwest Museum, Los Angeles.
———, National Anthropological Archives, BAE correspondence, Letters Received, 1879–1888. Smithsonian Institution, Washington.

26. "General Map of the Pueblo Region," by Victor Mindeleff

See entry for Map 27.

27. "Plan of Zuni Pueblo, 1881," by Victor Mindeleff

Mindeleff, V., "A Study of Pueblo Architecture: Tusayan and Cibola," *Eighth Annual Report of the Bureau of Ethnology*; Washington, 1891.

28. "Map Showing the Position of the More Important Ruins Near Zuni," by Jesse Walter Fewkes

Fewkes, J. W., "Reconnoissance of Ruins in or near the Zuni Reservation," *Journal of American Ethnology and Archaeology* 1, pt. 3 (1891): 93–132.

29. "Part of New Mexico, Showing the Location of Modern Zuni Towns, Ruins of the Seven Cities of Cibola and Other Ruins," by Washington Matthews, 1893

Matthews, W., "Human Bones of the Hemenway Collection in the United States Army Medical Museum," *Memoirs of the National Academy of Sciences*, vol. 6, pt. 7, Washington, 1893.

30. "Zuni Houses and Clans, 1916," by A. L. Kroeber

Kroeber, A. E., "Zuni Kin and Clan," *Anthropological Papers of the American Museum of Natural History,* vol. 18, pt. 2, New York Trustees, 1917.

31. Non-Zuni Settlement in the Zuni Area

Ferguson, T. J., "Zuni Settlement and Land Use: An Archaeological Perspective," written testimony submitted to the U.S. Court of Claims in behalf of the Zuni Indian Tribe; *Zuni Indian Tribe of New Mexico v. United States*; Docket 161-79L, 1980.

Hart, E. Richard, "Boundaries of Zuni Land: With Emphasis on Details Relating to Incidents Occurring 1846–1946;" Expert Witness Testimony Submitted December, 1980, to the U.S. Court of Claims on behalf of the Zuni Tribe, 2 vols.; *Zuni Tribe v. United States of America*; Docket 161-79L, 1980.

32. Area and Dates of Zuni Land Taken

Ferguson, T. J., "Zuni Settlement and Land Use: An Archaeological Perspective," written testimony submitted to the U.S. Court of Claims in behalf of the Zuni Indian Tribe, *Zuni Indian Tribe of New Mexico v. United States*, Docket 161-79L, 1980.

Hart, E. R., "Boundaries of Zuni Land: With Emphasis on Details Relating to Incidents Occurring 1846–1946," Expert Witness Testimony Submitted December, 1980, to the U.S. Court of Claims on Behalf of the Zuni Tribe, 2 vols., *Zuni Tribe v. United States of America.*

———, *The Zunis: Experiences and Descriptions.* Zuni, N.Mex.: Pueblo of Zuni, 1973; 28 pp.

33. Zuni Reservation Changes: 1877–1900

Hart, E. R., "Boundaries of Zuni Land: With Emphasis on Details Relating to Incidents Occurring 1846–1946," Expert Witness Testimony Submitted December, 1980, to the U.S. Court of Claims on Behalf of the Zuni Tribe, 2 vols., *Zuni Tribe v. United States of America.*

———, *The Zunis: Experiences and Descriptions.* Zuni, N. Mex.: Pueblo of Zuni, 1973.

34. Zuni Reservation Changes: 1900–49

Hart, E. R., "Boundaries of Zuni Land: With Emphasis on Details Relating to Incidents Occurring 1846–1946," Expert Witness Testimony Submitted December, 1980, to the U.S. Court of Claims on Behalf of the Zuni Tribe, 2 vols., *Zuni Tribe v. United States of America.*

———, *The Zunis: Experiences and Descriptions*, Zuni, N. Mex.: Pueblo of Zuni, 1973.

35. Zuni Reservation Changes: 1949–82

Hart, E. R., "Boundaries of Zuni Land: With Emphasis on Details Relating to Incidents Occurring 1846–1946," Expert Witness Testimony Submitted December, 1980, to the U.S. Court of Claims on Behalf of the Zuni Tribe, 2 vols.; *Zuni Tribe v. United States of America.*

———, *The Zunis: Experiences and Descriptions.* Zuni, N. Mex.: Pueblo of Zuni, 1973.

36. Development of the Zuni Reservation

Ferguson, T. J., "Zuni Settlement and Land Use: An Archaeological Perspective," written testimony submitted to the U.S. Court of Claims in behalf of the Zuni Indian Tribe; *Zuni Indian Tribe of New Mexico v. United States;* Docket 161-79L, 1980.

Hart, E. Richard, "Boundaries of Zuni Land: With Emphasis on Details Relating to Incidents Occurring 1846–1946;" Expert Witness Testimony Submitted December, 1980, to the U.S. Court of Claims on behalf of the Zuni Tribe, 2 vols.; *Zuni Tribe v. United States of America*; Docket 161-79L, 1980.

37. Grazing Units on the Zuni Reservation

Holmes, B. E. and A. P. Fowler, *The Alternate Dams Survey: An Archaeological Sample Survey and Evaluation of the Burned Timber and Coalmine Dams.* Zuni, N. Mex.: Zuni Archaeology Program, 1980.

BIA, Grazing Unit Map, Zuni Agency, Albuquerque Area Office.

38. Geology of the Zuni Reservation

Department of the Interior, "Zuni Oil and Gas Development, Comprehensive Environmental Assessment," Bureau of Indian Affairs, Albuquerque Area Office, 1981.

Maxwell, C. H., and L. G. Nonini, "Status of Mineral Resource Information for the Zuni Indian Reservation, New Mexico," U.S. Geological Survey and U.S. Bureau of Mines, Administrative Report BIA-32, 1977.

39. Aquifers Underlying the Zuni Reservation

Orr, Brennon R., "Water Resources of the Zuni Tribal Lands, McKinley and Cibola Counties, New Mexico," Water Supply of Indian Reservations, Geological Survey Water Supply Paper (open file); GPO, Washington; 1982.

40. Wells, Ponds, Springs, and Wet Spots

Department of the Interior, Map Atlas: Soil and Range Inventory of the Zuni Indian Reservation, Branch of Land Operations, BIA, Albuquerque Area Office.

41. Mineral Extraction on the Zuni Reservation

Maxwell, C. H., and L. G. Nonini, "Status of Mineral Resource Information for the Zuni Indian Reservation, New Mexico," U.S. Geological Survey and U.S. Bureau of Mines, Administrative Report BIA-32, 1977.

42. Mineral and Energy Resources on the Zuni Reservation

Maxwell, C. H., and L. G. Nonini, "Status of Mineral Resource Information for the Zuni Indian Reservation, New Mexico," U.S. Geological Survey and U.S. Bureau of Mines, Administrative Report BIA-32, 1977.

43. **Soil Associations on the Zuni Reservation**

Maker, H. J., H. E. Bullock, Jr., J. U. Anderson, "Soil Associations and Land Classification for Irrigation, McKinley County," *Agricultural Experiment Station, Research Report 262,* 1974.

Maker, H. J., L. W. Hacker, and J. U. Anderson, "Soil Association and Land Classification for Irrigation, Valencia County," *Agricultural Experiment Station, Research Report 267,* 1974.

44. **"Zuni Pueblo, 1972,"** by Perry E. Borchers

Borchers, P. E., Photogrametric Map of Zuni Pueblo; Historic American Building Survey, Washington, 1972.

United States Geological Survey, Zuni Pueblo, 7.5 Minute Quadrangle, 1972.

INDEX

Note: numbers in italics are map numbers.